Deadwood
and Shakespeare

Deadwood and Shakespeare
The Henriad in the Old West

SUSAN COSBY RONNENBERG

McFarland & Company, Inc., Publishers
Jefferson, North Carolina

LIBRARY OF CONGRESS CATALOGUING-IN-PUBLICATION DATA

Names: Ronnenberg, Susan Cosby, 1967– author.
Title: Deadwood and Shakespeare : the Henriad in the old west / Susan Cosby Ronnenberg.
Description: Jefferson, North Carolina : McFarland & Company, Inc., Publishers, 2018. | Includes bibliographical references and index.
Identifiers: LCCN 2018024790 | ISBN 9781476665757 (softcover : acid free paper) ∞
Subjects: LCSH: Deadwood (Television program) | Shakespeare, William, 1564–1616—Histories. | Shakespeare, William, 1564–1616—Influence.
Classification: LCC PN1992.77.D39 R66 2018 | DDC 791.45/72—dc23
LC record available at https://lccn.loc.gov/2018024790

BRITISH LIBRARY CATALOGUING DATA ARE AVAILABLE

ISBN (print) 978-1-4766-6575-7
ISBN (ebook) 978-1-4766-3095-3

© 2018 Susan Cosby Ronnenberg. All rights reserved

No part of this book may be reproduced or transmitted in any form or by any means, electronic or mechanical, including photocopying or recording, or by any information storage and retrieval system, without permission in writing from the publisher.

Front cover image based on the Flower portrait of William Shakespeare, circa 19th century (Royal Shakespeare Company)

Printed in the United States of America

McFarland & Company, Inc., Publishers
 Box 611, Jefferson, North Carolina 28640
 www.mcfarlandpub.com

For Clint, my Ellsworth, and Kate

Acknowledgments

This book would not exist without the encouragement and support of many people. I would like to especially thank Diana Stetler, Kelly Samuels, Kyle Jennings, and Ivy King for reading chapter drafts at various stages and providing feedback, along with encouragement.

Portions of Chapters 1, 2, 3, and 4 were presented, in a very condensed single paper version, at the 2010 National Popular Culture Association conference, with a focus on only *1 Henry IV* parallels to *Deadwood*. That draft was reviewed by Kelly Samuels and Rolf Samuels, who provided very detailed and useful feedback that ultimately led to the book proposal.

Thank you to Viterbo University's Faculty Development Grant program, which supported my continued attendance and participation in the National Popular Culture Association conference and the Midwest Popular Culture Association conference.

Thanks to Justin Charron for the year-long conversations on the value of comparing texts, which helped with both of our projects.

Thanks, too, to friends and family for offering unwavering and enthusiastic support for the development of this project, especially Clint Ronnenberg, my Hendrix College Labor-Day-Weekends alum group, and the S.F.S.G. I cannot convey how much your excitement over this work helped me complete it.

Finally, I've never been so glad that my parents shared their love of John Wayne and John Ford films with me during my childhood, which my sister balanced out with her love of Shakespeare.

Table of Contents

Acknowledgments vi
Preface 1
Introduction 3

1. Genres, Settings and Themes: Historical and Political Worlds in Transition 9
2. Seth Bullock as "Hotspur" and Prince "Hal" 36
3. Al Swearengen as Bolingbroke/Henry IV and Falstaff 59
4. Father-Son Relationships 81
5. Women's Marginalization 103
6. Managing Audience Responses through Narrative Space and Events 129
7. Managing Audience Responses through Character 158

Conclusion 174
Appendix: Deadwood *Episodes* 177
Chapter Notes 179
Bibliography 187
Index 193

Preface

HBO's critically-acclaimed Western series *Deadwood* was cancelled in 2006, but interest in the show has continued with its viewership consistently increasing, thanks to its streaming access and marathon television airings in recent years. In 2014, articles appeared on *Slate, Slant, Yahoo, Mental Floss, UpRoxx,* and *Television* observing the tenth anniversary of the series premiere. The year 2016 marked the tenth anniversary of the series' cancellation and another round of accolades and analyses about the show and the possibility of reviving it in some form. In January 2016, HBO greenlit script development from the series creator, David Milch, for one to two television movies to return to *Deadwood*'s incomplete narrative arcs.[1] The show has been ranked in the top ten dramatic television series by a number of television critics and media sites, including *IndieWire*'s list of "The 25 Best TV Dramas Since *The Sopranos*," from February 2016, which lists *Deadwood* at number two, second only to *The Wire*.

Ten books and numerous articles published since the series ended—promoting the show and analyzing aspects of it—reflect continuing critical and popular interest in the drama.[2] Obviously, these texts focus on a broad range of topics related to HBO's *Deadwood* series, with an emphasis on its use of violence and profanity, gender roles, and disability studies, as well as how it adheres to or challenges the conventions of the Western in literature, film, and television. Several studies, such as Alan Sepinwall's *The Revolution was Televised* (2013) and Kim Akass and Janet McCabe's *Quality TV: Contemporary American Television and Beyond* (2007), also include *Deadwood* and Milch as part of the American television revolution brought about by cable networks at the beginning of the 21st century. A few articles examine how historical figures and events, as well as cultural practices, of the real 19th century Deadwood are portrayed. Several articles address the extraordinary mixing of language, both high and low, in the series; many reference Shakespeare or Dickens for comparison, but do so only vaguely, with a nod to the influence of these texts—specifically the soliloquy and the dramatic monologue—and the language of the Bible in characters' dialogue on a regular basis.

None of the articles or books on *Deadwood* offer concrete comparisons between specific aspects of William Shakespeare's plays and the television series, however. While I enjoyed the extraordinary language play on the series, I was struck by how Seth Bullock's admirable qualities were offset by his intense and frequent anger, which often manifested in out-of-control violence. He reminded me of Hotspur from *1 Henry IV*, who has a similar problem; once I saw this association, I couldn't unsee it. The goal of this book is to explore correspondences between William Shakespeare's first set of history plays, consisting of *Richard II*, *1 Henry IV*, *2 Henry IV*, and *Henry V*, and the Western series *Deadwood*.

Other character parallels also seemed to fit; the other male lead character, Al Swearengen, shares a few traits in common with Falstaff and Henry IV, also in *1 Henry IV*. This character alignment then readily lent itself to looking at the relationship between Bullock and Swearengen through the lens of the son- and father-figure relationships of Prince Hal/Hotspur and Falstaff/Henry IV in *1 Henry IV*. I presented a paper on this subject at the National Popular Culture Association's conference in 2010 as part of an excellent "Masculinity Studies on Television" panel; the positive response it received encouraged me to continue expanding the study to other plays in the tetralogy, starting with *2 Henry IV* and *Richard II*. At the time, few of the *Deadwood* studies explicitly addressed in-depth the nature of the father-son relationship that emerges between *Deadwood*'s chief protagonists, Al Swearengen and Seth Bullock.

The unusual structure of *Richard II* is paralleled in *Deadwood*—particularly in relation to how the audience's response to Swearengen shifts as the series progresses. Few of the studies of the HBO series analyze the structure of the series regarding opening and closing framing shots, how the camera directs our attention to specific details in its sharpening focus, and how the juxtaposition of locations tells us something about the relationship between characters and events unfolding in the series. Like *Deadwood*, the Henriad emphasizes communities dealing with internal versus external threats, the creation of a unified community under threat, and the role of women, marginalized as they are in this set of history plays and, to a lesser degree, on the *Deadwood* series. Finally, studies on the Western genre in film for comparison with conventions of Shakespeare's history sub-genre offered a surprising number of similarities for further analysis, including a focus on father-son relationships and the marginalization of women. Both sets of work contain structural devices that disrupt the narrative to direct audience attention; Rumor, Epilogue, and the Chorus directly address the audience in *2 Henry IV* and *Henry V*, comparable to the ways that camera angles, focus, and close-ups direct audience attention in the filmed performance of these texts.

Introduction

From a traditionalist perspective, Shakespeare's work is broadly adaptable, offering timeless and universal truths to a range of cultures and situations. Harvard Shakespeare scholar Marjorie Garber notes, "Every age creates its own Shakespeare.... Shakespeare serves a wide variety of cultural purposes, from political nationalism around the globe to modern-day instruction in 'leadership' for business and corporate culture."[1] Many people view this universality and adaptability as two of the great strengths of the bard's work. A wide variety of popular culture works reflect Shakespeare's influence[2]; in the following chapters I'll make the argument that the HBO Western series *Deadwood* specifically reflects the influence of Shakespeare's second history tetralogy, known as the Henriad, through its simultaneous contribution to and critique of national mythology, its use of the past to meditate on the present, its acknowledgment of masculinity and gendered roles, its marginalization of women, and its narrative complexity designed to control and shift audience responses.

Deadwood, winner of the American Film Institute award for TV Program of the Year in both 2005 and 2006, has been described as having "grand schemes and Shakespearean motives" and as being "a Shakespearean epic in spurs."[3] Many comparisons have been raised about Shakespeare's influence on the series, primarily in terms of its language[4]; as one critic has noted, "viewers are not lulled passively into the story, both because the language calls attention to itself and because they must work to make sense of what is being said."[5] Few studies have explored any explicit parallels between particular plays and the television series. While it's not necessary to recognize the influence of Shakespeare on the series to enjoy the Western, it has been noted, as by media scholar Jason Mittell, "Many of the best complex television series work on numerous levels, providing both surface pleasures and deeper resonances for different groups of viewers."[6] Acknowledging the multiple parallels between the two sets of works can increase viewer engagement and enjoyment of the series. The goal of this book is to explore parallels between William Shakespeare's second set of history plays, consisting of *Richard II, 1 Henry IV, 2 Henry IV,* and *Henry V,* and the Western television series *Deadwood.* Part of the pleasure many viewers take in the series includes recognizing a variety of literary, film, and television influences interwoven throughout its run. Series creator David Milch has said, "you just [stop] questioning the fact that your work is part of a conversation, with everybody, with the work that has preceded you and you can pray humbly that it still be part of the conversation which ensues"; English and American Studies professor Melody Graulich adds, "That's part of the real pleasure for the reader, from a literary standpoint, to see that conversation going on in *Deadwood*."[7] For me, the loudest conversation of the series has been with Shakespeare's second history tetralogy.

This comparison draws upon textual analysis and cultural studies approaches to determine what the plays and the series "might be saying about identity and how representations fit within broader cultural assumptions and contexts,"[8] understanding culture to be "a site of negotiation and struggle."[9] In practicing textual analysis, "researchers analyze the range of meanings encoded in texts ... highlighting how a text might privilege particular meanings through narrative structure or other formal elements."[10] The commonalities between Shakespeare's second set of history plays and the HBO series *Deadwood* are often surprising, drawing our attention first to cultural consistencies across time and space and then, more importantly, to differences that reflect cultural change and progress. Susan Stanford Friedman notes, "the decontextualization that comparison relies on as it moves beyond the particular and local also involves a recontextualization that is potentially illuminating."[11] She adds that comparisons "double back to highlight aspects of each [text under comparison] that might have gone undetected" otherwise.[12] Thus, textual comparisons can provide insight into both works' details that might have escaped observation when each is viewed separately in isolation.

Chapter 1, "Genres, Settings and Themes: Historical and Political Worlds in Transition," explores how both sets of works are essentially about the stories we tell ourselves regarding the origins of community in the process of change or challenge, exploring the question of how legal order is possible in the midst of chaos. Both portray authority as consistently, inevitably morally compromised. Both are conventionally propagandistic narratives used to challenge and critique the familiar national mythology. *Deadwood, Richard II,* and the Henry IV plays explore shifts in influence, power, and order in the face of competing and conflicting interests of personal profit, justice, and fairness and through the responsibility of community-building.

Chapters 2 through 4 explore how parallels in character behavior and personality provide opportunities for understanding of motivation and choices and provide insight into what each individual's privilege is and why. In Chapter 2, "Seth Bullock as 'Hotspur' and Prince 'Hal,'" young men in the process of becoming adult participants in governance, reflect a youthful nation also in the process of becoming. The role of honor—how to achieve it or at least the appearance of it, how to maintain it, or how to avoid dishonor, despite one's inclinations—emerges as an important motivator for many seemingly opposed male characters. Chapter 3, "Al Swearengen as Bolingbroke/Henry IV and Falstaff," observes modern culture's interest in the antihero (but not the anti-heroine), which has been fostered in part by the provision of a compelling backstory to explain such characters' motivations. This is a development of the popular medieval vice character beyond a one-dimensional allegorical figure into a more humanized role with strengths and weaknesses. If we look at Swearengen as Falstaff, the audience's increasing fondness toward him becomes easier to understand. David Milch said he based Swearengen on Falstaff, having recently read *1 Henry IV* before beginning writing for *Deadwood*; in other interviews, Milch has claimed that Falstaff is his favorite literary character.[13]

Chapter 4, "Father-Son Relationships," examines the longing for cross-generational connection, the challenges of clear and sufficient communication, and conflicting and competing personal interests that hover constantly over father-son relationships in *Richard II*, the Henry IV plays, and *Deadwood*. Recognizing their similarities in one dramatic portrayal can enable us to better comprehend how those same dynamics are playing out in others. The historical, scripted portrayals of conflicted father-son dynamics speak to a universal psychological experience—one that will always have an audience. These parallels also provide an initial framework for analyzing the two men's evolving relationship with one another and with the camp. Masculinity is presented as a characteristic granted to men by other men's regard of them and respect demonstrated toward one another, a lesson that the younger men are still learning to negotiate, with violence or threatened violence as an inevitable part of that negotiation.

Chapter 5, "Women's Marginalization," explores how women's roles in both genres are severely restricted to emphasize the private, emotional costs of men's political powerplays, men's failure to listen to women, and women's grief, hopelessness, and passivity. Similarities between the portrayal of women's roles in 16th century historical drama and 21st century televisual drama point out appallingly persistent and consistent misogyny and discrimination, while distinctions between the two highlight significant cultural changes, including growth, independence, and capabilities of female characters on the television series as a hopeful reflection of the culture producing them. Women supplant the young men in reflecting the growth and advancement of the young nation.

Chapter 6, "Managing Audience Responses through Narrative Space and Events," and Chapter 7, "Managing Audience Responses through Character," examine how complex narrative structures control and manipulate audience sympathies across a broad spectrum. Comparing commonalities helps viewers recognize how these genres deliberately portray the past in a specific way to confirm or challenge audience views of history. These comparisons should also make us think about the role of national myth in our collective consciousness and, hopefully, make us question its origins and accuracy in terms of inclusion and exclusion. Whose perspective is privileged? Whose is omitted, marginalized, or erased, and to what end? How is this story presented to viewers? How does the organization and method of storytelling shape our response to the story? In his study on complex television narratives, Mittell says that applying the label of "complex[ity]" emphasizes "sophistication and nuance," describing that which "grows richer through sustained engagement and consideration."[14] Not only can complex narratives engage audiences more deeply and pleasurably, rewarding critical thinking, they also provide practice with verbal and visual textual analysis. By reading these aspects of *Deadwood* through the lens of Shakespeare's Henriad, viewers gain a deeper understanding and appreciation of how politics, power, gender, and relationships are presented in the series. And hopefully some of that analysis of power relations also transfers to how we view the world around us, where historical progress or backsliding is occurring every day.

Viewing, analyzing, and discussing the complexities of a smart television drama such as *Deadwood* can transfer into questioning what we're seeing and hearing in other venues, how messages are constantly being presented to us, what we know or accept as truth versus what we assume, and if there is clear discontinuity in the image or audio or disruption of the narration; these kinds of awareness can help us practice and extend our critical thinking skills in everyday life.

Identifying parallels between a television drama and a 400-year-old history play asks viewers to make connections they might not otherwise make between their formal education and their leisure entertainment. Yet both the history plays and the TV drama are forms of entertainment that may also serve to educate and simultaneously challenge viewer assumptions about historical periods significant to national identity.

This book focuses on a comparison of these specific works' commonalities and distinctions, and what we can learn from them about gender roles, political power, the reciprocal nature of how the past influences the present and how the present shapes our view of the past, narrative structure, the human condition, and how/why each reflects and comments on the cultural conditions in which it was created. Are the commonalities intentional? I think some of them must be. Others may simply be the product of genre convention similarities.

The sheer number of parallels between the two suggests a connection. Can I assert that David Milch's narrative plan for *Deadwood* was influenced by his reading of the Henriad? Of course not. And likely he'd deny it, even if I made the claim. Does *Deadwood* bear markers of the influence of Shakespeare's Henriad? Definitely. Recognizing such influences increases viewer enjoyment in the series and encourages her or him to be alert for more of the same. Our knowledge of the Henriad can also help us better understand character behavior, defining traits of some characters, relationships in the series, the limited but growing role of women in Western culture, and the complex structure of the stories being presented episodically.

The goal of this book is to encourage *Deadwood* viewers to learn more about Shakespeare's history plays and how they parallel aspects of the series so that they may rewatch the series with the insight the plays provide into mythmaking, political power negotiations, gender roles, and performative texts' portrayal of a nation in transition. For Shakespeare fans, the goal of this book is to encourage them to consider *Deadwood* as a work of art dealing with many of the same themes found in the Henriad regarding establishing order out of disorder, the inevitable corruption of authority in this process, the complicated, conflicted importance of father-son relationships, the importance of honor, and the marginalization of women.

1
Genres, Settings and Themes: Historical and Political Worlds in Transition

"The establishment of any legal order, or whatever doctrine, even liberal-democratic and humanist, must be illegal, violent, unjust, and brutal, and a society must find a way to represent that fact to itself as a national memory."[1]

"[Shakespeare's history plays] lay out, in all their complexity and tenuousness, the devious paths by which the crown descended to Elizabeth."[2]

How does an early 21st century version of the Western in television series format align at all with late 16th century English history plays? That may seem like an extraordinary leap, but it's actually much less of one than you might suspect. Both sets of work take as their source national myths or legends, sanitized versions of how order was formed out of disorder. Such transitions, however, are inherently messy, as the two quotes introducing this chapter indicate. *Deadwood* and the Henriad critique the heavily edited stories we tell ourselves about national origins. Set in unstable political environments during or after civil conflict, these genres raise questions about legitimate political authority and the qualities of an effective leader. Both genres contribute significantly to national mythology, departing from strict adherence to historical accuracy in order to shape a commentary on the past and the culture in which the works are created; they address national anxiety prompted by threats to established order and identity by looking to the past. The English history play and the Western television series also explore the complex, often contradictory, nature of the human condition.

Settings and genre conventions are intertwined in these works, contributing to a commentary on the present, i.e., the time of the production of the series and the plays. O'Connor and Rollins state that while U.S. popular culture may appear chaotic, film scholars have noted "that Westerns are a touchstone to understanding the nation's concerns."[3] This book contributes to the extension of that claim to include this Western cable series as reflective of 21st century national concerns. A special edition of *The Journal of Popular Film and Television* in 2011 was dedicated solely to HBO's *Deadwood*, with a range of articles all "illustrat[ing] once again how Western films and television series have been used to define the present and discover the future by looking backward and reexamining America's mythic past."[4] The first question that study of the past raises is often directly connected to present concerns: how did we get to this point? Despite the decades between the settling of the Deadwood camp and early 21st century America and the centuries between the reigns of Richard II, Henry IV, and Henry V and Elizabethan England, each work speaks to issues present in the culture that created it. *Deadwood* creator David Milch says, "It's understood that all of the corruption of the past has to be absorbed if the present is to be understood as the present, that it contains all of our past sinfulness without remediation."[5] In other words, he suggests that we are in constant negotiation with the past as we exist in the present and attempt to move forward into the future. It's also significant to note that this Western and the history plays are both performative stories we tell about community origins, reliant on visual and audio delivery to contribute to audience understanding of the commentary they provide on both the past and the present.

Genres: The English History Play on Stage and Screen

Although plays focusing on English history existed before those written by William Shakespeare, David Bevington asserts, "the English history play as a recognizable form came into being with *Henry VI*" in the late 16th century.[6] Shakespeare's history plays feature prominent historical English male monarchs, tracing ascensions to power, threats to the monarch and/or the unification of the nation, and the monarch's fall from power. Influenced by Greek and Roman histories of rulers that explored the question of what qualities constitute a "good" ruler, Shakespeare's history plays were also restricted by being written under a Tudor monarch, Elizabeth I, whose claim to the throne was challenged by some. The initial instability of her reign resulted in a demand for propaganda reinforcing her claim to the throne; the role of providence leading to Elizabeth's reign was emphasized in English history plays, along with portraying her ancestors in a favorable light. Any criticism of the Tudor line or the current monarch in the history plays had to be extremely subversive. A revival performance of *Richard II* in 1601 was intended by the aristocratic patrons, specifically the Earl of Essex, who sponsored it to critique Queen Elizabeth I, aligning Essex with Bolingbroke. Historical documentation records Elizabeth commenting, "I am Richard II. Know ye not that?" to her archivist, William Lambarde, as they reviewed royal manuscripts together.[7] Even today, Shakespeare's plays continue to be staged as political protest under tyrannical regimes. History plays not only teach audiences about the past but also serve as a warning to the present, to learn from historical mistakes and choose more wisely to avoid the same in the future.

While the drama of early modern England was written to entertain, it was also intended for commercial gain and sought patronage of the wealthy and powerful to enable it to continue to be produced. The history plays appeal to the idea of a unified England under Elizabeth I, but they also appeal to a nostalgic longing for some aspects of its shared, formative past. Shakespeare's history plays use Richard III as an illustration of ruthless tyranny, serving as God's punishment upon the English for the excessive ambition of his father, Richard of York, laying claim to the English throne.[8] In Shakespeare's two history series, Richard III is counterbalanced by Henry V as the most nostalgically beloved monarch who unified England against outside threats, even reclaiming part of France and expanding the realm. Modern stage, television, and film adaptations of the history plays are a blend of creative, artistic re-imagining and profit-driven enterprises, seeking to engage an audience that is much more visually-focused, easily distracted, and less familiar with the original texts and with English history.

Genres: The American Western on Screen

Some critics might argue that most 21st century American cable television programs are intended solely for consumer entertainment and financial profit for investors. While it's certainly true that television series production and programming are commercial endeavors marketed to specific target demographics, that doesn't negate their potential power to influence viewers' perspective of the world around them and their place in it. Film and media studies scholar Jason Mittell argues that regular exposure to a specific view of history can challenge, and even alter, our own understanding of the stories we're familiar with regarding national origins and identity.[9] The same critics might also argue that television, and the Western, in particular, lack appropriate elevation and sufficient complexity for contributing in meaningful ways to the development of national historic identity or for actively engaging viewers intellectually. However, Mittell says that

> a new paradigm of television storytelling has emerged over the past two decades with a heightened degree of self-consciousness in storytelling mechanics, and demanding

intensified viewer engagement focused on both diegetic pleasures and formal awareness. For television, contemporary complex narratives foreground the skills of narrative comprehension and media literacy that most viewers have developed but rarely put to use beyond rudimentary means.[10]

My observations support Mittell's claim that some television series' complex narratives invite, if not require, viewer intellectual engagement, the transfer of textual analysis from the printed word on the page to the screen's visual and audio texts. As Mittell notes, "this form of complexity [offers] viewers a 'cognitive workout' that increases problem-solving and observational skills … [offering] a broader range of rewards and pleasures than does most conventional programming."[11] This description of greater depth of intellectual engagement sounds a great deal like what happens when people read or see a Shakespeare play, which has been proven to activate parts of the brain that aren't regularly engaged.[12] In the case of Shakespeare's plays and *Deadwood*, the rich, dense complexity of language challenges readers and viewers. Audiences are also often drawn into the worlds presented by these genres as initially familiar and inviting, and their interest is sustained when the familiar is defamiliarized through plot or character complexity, especially in relation to national mythology.

Established film criticism of the Western genre is useful in examining commonalities between *Deadwood* and Shakespeare's English history plays' relationship to national identity. American Philosopher Robert B. Pippin, writing on Hollywood Westerns and the American myth, interprets French film critic André Bazin's praise of the Western film as a powerful genre that explores multiple views of social issues,

> especially the problem of law and political authority. Bazin expressed great contempt for critics who thought that Western plots were "simple," and he insisted that the right way to understand such simplicity was by reference to the "ethics" of epic and tragic literature. The Western, he said, turned the Civil War into our Trojan War, and "the migration West is our *Odyssey*." (One could go even further, paraphrasing a German commentator: the Greeks had their *Iliad*; the Jews the Hebrew Bible; the Romans the *Aeneid*; the Germans the *Nibelungenlied*; the Scandinavians their *Sagas*; the Spanish the *Cid*; the British the Arthurian legends. The Americans have John Ford.)[13]

Plot similarities between the Western and the history plays, as well as social issues raised by them, are worth addressing, which I discuss in Chapter 6 as structural parallels. Pippin's and Bazin's claims about the importance of the Western film to America's national identity may initially seem audacious. As an heir to that rich film genre, though, *Deadwood* shares with Shakespeare's history plays an interest in exploring specific aspects of national origins or beginnings, particularly in transitioning from political instability within a community to a stability based on nebulous alliances among male citizens or subjects. Legendary director John Ford is known primarily for two kinds of film-making: World War II military propaganda short films commissioned by the U.S. government and the Western, both focused distinctly on U.S. identity.[14] Over time, his series of Western films, ranging from the silent *3 Bad Men* (1926) to *The Man Who Shot Liberty Valance* (1962), established and then played with the conventions of the Western, ultimately challenging some aspects of them, and complicating the audience's perspective of the protagonist as heroic. Ford's first Western with sound, *Stagecoach* (1939), revitalized the genre, becoming a box office and critical hit, as well as a film studied by directors ranging from Orson Welles to Steven Spielberg.

Performed texts, such as the history play and the television series set historically, provide an educational invitation to reassess the past. According to Alison Landsberg, some historians claim that "learning about the past through reading it" as "unnatural" seems to resonate "with some of the important claims made by historians interested in thinking about film and television as powerful and effective vehicles for the transmission of certain forms of historical knowledge."[15] Such claims encourage a reassessment of television and film representations of the past. The popularity of such television series as AMC's *Mad Men*, with its nostalgic representation of the cultural origins of big advertising in New York City, and the BBC's miniseries *The Crown*, tracing Elizabeth II's ascension to the throne, both set in the mid–20th century, suggests that viewers are interested in even more recent televisual performances of cultural history. Additionally, Wendy Witherspoon notes that *Deadwood*'s robust complexity owes much to "series creator David Milch's informed and adept ability to marshal seemingly disparate generic conventions."[16] A number of studies have examined the influence of American literature, gothic literature, film noir, modern cop shows, and, of course, the Western film and television, on the HBO series.[17] This study contributes to that conversation with its analysis of the influence of Shakespeare's history plays on *Deadwood*.

Other prominent historical representations of the American West have emphasized a connection between the English nobility and the American cowboy. Among these are the writings of Theodore Roosevelt and Owen Wister, as well as the paintings by Frederick Remington; Roosevelt, Wister, and Remington were friends, which may account for their unified emphasis on the West's alleged legacy of English elitism.[18] Michael J. Shapiro observes that Roosevelt's historical series on the American West was deliberately anti–Spanish in its praise of English imperialism and sustainment of ethnic purity against Spanish colonialism that mixed races; Wister, too, emphasizes English superiority in his fiction of an English nobleman in Texas who "adapts rapidly because of his superior horsemanship and marksmanship."[19] Remington "depict[s] [Roosevelt's and Wister's] invention of the cowboy as a legacy of the English aristocracy" through paintings such as the "*Last Cavalier* (1895), which shows a cowboy in the foreground against a background that consists of a 'faded panorama of historical horsemen of which the most prominent are generations of English knights.'"[20] Also friends with Roosevelt, the real Seth Bullock was the son of a retired British major, which may have reinforced Roosevelt's idealization of an English colonialist model in depicting the American West.

Historically-Based Genres

Both Shakespeare's Henriad and Milch's *Deadwood* take as their source historical figures and events. Shakespeare's second tetralogy of history plays focus on three English kings: Richard II, Henry IV, and Henry V. These plays present a usurpation of the crown by a more "fit" ruler followed by inheritance of the crown by a worthy heir. They also explore the constant shifts in alliances and threats to the monarch maintaining power. Shakespeare relies heavily on Edward Hall's *The Union of Two Noble and Illustre Famelies of Lancastre & Yorke*, also known simply as *Hall's Chronicle* (1548), and Raphael Holinshed's *Chronicles of England, Scotland, and Ireland* (1587). Harry Berger, Jr., writes that "Hall's chronicle was slanted toward glorification of the Tudors, correlated with an emphasis on divine providence and justice. The 1587 version of Holinshed has been called a political 'counterstatement' to Hall, but it contains frequent assertions of the same moral and ideological commitments."[21] Even the chronicles, or histories, upon which Shakespeare drew were not factually accurate; they, too, presented a biased perspective that took liberties with historical events and figures. Hall's and Holinshed's works were based on Polydore Vergil's work, *Historia Anglica* (1533), commissioned by Henry VII as a deliberately directed historical record supporting the Tudor reign. Shakespeare's second tetralogy is also influenced by Samuel Daniel's poem *The First Four Books of the Civil Wars* (1595), the anonymous play *Thomas of Woodstock*, which was sometimes known as *1 Richard II* (1591–1595), and *A Mirror for Magistrates* (1574), all of which portray a range of variations of historical figures and events featured in *Richard II*, the Henry IV plays, and *Henry V*.[22] Martha A. Kurtz notes that "The history play ... was an invention of the last twenty years of Elizabeth's reign,"[23] perhaps to allay anxiety about succession and political stability, given the Queen's continued unmarried status.

Milch takes as his source historical and folk accounts during Deadwood's transition from illegal mining camp in Indian territory to annexation as part of the state of Dakota, including John S. McClintock's *Pioneer Days of the Black Hills*, Watson Parker's *Deadwood: The Golden Years*, letters, diaries, and *Black Hills Pioneer* articles from the town's residents during this period.[24] He includes well-known historical figures such as the legendary "Wild Bill"

Hickok, his manager/friend Charlie Utter, "Calamity Jane" Canary, former U.S. Marshal Seth Bullock, and entrepreneur George Hearst, but also lesser-known individuals, such as saloon owner Albert Swearengen, businessman and politician Sol Star, Doctor Cochran, bar-keep Dan Doherty, businessman E.B. Farnum, General Samuel Fields, and the Rev. Henry Weston Smith, among others. Including well-known historical figures and events, such as Hickok's murder, that audience members would expect to see in Deadwood during this period provides a framework for the series while allowing Milch and company to depart from strict adherence to the facts, shaping the narrative in imaginative ways. Inclusion of the lesser-known figures permits even more narrative creative leeway for theme and story arc development through star-crossed romantic attachments such as Alma and Seth's, among others.

It's necessary, too, to consider the legal violations occurring in the settlement of Deadwood by non–Native Americans as part of U.S. history often glossed over in favor of presenting the Western expansion romantically. Mark L. Berrettini reminds us that

> the camp is a territorial violation of the 1868 Fort Laramie Treaty between the U.S. government and the Sioux Nation [which] stipulated "that no white person or persons shall be permitted to settle upon or occupy any position of [] Indian Territory; or without the consent of the Indians."[25]

While there are multiple references to the Sioux and their leadership, Spotted Elk and Red Cloud, throughout the first season of the series, only two members of the Sioux tribe are ever represented. One attacks Bullock for desecrating holy ground by passing through a burial ground while he's trying to honor his friend's death there; he's killed by the stunned former lawman. The other takes the form of the decapitated head brought to Swearengen for the bounty he promised after news of the Metz family's falsely alleged slaughter at the hands of the Sioux. This head remains with Swearengen, in a box, as a prop to which he soliloquizes frequently throughout the series, serving as a parallel to Hamlet's pondering on mortality at the sight of Yorick's skull in the graveyard. Amanda Ann Klein notes that *Deadwood*'s "opening credits foreground this opposition between civilization and savagery precisely because these concepts do *not* appear as oppositions within the series itself. They are, rather, the twin faces of America, past and present."[26] Often what we're shown is the foundation of savagery as justifiable or even necessary to establishing what comes to pass as civilization.

Deliberate Anachronisms with a Common Purpose

Anachronisms, "error[s] in respect to dates" or "the misplacing of persons or events in time,"[27] are used in Shakespeare's history plays and in the

Deadwood series to provide comic relief, to offer insight into character relationships, and to engage the audience. Anachronisms convey an "awareness of the difference and distance that separate a historiographic text from the history it purports to represent."[28] Phyllis Rackin says that

> What distinguishes the Renaissance [from the medieval period's use of anachronisms] is the ... recognition of temporal distance that alienated a nostalgic present from a lost historical past. Typically, medieval writers of history display no sense of anachronism, although they use it constantly. When a thirteenth-century Florentine chronicler reports that once when the wife of Catiline was at mass[29] in the church of Fiesole on Easter morning, a centurion went up and spoke to her, he uses an anachronism. When the Fool in *King Lear* says, "This prophecy Merlin shall make, for I live before his time" (III.ii.95), he expresses a sense of anachronism.[30]

Rackin's example clearly shows that occasionally Shakespeare playfully chose to draw attention to the anachronistic nature of the history plays, revealing his awareness of such fictional blending of the present with the past. Shakespeare wrote the plays now known as the second tetralogy, *Richard II*, *1 Henry IV*, *2 Henry IV*, and *Henry V*, between 1595–1599[31]; they are set in the period of the late 1300s through the mid–1400s. Rackin writes:

> Often, Shakespeare ... takes advantage of a customary poetic license ... telescoping two or three battles into one decisive encounter, altering the order in which events occurred, or manipulating the ages of historical characters to make a dramatic point.[32]

Shakespeare changes the historical record for specific purposes, creating competitive tension between Hotspur and Prince Hal as peers, and extending Queen Margaret's life so that she provides a direct connection to the preceding events in the *Henry VI* plays as well as a damning commentary on Richard III's actions. The medium of drama often licenses such fictional changes as practical and necessary.

Another example of an anachronism in *1 Henry IV* is when Prince Hal says that "The Douglas ... is reputed to be such a good shot that he can kill a flying sparrow with his pistol (II.iv.345–46). The Variorum edition of *1 Henry IV* reminds us that pistols were not yet invented in the days of Henry IV"[33]; the *Oxford English Dictionary* indicates that the term "pistol" was first used in English to refer to a small firearm in the late 16th century, when these plays were written. Of course, this also means that one of the characters shouldn't be named Pistol, either. Rackin notes that "Poins ... wears the peach-colored silk stockings that were a new fashion in sixteenth-century England, and ... Hal indulges in the sack that no one in England drank before the time of Henry VIII."[34] Rackin also observes that "In the Boar's Head Tavern, [Prince Hal] plays practical jokes and rubs elbows with a dissolute crew whose social rank is far beneath his own. He behaves, in short, like an aristocrat at an Elizabethan public theater."[35] Textual references in the plays draw attention to anachronistic weaponry, fashion, and behaviors familiar to the late 16th century audience, connecting the present culture producing the play to the setting of the play, eliding the historical distance between the two. Such elision makes the past more clearly relatable to the present to viewers who might not otherwise recognize parallels between the two. It's also often just entertaining when audiences recognize that an item is a recent innovation, yet they see it worn or used by someone in a prior century.

The *Deadwood* series aired from 2005–2007 on HBO; it was set in the late 1870s. In the first season, Sol Star tries to loosen up his anxious business partner Seth Bullock by telling him that "Coming out with your fly down might strike the wrong note" before they step outside their hardware tent to start hawking their wares ("Deadwood" 1.1). Zippers weren't used in pants in 1876[36]; Bullock's fly would have been open or closed, instead of up or down. This exchange adds humor to the scene and illustrates Star's familiarity with Bullock; he knows his friend is nervous about trying something new in trading his badge for entrepreneurism. Although the television series suggests that Bullock and Hickok arrived in Deadwood on the same day and spent several weeks in camp together, in actuality, Bullock arrived in Deadwood August 1, 1876, the day before Wild Bill Hickok was killed by Jack McCall. Hickok had arrived two weeks earlier. This change allows a friendship to develop between Bullock and Hickok, providing the impetus for Bullock to pursue McCall beyond the camp. Clothing and friendship anachronisms provide humor and emotional connections that influence viewer perceptions of Bullock, in particular.

Joanie Stubbs, a prostitute at the Bella Union who becomes brothel owner of the Chez Ami, is presented anachronistically as well. Linda Mizejewski notes that Stubbs fit the then-current televisual ideal of the femme lesbian, conventionally attractive, with few references to her sex life similar to lesbians on *The L Word*, debuting on Showtime in 2004.[37] Stubbs, Mizejewski claims, "exemplifies [the series'] movement toward modernity" through her transition from prostitute, "her work and identity tied to her body and gender," to becoming an independent businesswoman, "neither wife nor prostitute and thus not defined by a relationship to men."[38] Stubbs represents a modern figure, further blurring the lines between the prostitute Trixie and the wealthy wife Alma, and offering an alternative existence to either of these women with their dependence upon individual men, notable from the moment she participates in Swearengen's business conversation with Tolliver, especially when she quips in response to Swearengen's apology for his "French" (i.e. profanity), "Oh, I speak French" ("Reconnoitering the Rim" 1.3). Not only does Stubbs evolve in her dependence upon men, but she also develops a romantic relationship with Jane Canary. This revision of the Calamity Jane legend speaks to contemporary politics and culture; in the year that *Deadwood* debuted, 2004, Massachusetts was the first state to approve same-sex marriage.[39] Mizejewski adds that Jane's

> narrative trajectory, from Bill Hickok to Joanie Stubbs, delineates *Deadwood*'s narrative arc from traditional ideas and stories of the West, in which power resided in the body of the gunfighter, to the modern West, where power is decentralized, no longer phallic nor exclusively tied to the gun, the most obvious symbol of masculine power.[40]

Both story arcs, Joanie's and Jane's, trace a cultural shift in power and profit away from the body and onto the external, the communal, instead. Their relationship is presented as known and accepted by their friends, such as Charlie Utter, who provides them with the gift of Bill's buffalo blanket. In addition, one scene shows them walking arm-in-arm together down the main street of Deadwood, leading the children to the new school made possible by Joanie, while the procession is followed up by a heterosexual married couple, Seth and Martha Bullock, walking together. However, the romantic presentation of the two couples bookending the children is somewhat negated by Jane's near-constant drunken state and advancing cirrhosis, necessitating assistance from Joanie.

Departures from Documented History

The Henriad and *Deadwood* depart from strict adherence to those historical sources, fictionalizing multiple aspects of the setting, events, and historic figures. The bard freely adapts details to suit dramatic needs and to serve as Tudor propaganda. For example, it is accurate that Richard II was deposed by his cousin Henry Bolingbroke, with the help of the Duke of Northumberland and his son, Henry "Hotspur" Percy, then had to suppress rebellions, one of which was led by the Percy family. In Shakespeare's *Richard II*, the king makes a number of very articulate and powerful speeches, which I analyze in Chapters 3 and 6. In Holinshed's *Chronicle*, Richard II isn't documented as a skillful rhetorician[41]; however, this change allows Richard to articulate the lessons he has learned as a result of his fall from power, eliciting audience sympathy. Shakespeare appears to have combined Richard's two wives, Anne and Isabel, into one—a wife closer to his own age, like Anne, but from France, like Isabel. Unlike how they're presented in *1 Henry IV*, Henry "Hotspur" Percy and Henry "Prince Hal" Bolingbroke were not peers in age; Hotspur was several decades older than Prince Hal, closer to King Henry IV's age. Making Hotspur and Prince Hal peers allows Shakespeare to set up a number of contrasts between not only Hotspur and Prince Hal, but also Hotspur and Falstaff to emphasize and illustrate the necessary moderate qualities of a good king, which we see the short-lived Henry V emerge as. In addition, as Kurtz notes, the English history play served as "patriarchal Tudor historiography" focused on the public political male domain, which emphasized "power and conquest through aggression" and viewed women and the domestic sphere they occupied as "powerless."[42]

The conventions of the English history play, then, with its function of supporting the Tudor monarchy, limit the way the play presents the past to emphasize that which is favorable to the Tudor ancestors of Elizabeth I, the monarch under whose reign Shakespeare was writing these history plays, and the plays restrict protagonists to male historical figures. Of course, it was also strategic to avoid portraying female rulers in a critical light, unless they were foreign, given that such dramatic critique could easily be viewed as commenting on Elizabeth's reign. In addition, the English history play emphasizes public political conflict, minimizing or ignoring the domestic sphere. Women's marginalized but important roles in these genres are addressed more fully in Chapter 5.

Shakespeare's second history tetralogy traces the beginning of the Wars of the Roses, while his first history tetralogy follows the conclusion of them, which takes the form of Richmond's victory over Richard III on the battlefield, resulting in Richmond taking the throne as Henry VII, and Richmond's marriage to Elizabeth of York; they were Elizabeth I's grandparents. The play's ending suggests that order has been restored and it leads conclusively and undoubtedly to the reign of Queen Elizabeth I, omitting any references suggesting otherwise. While she is clearly Henry VIII's daughter, debate over the legitimacy of her birth lingered, since her father had named himself Supreme Head of the Church of England, which served to pressure the English clerical leadership to grant his request for an annulment from his first wife Katherine of Aragon in order to marry Anne Boleyn, Elizabeth's mother. The closest Shakespeare offers to a critique of monarchical pressure on clergy appears in *Henry V*, with the monarch demanding the bishops approve his claim to the throne of France before he embarks on a war to "reclaim" that land for England.

Milch also plays with history, keeping his Farnum and Swearengen single, making the Reverend Smith an epileptic and changing his roadway murder to a mercy killing, and changing Bullock's childhood sweetheart Martha to the widow of his elder brother.[43] He adds other non-historical figures, such as Trixie, Brom and Alma Garret, Cy Tolliver, Joanie Stubbs, and Whitney Ellsworth to tell the story he wants to tell focusing on Deadwood's shift from a lawless environment to a community bound by certain codes of behavior. Jason Jacobs notes, the series includes historical figures and events, but it refuses to be "confined" by them.[44] The focus of the narrative instead lies in developing individual characters' story arcs in conjunction with some adherence to historical legend or fact. Milch also makes Bullock and Swearengen eventual allies as opposed to adversaries who divided Deadwood into lawful and unlawful sections over which each asserted authority.[45] This allows the writers some dramatic license for exploring issues of character growth, shifting alliances, mundane personal conflicts, and humor, along with tracking larger-than-life historical figures and events.

In addition to departing from documented history, *Deadwood* challenges the established mythology of the American West. As Klein writes, Westerns "allow audiences to continually work through and thus 'naturalize' the violence of Manifest Destiny (Schatz 47)"; she adds that "The Western thus implies that, while the Westward expansion was a violent process, this violence was ultimately justified."[46] Such nostalgic representations of the Western hero invariably portray him as the fastest to draw a gun, but never the initiator of such confrontations.[47] Yet *Deadwood* shows us otherwise when the hero-figure Hickok does draw first, against Tom Mason, raising questions about the idealized image of the old West most of us carry in our memories from our school days. Joseph Millichap writes that "Milch's finest creations, especially *Deadwood*, employ a distinctive, diverse, and mannered style to delineate a harshly naturalistic vision of the dark and divided depths within the American national character, an identity simultaneously and paradoxically both innocent and corrupt."[48] This mix of innocence and corruption, redemption and damnation, is portrayed in every episode of the series through the interactions of its large cast of characters.

Settings: Unstable Political Environments

The historical settings of *Richard II*, *Henry IV*, and *Deadwood* feature a similar unstable political climate. Civil war or rebellion is a common theme in the *Richard II* and the *Henry IV* plays, tracking the origins of the Wars of the Roses, the familial political conflict between cousins. This conflict lasted until 1485, with the Tudor rule uniting the two warring branches of the family. Most American Western films are set in the years just following the Civil War; so, too, is *Deadwood* in the 1870s. Garber describes "The England of *Henry IV* [as] a fallen world, a world, we might say, made up too much of politics and plotting, and not enough fellowship and love."[49] This description of setting is also applicable to Deadwood, which is in the process of defining itself, becoming an ordered community and doing so in the wake of Civil War divisions. As such, the focus of the series is often on strategic alliances among the men and efforts to sustain some kind of independence or power through the shifting status of Deadwood from mining camp to annexation as part of the United States. As Daniel Salerno notes, "*Deadwood* is ... about what Foucault called *governmentality*—the need for the few to govern the many—and about the role of both actions and language in this 'strange discourse' of power."⁵⁰ *Deadwood*, like *Richard II* and the *Henry IV* plays, explores shifts in influence, power, and order in the face of competing and conflicting interests of personal profit, justice, fairness, and the responsibility of community-building.

Both *Richard II* and *Deadwood* open with historic images related to justice that are familiar to English and American viewers and that speak to national mythology. The play's opening features a conflict of honor and justice between two noblemen brought before a king as the arbitrator of conflicts. The television series opens with a marshal, an agent of justice, writing something while a jailed prisoner watches him. In both opening scenes, we initially see exactly what we might expect to see in these historically-set works, with recognizable scenarios and stock characters. Even the street scenes in *The Hollow Crown's Henry IV* plays and *Deadwood* are surprisingly and strikingly similar: crowded, muddy, and lined with vendors under tents, some holding up knives and freshly butchered animals. Both provide an atmosphere of dirty, bloody, overcrowded, and temporary commercial competition. Both suggest opportunity and danger simultaneously, given the presence of crowds mixing the social classes, and the goods and money present. In the history plays, the king's court is the center of power and in productions the throne is often elevated so that the king sits at a level higher than his advisors or courtiers. The throne is usually raised so that the king, although seated, remains at eye-level with courtiers who are standing. In *Richard II*, when Bolingbroke and Richard meet again after Bolingbroke's banishment, Richard is in Bristol castle, on an upper outdoor level looking down on Bolingbroke's approach, signifying the initial positions of power each occupies. Even when Falstaff and Prince Hal take turns role-playing as King Henry IV in the tavern in productions of *1 Henry IV*, whoever is playing the king is often seated atop a table, elevating him above the individual playing his son and the crowd watching. Elevated location also signifies power in *Deadwood*, in that "the men own the town from the balconies," watching interactions in the thoroughfare; "these settings indicate a concern for surveillance, control and power" in addition to emphasizing "the series' obsession with point of view."⁵¹ Perspective plays an important role in both series' themes, as I discuss later in this chapter.

Shakespeare's second tetralogy, like his other history plays, raises questions of legitimate political authority as it explores the characteristics of a "good king." But these plays also deliberately complicate that question, leading as they do into the beginning of the Wars of the Roses, the struggle for the throne of England between Lancaster and York, two rival branches of the royal House of Plantagenet, which occurred from 1455 to 1485. Michael Hattaway notes that in his history plays Shakespeare "was concerned not just with chronicle and personality but with institutions: in particular, with the fissures of court politics."⁵² Both sets of his history tetralogies "move from an outbreak of civil faction to the eventual triumph of political stability,"[53] but Shakespeare chooses to tell this historical tale in reverse order, as his first tetralogy (*Henry VI* and *Richard III*) provides the conclusion to the Wars of the Roses.

The second tetralogy follows the beginning of these wars. *Richard II* features an ineffectual, corrupt monarch deposed by a forceful cousin leading an army, with an apparently justified claim of righting a wrong. Henry Bolingbroke's strategy is a clever and effective one, seemingly motivated by a legitimate claim to his usurped inheritance. Although Bolingbroke is banished for a set period of time that has not yet run its limit, his father, John of Gaunt, dies, and Richard seizes Gaunt's property, which should pass to his eldest son, per the law of primogeniture. Bolingbroke claims to have broken his banishment only to reclaim what was rightfully his. This play asks under what conditions is it acceptable for a legitimate monarch to be deposed by force. It's a risky question to raise in late 16th century England, where some subjects question Elizabeth I's claim to the throne. *Deadwood* raises the question of what conditions warrant collective violence and by whom is such a response authorized; it raises these questions in the wake of the 9/11 terrorist attacks on the United States. Both sets of work use historical settings to explore the answers to questions in their current culture.

Once Bolingbroke has become King Henry IV in the plays of the same title, he remains haunted by his role in Richard's deposition and regicide as possible precedent for challenges to his own monarchy. In *2 Henry IV*, his remorse keeps emerging in lines like these: "God knows, my son, / By what bypaths and indirect crook'd ways / I met this crown…" (4.5.182–184), "For all the soil of the achievement goes / With me into the earth" (4.5.188–189), "It seemed in me / But as an honour snatched with boist'rous hand," (4.5.189–190) and "How I came by this crown, O God forgive" (4.5.217). He is also worried about his legacy and England's future, given the uncertainty of succession with a seemingly wayward heir, despite his advisor's reassurance that the prince will ultimately "[Turn] past evils to advantages" (4.4.78). Concern about succession was also an issue during Elizabeth I's entire reign, since she was an unmarried female monarch with no surviving legitimate siblings, nephews, or nieces. Although the two plays are titled *Henry IV parts one* and *two*, they focus more on Prince Hal than his father, as the line count per character easily illustrates. In part one, King Henry IV has 341 lines to Prince Hal's 551 and Hotspur's 562.[54] In part two, King Henry IV has 296 lines compared to Prince Hal's 292 lines.[55] Falstaff has more lines than either of them; in each play, his line count runs over 600.[56] Obviously, King Henry IV is not the sole central figure in these plays that bear his name, rather his legacy and heir—as well as competing influences on him—are an equal or even more elevated focus.

If Shakespeare's second tetralogy opens with the recognizably historical image of two knights appearing before a king to settle a dispute, *Deadwood*'s first episode introduces an equally recognizable and distinctly American historical figure: the gunfighter. Soon-to-be-ex–Marshal Seth Bullock's gunslinger status is made apparent by his costuming in a trim, dark, three-piece suit and hat with gun holster at his hip, his capability with a gun, and his quick ability to identify threats to social order. Wild Bill Hickok, an already legendary gunfighter at the end of his career, comes to Deadwood to pursue his fortune. These two men recognize almost immediately these similarities they share, beyond their past work as U.S. marshals. They both possess the "'gunfighter' understanding of how the world works," that "the world is a hostile place, human motives are rarely good, and outcomes depend not on right but on the proper deployment of might"; they also both express a strong sense of irony and self-deprecating humor which furthers their friendship quickly.[57] Drawing on Slotkin's study of the gunfighter on film, Witherspoon observes, "the morally righteous and often aristocratic gunfighter is suggestive of a (mythical) historical moment of social stability (*Gunfighter Nation* 401)."[58] *Deadwood*'s first season moves toward and past the murder of Bill Hickok, suggesting a transition is taking place; the gunfighter belongs to the past already. Even our introduction to Hickok foreshadows his fate; we first see him laid out in the back of a wagon like the corpse he is soon to become. In addition to cultural change symbolized in the end of the gunfighter era with Hickok's death, Nicolas S. Witschi observes that "just about every one of *Deadwood*'s thirty-six episodes features a significant arrival or departure from the camp."[59] This revolving door of inhabitants as the camp continues to grow also means a constantly shifting social and political dynamic as the camp transitions to a town and then to part of the U.S.

The struggle of cultural change from individual pursuits of honor to communal collaboration is emphasized in *Deadwood*'s three seasons; in season two, Swearengen observes, "Who impressed me at that meeting was Bullock, that avoided putting his pet interests—innocence, so forth, guilt, fucking who did what to fucking who—before the needs of the fucking camp" ("E.B. was Left Out" 2.7). That same struggle and form of narrative can also be seen in the classic Western films *Red River* (1948) and *The Man Who Shot Liberty Valance* (1962). Pippin describes both films as "involv[ing] a multilayered reflection on what it would mean to submerge the drive to distinction, honor, glory, and aristocratic independence to the demands of security, cooperation, and peace."[60] With a large cast of recurring characters, multiple and shifting narrative points of view that also shift viewers' attention from the personal to the communal and back again, and compromises of personal gain to achieve collective stability, *Deadwood* is an obvious heir to the classic Western films that precede it in some ways.

The Western film genre often features emerging communities in the process of change or challenge. Pippin notes that "many great Westerns are ... about" foundings, "societies in transition—in situations of, mostly lawlessness (or corrupt and ineffectual law) that border on classic 'state of nature' theories. The question often raised is that of how legal order ... is possible, under what conditions it can be formed and command allegiance."[61] For the history plays, the question usually raised asks what characteristics constitute a "good king" and the plays present both exemplary models, Henry V, for an example, and corrupt ones, Richard III, as another. The Western film "[p]resent[s] mythically, the problem [of] the transition from the feudal patriarchal authority that arose in the pre-legal situation of the frontier to a more fraternal, modern form; and the films are about the psychic costs of such a transition."[62] Shakespeare's history plays focus on disruptions to established monarchical rule, civil war, regicide, and a temporary political instability as the emerging victor in the battle asserts, or reasserts, his authority with the support of his subjects. The resolution following such disruptions is not always simple or complete. Often, a sense of unease and unanswered questions accompany it.

Using the Past to Meditate on the Present

Performance art, in the form of films, television shows, plays, and musicals, often focuses on the past, because we use the past to help us understand the present and attempt to predict the future. Although some aspects of the past may seem distant and removed from our present, writers frequently look at how similar events, figures, or issues have emerged in the past, how they were discussed, debated, or fought over, and what resolution, if any, came out of the conflict. A more recent example of this kind of artistic exploration between past and present is Lin-Manuel Miranda's Broadway phenomenon *Hamilton* (2015), which uses a figure from the United States' founding to raise questions about race, social and economic status, immigration, education, communication, sex, friendship, influence, gender, and power in the present. Such texts also often present the personal as a microcosm of the national. One of the purposes of the American Western film, according to some critics, is to anatomize history, revealing gaps and contradictions in the commonly accepted and rarely questioned established mythology of the American frontier. David Drysdale writes that Bazin declares the Western's objective isn't to just "reconstruct history," but to "deconstruct" it, "expos[ing] its inconsistencies" and "emphasiz[ing] the Western's mythic role ... help[ing] audience[s] internalize historical matters."[63]

In particular, late 20th and early 21st century Western films, such as *Unforgiven* (1992), *3:10 to Yuma* (original 1957; remake 2007), and *True Grit* (original 1969; remake 2010) have offered a critical meta-commentary on some conventions of the traditional Western genre. It's worth noting that two remakes of popular Western films emerged roughly fifty years later, both offering significant changes from the original films. Writing about *Deadwood*, Jacobs says that "Like many revisionist Westerns, it is interested in the very nature of history as a 'lie agreed upon,'"[64] a description that is also used as the title for two episodes of the series. In addition, a couple of studies have examined *Deadwood* as having been Milch's response to 9/11,[65] seeking removal from the present given horrific national trauma, but choosing an historic setting that would still permit exploration of some aspects of national anxiety regarding American values and identity related to that event. This suggests that we turn to art, not just a means of comfort in times of crisis, but also as a means of meditating simultaneously on the past and the present, with the hope of making better decisions for our collective future.

We can see a similar metacriticism at work in Shakespeare's *2 Henry IV*, which features the allegorical figure of Rumor spreading false information at the play's opening and a comic and apologetic epilogue figure at the play's end, directly deflecting speculation that Falstaff is based on a real person, Sir John Oldcastle. *Henry V* includes a recurring chorus commenting on the limits of stage drama to represent war scenes, interrupting the action repeatedly, asking for the audience's participation to imagine more than is presented on stage, and acknowledging a keen self-awareness of how this beloved monarch is being presented. In the prologue, the Chorus invites the audience to "Piece out our imperfections with your thoughts" (*Henry V* 0.0.23) and, later,

> Vouchsafe to those that have read the story
> That I may prompt them; and of such as have,
> I humbly pray them to admit th'excuse
> Of time, of numbers, and due course of things,
> Which cannot in their huge and proper life
> Be here presented [*Henry V* 5.0.1–6].

The Chorus warns that historical details have been left out of the play, notes that some events and time frames have been condensed or omitted, and acknowledges that there is much that the audience's imagination will have to fill in. The Chorus opens and closes the play, as well as interrupts it three times, calling attention to the limitations of theater and of history itself, to include the whole truth in its complex entirety.[66] In the epilogue, the Chorus describes the play as "In little room confining mighty men, / Mangling by starts the full course of their glory" (3–4), with a play on the use of stanzas, Italian for "little room," attempting to contain larger-than-life powerful historical figures and damaging in abrupt movements the fullness of their achievements. The role of creativity in national myth-building is nothing new, even in Shakespeare's time. As Phyllis Rackin and Jean Howard note:

> Nations are artificial creations, and the unity of a nation is a carefully constructed fiction. In Benedict Anderson's telling phrase, nations are "imagined communities," that is, they are communities that are imagined into being by certain cultural practices and ideas [Anderson 1983:14–16].[67]

They add that "discursive innovations such as mapmaking, linguistic standardization, and the development of a self-consciously national literature also contributed to the nation-building process. It is important to recognize, however, that an imagined community can never be as unified as it is represented as being."[68] At best, stories of wholly unified nations historically convey a longing or anxiety in the present culture, seeking models of stability from its past and creating them where none exist. Rackin and Howard also observe that the history plays served to reinforce a providential perspective of the Tudor dynasty. As such, they selectively presented historical figures and events that flattered Tudor ancestors and foreshadowed, so to speak, the current sovereign under whose reign Shakespeare was writing. They also sought to alleviate anxieties and contradictions regarding the monarch's claim to the throne, marginalizing or altogether erasing some figures and events that complicated the providential view of the Tudors.

All of the characters in *Deadwood* are in the mining camp to start anew or to take advantage of those who are, yet they carry with them the psychological baggage of their past. As Dudley points out, *Deadwood*'s main characters all seem to be "defined by the trauma of lost or inadequate" family members or lovers and find themselves "repeatedly confronted with instances of the abject—thrown back, against their will, to their own painful past."[69] As much as they—and Henry IV—try to leave the past behind them, they find they are unable to do so; their present is predicated on their pasts, forcing them to return to their own personal histories in an attempt to negotiate their problems in the present. Jacobs writes that humans inherently seek to better understand the present by looking to "patterns of the past," making *Deadwood* not so much about "the absence" of community, order, or law, "but about the continued entangling presence of the past, and our efforts in the here and now to live it."[70] This "continued entangling presence of the past, and our efforts in the here and now to live in it" is applicable to issues raised in the English history plays and the *Deadwood* series, issues of legitimate versus illegitimate political authority, consequentialism, the personal versus the public good, and personal sacrifice or compromise to benefit others. Worden notes that the nostalgia that colors most art depicting the historic West is contradicted by scholarship recognizing how Western texts inevitably reflect the time and culture of their creation just as much their historical setting; he adds that "This historicist view [emphasizes] the Western genre itself [as] politically conservative: at best a justification for nationalism, at worst an alibi for American imperialism, racism, paternalism, and violence."[71] The classical Western, then, has often seemed to justify nationalism or make excuses for American domination, discrimination, and violence as various aspects of particular films or television series have reflected current events in the culture that has produced them. The revisionist Western, however, offers something more, challenging and critiquing some aspects of the traditional Western conventions as it includes references to parallels in the culture that created it.

Because of the television series *Deadwood*'s unstable political setting, not to mention opening with "the insufficiently harnessed ambitions of ego and vanity" for many of the men seeking to advance their status, it occupies a position "[that] allows it to meditate on the nature of settlement and its relationship to contemporary society."[72] Developed in the age of the burgeoning obsession with social media presentations of the self and its new venues for narcissistic displays, *Deadwood* offered a prime opportunity for an analysis of capitalism, technology, ambition, and the remaking of the public self. Swearengen's astute use of knowledge as power over others becomes limited when the camp becomes more populated, more developed, and when the telegraph wires and poles are installed. These changes all speak to an historic culture in transition. Horace Newcomb and Paul Hirsch claim that television drama formats and genres soften, distance, and make more palatable to viewers a reflection of "conflicts ongoing in American social experience and cultural history."[73] The setting of the past offers a deliberate distancing to analyze political conflict and/or social issues in modern American culture. Sarah Hagelin argues that

> those elements that make the show difficult for some viewers—baroque language, the absence of episodic structure, seemingly incomprehensible plots about treaties and land annexation—allow *Deadwood* to say something about the violence that haunts the founding of America as a nation and that drives its westward expansion.[74]

This violence haunting America's origins lingers at the edges, and sometimes even the center, of historical records of slavery, broken treaties, attempted genocide, racism, and imperialism in the name of progress, under the guise of Manifest Destiny.

Shakespeare's second tetralogy attempts to create a unified, positive, and providential portrait of the past leading to the rule of Elizabeth Tudor. Cohen claims that "[i]n the Henry plays, history ... is a means of negotiating with the present. The retrospective mode animates the present, and the past is a felt and perceptible force that directs and positions that present."[75] The attempted "reconstructions of the past" found in the history plays, Cohen goes on to say, "reflect the persistence of a need ... to construct something whole out of something inherently fragmented. The past is known only in bits and pieces."[76] Cohen also claims that *"Henry IV* describes the inevitable process by which real events are transmogrified into myth and, hence, national consciousness."[77] *Henry V* is even more self-conscious about its role and its shortcomings in English mythmaking, necessitating direct, explicit prompts for audience participation.

Audiences watching *Deadwood* know that the camp eventually becomes part of the state of South Dakota. Ina Rae Hark observes that

> Since annexation is inevitable, the first two seasons of *Deadwood* deal with the camp positioning itself to be annexed on terms most favourable to its interests. Secondarily, members of the camp contemplate the changes that individuals may undergo as they create or renew their identities as Americans.[78]

This reading suggests a dual historical view of the community's transition and individual characters' transformation as they work together, determining their individual places in this new environment they are assisting in creating and defining. The characters' and community "transformations don't point so much to America requiring a conformity of appearance and behavior but rather to the capacity to reach beyond insular, parochial identities and alliances."[79] The common good comes to prevail over individual benefit, at least temporarily, to achieve communal progress or advancement. As Patrick McGee asserts regarding the ending of the Howard Hawks directed classic Western film *Red River*, it

> holds in some kind of imaginary resolution the contradiction at the heart of American democracy between the tendency toward authoritarian political figures who would monopolize the use of violence (both nationally and internationally) and the democratic quest for communal solutions to social problems, between radical individualism and collective interests.[80]

Like many other historically-based artistic forms, *Red River* creates the resolution audiences seek where there is none. The contradictory desire of democracy for strong leaders who aren't hesitant to use force *and* for communal solutions to social problems doesn't allow for easy or quick compromise between the two. Instead, art can present what such resolutions might look like, in many different forms, including recognition of interconnectedness as a necessity and strength to be fostered and through which we might find solutions.

There are a number of ways that critics and audiences have perceived *Deadwood*'s relationship with the present. Drysdale claims that, in its exploration of Bullock's complicated alliances in the camp, "*Deadwood* interrogates the position of the Western hero, and, by proxy, that of the USA in contemporary politics," ultimately as one in which "authority is consistently morally compromised."[81] This cynical perspective of political power and corruption offers little hope for non-corrupt leadership's facilitation of significant community progress. Other critics examine how *Deadwood* emphasizes the role of capitalism as a driving force in community development. Worden claims that "*Deadwood* revises the Western by focusing on the marketplace" with even the pilot episode emphasizing economics as core to the initial community-building in the camp.[82] Throughout the series we see characters coming to Deadwood to start over, to start a new business, and to expand business interests; we also see alliances formed and conflicts between competing marketplace interests, most notably the Gem Saloon and the Bella Union Saloon over prostitution and games of chance. Much of Al Swearengen's concern in the initial season of the series is over the possibility of other such competitors emerging in the camp, taking business away from the Gem.

By the third season, though, the threat to the entire community comes from an outside financial force in the form of George Hearst. Worden observes that "*Deadwood* offers numerous examples of how strategic alliances grow increasingly complex when determined by entrepreneurial self-interest."[83] Former adversaries put aside their differences in the face of an outside threat to the entire community and pledge to work together, at least temporarily, to achieve a common goal, much like we see with the unified forces of the Scottish, Welsh, Irish, and English fighting against France in *Henry V*. With capitalism presented as a significant driving force in Deadwood, McGee says, "If anyone challenges the force that justifies the right to wealth, they must somehow do it without the use of force or end up validating the very principle that justified social inequality in the first place. Yet it seems impossible to challenge force without force."[84] But we see the shrewd Swearengen do just that in season three of *Deadwood* by having Mrs. Ellsworth complete her walk to the bank and through his encouragement of the publication of Bullock's letter about the murdered Cornish miners, as I address in Chapter 3. These actions and their relative success suggest the possibility of growth and non-violent resolutions to communal conflicts.

Another means of connecting the past to the present in both the history plays and the television series comes through the interplay of cultures featured, suggestive of the beginnings of an intercultural, global exchange. In *Richard II*, we see Richard addressing England's conflicts with Ireland and his reliance on Welsh troops to face the threat of Bolingbroke; in the Henry IV plays we're shown England's battles with Scottish troops led by the Douglas and Welsh troops led by Glendower and Hotspur. *Henry V* pointedly presents the king leading combined troops from Scotland, Wales, Ireland, and England against France. The plays present a positive perspective on England's ambitious expansion and domination of these other cultures in its past, reinforcing England's right under Queen Elizabeth I to extend its reaches even further abroad through imperialism. In *Deadwood*, with its focus on capitalism and the marketplace, George Hearst's multinational business interests include importing Chinese prostitutes and Cornish miners to the Deadwood camp and exploring the potential of Liberian gold mines, as well as the gold mines in Deadwood, not yet part of the U.S.[85] Viewing *Deadwood* in this way emphasizes its critique of unregulated capitalism, specifically in the form of multinational corporations' dehumanizing treatment of workers as a means to the profitable end. The brutal consequences of such treatment threaten the entire existence of community. Such a reading of *Deadwood* obviously emphasizes its connection to present concerns about human rights, racism, immigration, human trafficking, and outsourcing.

Worden also says that one of *Deadwood*'s strengths is the television series' ability to allegorize, to defamiliarize and mingle the past and the present symbolically in order to draw viewers in and "reframe" their understanding of both; in particular, he sees the language of the series doing this work, mixing high and low registers, eloquent and articulate one minute, base and vulgar the next.[86] It keeps viewers off-balance and attentive. One of *Deadwood*'s stylistic visual features serves a similar function. The rack-focus shot, where the camera focus shifts from the foreground to the background, forces viewers to look closer, seeing what has been hidden from them initially, often that one character has been observing another, unnoticed, or shifting from one character's facial expression to another's, revealing a completely different reaction. It emphasizes that our focus may limit our perspective; there is often much more happening in a scene than we realize because of that limited perspective. It's also a perfect metaphor for how the series engages with the present by its address of the past.

With a slight, but important, shift in focus, a scene or an episode is no longer just presenting an historical issue, but a current one, as well. Although the two characters may occupy the same space, they are distinctly separate from one another. In the first episode, we're given multiple examples of this, starting with a shot focused on the marshal, seated at his desk, writing something, his other arm in a sling; the shot then adjusts its focus to the prisoner in the cell, standing, behind the lawman, watching him closely, searching for an angle out of the situation he's in. The prisoner is loquacious, as he attempts to persuade the marshal to free him; the lawman, as befits a Western, is taciturn, but astute, as he recognizes the prisoner's objective. A second rack-focus shot comes in the No. 10 Saloon, with Ned Mason declaring he isn't risking his scalp to ride out to where the Metz family were slaughtered; the focus then shifts to the back of the bar and Wild Bill Hickok standing to offer protection against further Indian attacks ("Deadwood" 1.1). The imposing and legendary gunfighter's response shifts the tension in the bar and makes it impossible for Mason to refuse. This scene also initiates the friendship between Bullock and Hickok, linking their shared experience at quickly assessing a questionable situation or figure and responding immediately.

Universal Themes: Exploring the Human Condition

Both the television series and the plays explore the question of what it means to be human, to love, to possess ambition, to reflect on the positive and negative consequences of power, to acknowledge the often unforeseen difficulty of keeping power once it has been attained, and the difficult necessity of collaborating with others in establishing communal standards and civic authority. Freud famously "used Shakespearean characters as the models for some of his most influential case studies and theories about human behavior."[87] Melody Graulich claims that "despite its grisly subject matter, *Deadwood* fits Hawthorne's definition of the 'romance,' far more concerned with 'the truths of the human heart' than with fidelity to facts"[88] and that the series' themes include "surveillance, deception, disconnection, interpretation," and "insight into human nature."[89] One example of the series' emphasis on the "truths of the human heart" is the episode "Jewel's Boot is Made for Walking" (1.11), featuring Jewel's pursuit of a brace for her leg; we're shown her resilience in negotiating the treacherous terrain of the Deadwood thoroughfare to seek Doc Cochran out privately, her initiative in presenting the idea to him, and her persistence at persuading him to collaborate with her on it. We're also shown that she recognizes Doc's insecurities, too, and encourages him to think positively of himself, when they dance and she asks him to say, "I'm as nimble as a forest creature" in the first person, describing himself rather than her ("Jewel's Boot is Made for Walking" 1.11). Emphasizing these themes reflects another similarity with some of Shakespeare's more widely-known plays; "surveillance, deception, disconnection," and "interpretation" make me think immediately of *Hamlet* and *Much Ado About Nothing*, both of which focus on these same ideas but in very different ways given their respective genres of tragedy and comedy. In *Deadwood*, Al Swearengen has an elaborate system of surveillance utilizing a number of agents across the camp; E.B. Farnum reports on wealthy hotel guests Alma Garret and George Hearst, Trixie reports on potential economic threats from Alma Garret and Bullock and Star's hardware store, and Silas Adams reports on political threats from Claggett and Yankton.

Several critics agree that *Deadwood* explores what motivates people to make the choices they do, especially in relation to the violence that is a central characteristic of the Western genre. Jennilyn Merten states that this isn't a mindless violence, but one prompted by characters' inner lives and often only in reaction to the actions or words of others; she adds, too, that "Rather than sever[ing] intimacy, the varied forms of violence regularly become catalysts or disguises for kindness, empathy, and a developing solidarity between" a number of characters.[90] There are multiple examples of violence followed by collaborative support throughout the series, among them: Swearengen and

Bullock's supportive alliance, strengthened after their physical brawl in season two, Cy Tolliver and Charlie Utter's assistance of Joanie Stubbs, post-bloodbath at the Chez Ami in season two, and Dan Dority and Swearengen's moving exchange after Dority's public fight with Captain Turner in season three.

In *Richard II*, in addition to the political usurpation of the throne, more personal lessons are being learned by the protagonists and those watching them; "While Richard is learning the true nature of his limited human condition, 'great Bolingbroke' forgets his place in the order of things."[91] Richard is the rightful king of England, however, his behavior is decidedly not kingly, but selfish. As his political fall occurs, his character grows, demonstrating remorse and wisdom gained about the human condition and his own mortality that encourage audiences to sympathize with him, as I discuss in Chapter 6. Audiences are given insight into this change in Richard's perspective that allow us to view him differently than we initially might have. Viewers are given a similar opportunity when it comes to Al Swearengen on *Deadwood*. Clearly introduced as a violent and dangerous force, a villain to counter Seth Bullock's heroic introduction, Swearengen's monologues reveal traumatic life events that shaped his perspective, providing audience insight into his past, which I discuss further in Chapter 3. Swearengen also experiences a debilitating illness—kidney stones—that serves to humanize him further. As his power in Deadwood diminishes and his physical health fails—first with his eyesight, requiring reading glasses—his likeability increases. Drysdale writes that, in the series, "neither 'good' nor 'evil' exist as absolute categories," noting that sometimes "the heroes' actions can be as suspect as the villains," thus allowing the series to engage in the deconstruction of the Western hero ("Deadwood").[92]

Deadwood doesn't present a romanticized version of its Western story. Some men, like Al Swearengen, commit heroic actions under dubious ethical motivations; other men, like Seth Bullock, commit despicable acts with good intentions. The women, per the Western genre, are portrayed as inherently good, which I discuss further in Chapter 5. Jacobs suggests that part of *Deadwood*'s brilliance lies in "its mixing of associations, probing for the feeling that moves the characters, the scene, us, without making them hostage to an insistence on clear meaning."[93] Much is left to viewer interpretation when it comes to what has motivated a particular action or restraint for a character. As Diane Cook notes, as the series progresses most if not all of the characters are shown as "conflicted," often over a moral dilemma wherein "their weaknesses [triumph] over [their] best intentions and better judgment."[94] Milch emphasizes human fallibility repeatedly. Similarly, Shakespeare presents ambivalent portraits of both Henry IV and Henry V as wholly ethical leaders.

Complex Narratives Featuring Moral Ambiguity

More sophisticated audiences also mean an expectation for increasingly complex and modern storytelling in both the history plays and the television drama. Compare the clearly delineated identification of the heroic Richmond and the villainous Richard III in *Richard III* with the morally ambiguous presentations of both Bolingbroke and Richard II in *Richard II*. These plays may have been written only a year apart, but they demonstrate Shakespeare playing with audience expectations and deliberately confusing—and controlling—audience sympathy toward lead characters in positions of power. While *Richard III* may satisfy the audience's desire for punishment of the villains and restoration of a stable and fair ruler to the throne, *Richard II* raises uncomfortable questions about legitimate authority that are never quite resolved. David Scott Diffrient notes the conflict between Al Swearengen and Seth Bullock also illustrates larger, universal, and complicated themes that blur boundaries between categories. He writes that *Deadwood*:

> torn between the chaos and order respectively personified by Swearengen and Bullock (who are constantly locking horns), oscillates between the earthy and the transcendent. Yet archetypal dichotomies and clearly delineated heroes and villains in this ultimately deconstructive Western give way to infinite shades of gray.[95]

Just as the television series features characters and plot arcs that blur boundaries between the bad and the good, the villain and the hero, activity and passivity, and masculinity and femininity, Shakespeare's Henriad, too, offers ambivalent portraits of rulers, fallen rulers, and the interplay between men in political and personal conflict with one another. Some scholars have pointed to the feminization of both Hotspur and Falstaff as counterpoints to Prince Hal's masculinity.[96] Shakespeare's presentation of Henry Bolingbroke's claim to the throne and his son's aggressive actions toward France once he himself is king raise ethical questions about the political choices made by both men. David Milch has said that "seeming absolute contraries contain each other,"[97] suggesting that a more complex portrayal of individuals in conflict with one another should provide a range of behaviors within any one character.

If one character serves as the voice of reason in the midst of conflict or crisis in either of these narratives, the histories or the television series, it would have to be the Duke of York in *Richard II* and the Reverend Smith in *Deadwood*.[98] York walks a delicate line in *Richard II*, continuing to observe policies and practices in serving the king and reminding others of the complex reality of the situation when the authority figure who should be fairly administering justice is its violator instead; he protests directly to the king when the monarch violates custom and perhaps sets dangerous precedent for others to do so as well, and, finally, York switches his loyalties when the times seem to call for it. Similarly, Westerfelhaus and Lacroix claim that

"Smith serves the community as its sole prophetic voice ... [extoling the necessity of community] to a community that is indifferent to or actively hostile towards those values."[99] One of the problems with this difficult position of speaking truth to power, though, is that it cannot be sustained in either of these narratives. York has no place in the *Henry IV* or *Henry V* plays. Instead, his role of reasonable mediator of conflict seems, in some ways, to be inherited by Prince Hal/Henry V himself. On *Deadwood*, Al Swearengen, "in an act of uncharacteristic kindness," gently smothers the Reverend Smith to put the debilitated and suffering man out of his misery; thus, "by the conclusion of *Deadwood*'s first season, the town has lost the man who had functioned as its moral conscience."[100] Some critics claim that Bullock inherits this role, eventually becoming "the narrator of the community conscience," evident in his letter to the family of Hearst's murdered mineworker in season three.[101]

The Western film under the direction of John Ford, Howard Hawks, or Sam Peckinpah, just to name a few, complicated the original Western moral formula that clearly delineated good guys from bad guys. As Pippin observes,

> what is true is that their presentations of conflict, hesitations, ambiguity, and crises largely concern characters trying to resolve issues of right, justice, responsibility, honor, and the claims of the public world versus the private, and that these situations are presented in both historical and psychological terms that greatly complicate any neat moral dividing line between characters, any straightforward assessment of events.[102]

Reflecting the complexity of the human condition, that each character contains both good and bad traits, the capacity for both good and evil acts, complicates easy moral categorization of characters. "At [*Deadwood*'s] core," writes Cook, "lies a profound empathy and respect for humanity in all its nobility *and* reprehensibility."[103] Merten says *Deadwood* is "a Western about being a Western ... neither in love with the Western nor out to teach it a lesson"[104]; she describes it as "a blunt, daring, and achingly curious exploration of the genre's preoccupation with violence from an endless and overlapping set of lenses."[105]

Some critics have seen connections between the American Western and an exploration of the human condition. Westerfelhaus and Lacroix describe the American Western as a genre that deliberately emphasizes "the division between civilization and so-called savagery" in order to explore the problem of "how to distinguish the former from the latter, in ourselves as well as in others."[106] The conflicts Milch highlights in *Deadwood* also explore this question, emerging from a setting in "genesis," in which we see how individuals in such a setting outside the boundaries of civilization or law must negotiate with one another repeatedly, forming and dissolving alliances to achieve common goals; in addition, this exploration also provides "a generically ripe historical setting as the stage for the fictional exploration of human nature itself."[107] If community is necessary not just to survival but to advance a culture, Milch's series explores the question of how community is formed among disparate individuals from all social and economic levels, with competing personal interests.

Audiences are given varied points of view on this process over the course of the series. Milch provides a range of characters' perspectives on tensions and events unfolding in the Deadwood camp, including the powerful, exemplified in Swearengen and later Hearst, too, and the seemingly powerless, seen in the prostitute Trixie, stable-keeper and blacksmith Hostetler, and cook-custodian Richardson, to name a few. Shakespeare often presents a range of humanity in his plays, especially in juxtaposing court scenes featuring the aristocracy and royalty with those of the tavern or street scenes featuring commoners, as we see in the *Henry IV* plays in particular. By being presented with multiple perspectives on events, audiences are encouraged to question their first impressions of these events and recognize the fragmented nature of the narrative. Repeatedly the idea of a single, unified perspective is challenged and resisted. As Cook observes, the series' "emphasis on the social and/or psychospiritual efficacy of understanding others' points of view is at least as important to story" as other aspects of the show.[108]

Conclusion

The Henriad and *Deadwood*, despite their distinct generic categorizations and the genre conventions each follows to some degree, share a surprising number of commonalities in their reshaping of national origin stories and their use of the past to meditate upon the present and the human condition. Analysis of genre conventions of the history play and the Western, settings of political instability and transition, and themes provides a macro-level perspective of initial parallels between Shakespeare's Henriad and *Deadwood*. However, at the micro-level, specific character alignments between the two offer a more striking means of understanding the two lead characters in the television series and their evolving relationship toward one another.

The first episode of HBO's *Deadwood* opens with Seth Bullock in Montana and closes with Al Swearengen in Deadwood—we've been given our framing devices of the two most important characters to watch as the series unfolds. Bullock and Swearengen are introduced as protagonist and antagonist in the pilot episode, but as the series progresses, the viewer learns that there is more to both of these men than that simple dichotomy. Their complicated relationship with one another can be better understood by viewing it through the lens of their counterparts in Shakespeare's *Henriad*. Chapter 2 analyzes Bullock as an amalgam of Henry "Hotspur" Percy, noted for his quick temper and honor, and Prince Hal/Henry V, with his apparent aversion to taking responsibility for the kingdom, as its heir.

2

Seth Bullock as "Hotspur" and Prince "Hal"

> SETH BULLOCK: *"What kind of man have I become, Sol?"*
> SOL STAR: *"I don't know. The day ain't fucking over yet."* ("Sold Under Sin" 1.12)

Seth Bullock is presented as a contradiction even in the pilot episode, enforcing the law in an unorthodox manner. If we interpret him as an amalgam of two young male characters who are foils to one another in Shakespeare's Henry IV plays, these contradictions begin to make more sense. Bullock is similar to Henry "Hotspur" Percy, from Shakespeare's *1 Henry IV*, in several ways: a young man associated with honor through his own actions and in the esteem of others, but one whose temper gets the best of him repeatedly and whose emphasis on honor sometimes comes across as self-righteous arrogance. Like Hotspur, Bullock is a man of action, stepping up when circumstances call for it, however this trait, combined with his emphasis on honor and his temper, often leads to uncontrolled violence. Because of this combination of characteristics, he is not suited for the role of politician. But, like Prince Hal, initially Bullock actively avoids serving the community of Deadwood in the most obvious way, as its sheriff, before stepping up to take on that responsible role in the community. Both Prince Hal and Bullock marry out of a sense of duty and obligation, for the care of others. Both Hotspur and Bullock are sexually drawn to women other than their wives. However, unlike Hotspur and Prince Hal, Bullock exhibits a sense of self-awareness and capacity for growth and change. All of these young men are in the process of becoming adult participants in public discourse, demonstrating the potential for leadership but in need of the right kind of older male guidance to achieve that potential. As such, they can also be seen to represent their nations, in that process of becoming, growing, in transition. These character comparisons provide striking parallels between the young male figures that also aid in identifying distinctions among them, helping us to view each of them more clearly.

While Hotspur is presented in Shakespeare's *1 Henry IV* as a static character, one who doesn't learn and grow, despite the advice of his elders, one who fails to know himself well, Prince Hal is portrayed as contriving to *appear* dynamic; revealed to the audience through soliloquy, he strategizes as to how to appear a reprobate who then reforms in order to win the people's support. He deliberately cultivates the appearance of growth, which demonstrates his political acuity. Unlike either Hotspur or Prince Hal, Seth Bullock demonstrates real growth, maturing as the series progresses, recognizing he is in need of some guidance and seeking out older males who can provide what he lacks.

Held in High Esteem by Others

The first mention of Hotspur is Westmoreland's praise to Henry IV at how the young man handled himself in battle defending the king against Glendower and his Welsh forces; he commends "the gallant Hotspur there, / Young Harry Percy" (*1 Henry IV* 1.1.52–53). The king refers to the prisoners of name taken by Hotspur in that battle as "an honourable spoil" and "a gallant prize," using the same language as Westmoreland (*1 Henry IV* 1.1.74–75). Westmoreland's reply, "it is a conquest for a prince to boast of," initiates the comparison between the two young men (*1 Henry IV* 1.1.76). King Henry acknowledges his envy that Northumberland "should be the father to so blest a son" (*1 Henry IV* 1.1.79). Shakespeare wants us to see Hotspur's *potential*: he is viewed by these older noblemen as honorable, brave, and loyal, and as perhaps a worthier heir to the throne than the prince himself.

Shortly thereafter, King Henry refers to his eldest son in a negative manner, as one upon whom "riot and dishonour stain the brow" (*1 Henry IV* 1.1.84). Even Hotspur later mockingly asks about the location of "the nimble-footed madcap Prince of Wales, / And his comrades, that doffed the world aside / and bid it pass" (*1 Henry IV* 4.1.95–97). The two young Henries are set up from the beginning of this play as being opposite in character, Hotspur exceeding the expectations of his elders and Prince Hal failing to meet them at all.

Late in the play, Prince Hal praises Hotspur to Worcester, Vernon, and the king in a speech that shows Prince Hal's awareness that others hold Hotspur in high esteem and acknowledges his own admiration for the young nobleman, excepting for his participation in the rebellion. The syntax of his speech is also a reprimand, beginning with "your nephew" (*1 Henry IV* 5.1.85) emphasizing Worcester's relationship to Hotspur, then asserts Hal's title "The

Prince of Wales" (*1 Henry IV* 5.1.86) in third person, rather than the more informal first person pronoun, and, lastly, names Henry Percy by his name, not his nickname. This offers praise of a nobleman, while at the same time asserting his own claim to the title of heir to the throne of England. Prince Hal praises Hotspur specifically for his bravery, daring, boldness, and two odd phrasings: "active-valiant" and "valiant-young" (*1 Henry IV* 5.1.90), emphasizing simultaneously Hotspur's propensity for quick, bold action and his youth, perhaps encouraging his father to forgive Hotspur's role in the rebellion. He uses "valiant" twice, noting Hotspur's strength and courage. The prince is also keenly aware of his own reputation in the eyes of the public and of Hotspur when he says, "For my part, I may speak it to my shame, / I have a truant been to chivalry; / And so I hear he doth account me too" (*1 Henry IV* 5.1.93–95). The language he applies to himself also suggests his own youth, a certain schoolboyishness, referring to himself as "truant" when it comes to manners and royal protocol and placing no blame on Hotspur for holding this negative view of Prince Hal.

When this news reaches Hotspur, he's skeptical, asking Vernon and Worcester how Prince Hal issued a challenge to him, "Seemed it in contempt?" (*1 Henry IV* 5.2.50). Vernon quickly corrects that assumption, using some form of the word "praise" four times in his brief response, noting that Prince Hal spoke of Hotspur like a history ("chronicle"), claiming that the praise circulating about Hotspur wasn't sufficient to the praise he deserves but also perhaps carrying a veiled threat in referencing Hotspur as a "chronicle," that which is past or over already (*1 Henry IV* 5.2.54–59). Vernon, however, emphasizes Prince Hal's sincerity. He also notes a drastic reformation of character in the prince's demeanor through self-correcting his youthful faults (*1 Henry IV* 5.2.61–64). He adds, "If he outlive the envy of this day, / England did never owe so sweet a hope, / So much misconstrued in his wantonness" (*1 Henry IV* 5.2.66–68). Vernon notes the prince's *potential* here, also using the language of youth in referring to the prince's "blushing cital," i.e., "recital" of himself, and how he "chid his truant youth" (*1 Henry IV* 5.2.1–64). He refers to Prince Hal as one simultaneously teaching others while learning himself. It's clear that he's impressed with the apparently reformed young man. He says that the prince has been "misconstrued in his wantonness," or misunderstood, as being "reckless, willful, or wild," "unruly, naughty, disobedient," or behaving with "extravagance or self-indulgence in appetite or imagination."[1] All of these definitions connect Prince Hal's reputation with Hotspur's own behavior when in an unprovoked rage, indicating the play's subtle chiasmus in how Vernon views both of these young men, and the effectiveness of Prince Hal's plan to present himself as a reformed reprobate.

After Prince Hal keeps his word, fighting to defend the king and even protecting him from an attack by the Douglas on the battlefield, King Henry

IV tells him "Thou hast redeemed thy lost opinion, / And showed thou mak'st some tender of my life / In this fair rescue thou hast brought to me" (*1 Henry IV* 5.4.48–50). The prince has proven himself loyal to his father and brave in battle in defending him.

After Prince Hal defeats Hotspur in battle (and kills him), he provides a surprisingly respectful eulogy (*1 Henry IV* 5.4.87–101). His impromptu eulogy begins with respect for his opponent's "great heart," noting his negative quality of "ill-weaved ambition" has diminished (*1 Henry IV* 5.4.87–88). He comments again that the kingdom was too small to contain such a great spirit, but absent that element, the body fits within two steps of earth. His comments focus on transformation, specifically reduction of his peer's greatness, although he calls for only Hotspur's strengths to be remembered and his flaws forgotten. The transformation of Hotspur also serves as a catalyst for the transformation in public perception of Prince Hal, who has acted courageously and admirably in defending his father's (and his own) claim to the throne. He has begun to prove himself a reliable, responsible heir to the crown.

On *Deadwood*, Seth Bullock is introduced as a highly responsible, reasonable, and amiable marshal. He's seated at a desk, pausing in writing something to think, in a jail with a prisoner behind bars watching him. He's neatly dressed in dark multiple layers. Our first impression of him is one of controlled, assured, capable, and reasonable authority, perhaps stoic, too, given the injury sustained in capturing the prisoner. Injured and outnumbered, he relies on his position of authority to enforce the law, regardless of the fact that he is leaving the badge behind immediately. He tells the drunken, rowdy, and armed mob gathered outside, "I'm executing sentence now and he's hanging under color of law" ("Deadwood" 1.1). Obviously, he takes his responsibility of enforcing the law seriously, even in circumstances that would easily excuse him from it.

Once he and Sol Star have set up their hardware tent for business in Deadwood, he offers a guarantee on goods to prospective buyers when he says, "We stand by our stock. Any item that don't do what it's supposed to do will be exchanged for one that does. And we'll be here for you to find us" ("Deadwood" 1.1). He also recognizes the soap hawker's game, warning him quietly to move his scam away from their legitimate business ("Deadwood" 1.1) and the man respectfully does so, tipping his hat to Bullock. He is presented as serious, fair-minded, and capable of supporting his threats toward others.

Bullock is also presented as a brave, active defender of the vulnerable against harm. When he first hears Ned Mason's story about the Indian massacre, he recognizes that it doesn't seem accurate. He forces Ned to tell the story in the No. 10 Saloon, emphasizing the part about a possible surviving child, and he offers to ride out to check for the child at the massacre site.

After he and Hickok have identified one another as former U.S. marshals, he confides in Hickok his doubts about Ned's tale ("Deadwood" 1.1). It's Seth Bullock who locates the surviving child and carries her as the men ride back toward camp. In camp, it's Bullock who dismounts and walks slowly but purposefully toward Ned Mason, who eyes him warily. The intention in Bullock's approach leads Hickok to ask Star how Bullock is with a gun before joining him to hold Mason accountable. Bullock calls Mason out for having committed the massacre, looking to rob the Metz family; he warns Mason, "Get down off your horse or face the consequences" ("Deadwood" 1.1). When Hickok asks, after Mason is shot off his horse which of them is responsible for the accurate hit, Bullock defers to Hickok's seniority and expertise ("Deadwood" 1.1). Our introduction to Bullock shows him to be highly responsible, confident and capable with a gun, an astute assessor of ill-intent in others, trusting of other former marshals, respectful, and protective toward the vulnerable and innocent.

Bullock is quickly held in high esteem by other men in the camp. As he's building a casket for Ned Mason, the Reverend Smith tells Johnny Burns that "Men like Mr. Seth Bullock raise a camp up" ("Deep Water" 1.2); Burns questions that, reminding Smith that it was Bullock who made the casket a necessity, to which Smith defends Bullock as reacting to events rather than initiating the violence and observes that Bullock paid the minister to provide a coffin and Christian burial for Mason ("Deep Water" 1.2). We see something similar said of Hotspur, after his death. In *2 Henry IV*, Morton says to Northumberland, Hotspur's father, that his son's "spirit lent a fire / Even to the dullest peasant in his camp" (1.1.112–113). Hickok himself tells Bullock that "Charlie encourages me being in your company. He feels you're a positive influence" ("Reconnoitering the Rim" 1.3). He also refers Bullock to Alma Garret as a resource for locating an honest assayer of her gold claim. He tells her, "You can trust him to see to your interests" ("Here Was a Man" 1.4). In both cases, the young man, his passion, and his potential, serve to inspire or motivate others in his community.

Association with Honor

Honor appears as a frequent theme in Shakespeare's plays. Many critics have noted that honor is clearly a defining characteristic of Hotspur in *1 Henry IV*. Hotspur's own words regarding the state of honor suggest his belief that it is in need of recovery:

> By heaven, methinks it were an easy leap
> To pluck bright honour from the pale-faced moon,
> Or dive into the bottom of the deep,

> Where fathom-line could never touch the ground,
> And pluck up drown'ed honour by the locks,
> So he that doth redeem her thence might wear,
> Without corrival, all her dignities [*1 Henry IV* 1.3.199–205].

Hotspur speaks of recovering a seemingly lost honor, perhaps a critique of the state of England under Henry IV's rule. His motives for recovering the lost honor he speaks of above are self-serving, to enhance his own image, not that different from Prince Hal's attention to enhancing his own image.

When Prince Hal and Hotspur come face-to-face in battle, late in *1 Henry IV*, Hotspur attempts to identify his counterpart by his name, "Harry Monmouth" (5.4.59) disrespectfully, which Hal picks up on, responding first with "Thou speak'st as if I would deny my name" (5.4.60) and then with his royal title and a rebuke for Hotspur:

> I am the Prince of Wales; and think not, Percy,
> To share with me in glory any more.
> Two stars keep not their motion in one sphere,
> Nor can one England brook a double reign
> Of Harry Percy and the Prince of Wales [*1 Henry IV* 5.4.63–67].

He notes that England is not big enough to hold the reign of both Henries, but he refers to Percy by his name and himself by his title, asserting his claim to the throne twice in only five lines.

Early in the first season of *Deadwood*, Bullock is repeatedly associated with honor, as Wild Bill Hickok assures Alma Garret, "Bullock is honorable" when he refers Bullock for assaying her claim ("Here was a Man" 1.4). In a later episode, we hear Bullock describing his fight to the death with an Indian to his friend Sol Star. Bullock says, "He was just trying to live, same as me, and do honor to his friend" ("Bullock Returns to the Camp" 1.7). The role of honoring a dead friend is something Bullock obviously identifies with, given that when this happened he was pursuing Jack McCall to hold him accountable for the murder of his friend Wild Bill Hickok. He identifies strongly with the Indian he has killed. We see further evidence of his claims to value honor in his challenge to Swearengen about attempting to fleece the Garrets over the gold claim in the pilot and his complaints about Con Stapleton being named Sheriff ("Jewel's Boot is Made for Walking" 1.11). In season two, he defers to Alma Garret to decide the future of their romantic relationship, giving her two options: they remain in camp but stop their affair or they continue the affair and leave the camp together, out of respect for his wife's feelings. He even admits that he does not trust himself to make this decision. The letter he writes in season three to the family of Hearst's murdered Cornish mineworker, expressing condolences for the family's loss, is a sincere and genuine attempt at honoring the dead man. Repeatedly, Bullock expresses a concern for honor and respect toward those he deems deserving, which are often the more vulnerable in camp in addition to his peers.

Association with Anger/Temper

In Shakespeare's *1 Henry IV* others' awareness of Hotspur's anger as a flaw is evident. Even Hotspur seems to recognize this, but proves incapable of self-control over his fury when he denies the king's second demand to turn over his prisoners, declaring, "I will not send them," swearing he will even tell the king so to his face, "for I will ease my heart, / Albeit I make a hazard of my head" (*1 Henry IV* 1.3.126–128). He is aware of the possibility of deadly consequences but he wants to deny the king's demand anyway. He lets passion, driven by a sense of honor, rule over reason. We see immediately that he would not make a good king because of this inability to govern himself reasonably. Northumberland, his father, chides him with "What, drunk with choler? Stay and pause awhile" (*1 Henry IV* 1.3.129), but Hotspur is on a tear and won't listen. He goes on to declare his defiance of the king's order not to speak of his cousin, taken prisoner by the Welsh, with a rant naming Mortimer twice and insulting the king, whom he refers to as an "unthankful king" and "this ingrate and cankered Bolingbroke" (*1 Henry IV* 1.3.130–137). With his declaration that he'll be loyal to Mortimer or he'll slit his own wrists and empty his blood into the dust he shows that he is given to passionate, verbal excess, completely uncalled for in this scene. Northumberland tells his brother, "the King hath made your nephew mad" (*1 Henry IV* 1.3.138), to which Worcester asks, "Who struck this heat up after I was gone?" (*1 Henry IV* 1.3.139). Once Hotspur suspects an insult, he dwells on it, allowing his emotional response full reign, rather than asserting reason to temper and control that response.

After he has received an explanation of why King Henry IV may be particularly sensitive about the possibility of Mortimer rebelling, given that Richard II named Mortimer as his heir, Hotspur understands his response, saying "Nay, then I cannot blame his cousin king" (*1 Henry IV* 1.3.158). Hotspur's understanding is only momentary, though, as he then works himself back up into a rage, for no apparent reason. Hotspur declares carelessly, in an extended fit of rage against the King,

> Send danger from the east unto the west,
> So honour cross it from the north to the south,
> And let them grapple. Oh, the blood more stirs
> To rouse a lion than to start a hare! [*1 Henry IV* 1.3.195–198].

He says that he's more interested in honor than danger; he doesn't care what the risk is so long as action is determined by honor. His speech makes the sign of the cross, welcoming danger from throughout the life cycle, from the east, symbolizing birth, to the west, symbolizing death, so long as honor intersects it. He references his stirred blood or strong emotional response, comparing it to that which it takes to rouse a lion, often associated with the sun, kings, and courage, a predator, king of the beasts, rather than to put fear into a hare, often associated with the moon, rebirth, and resurrection, associated with being prey, or the hunted, able to survive primarily by breeding often, which makes it also associated with fertility and sensuality. Hence, it's enough provocation to move the cautious, stately lion to react, as opposed to something dismissible that could start a, one assumes, mad March hare, given to jump at nothing during the season of its mating. However, in early modern England both of these creatures were believed to sleep with at least one eye open, constantly on guard, alert, aware. He's beyond wary, into paranoid, another excessive response. His reference to the lion suggests his identification with a noble leader in the animal kingdom, per the great chain of being concept of the world, however, later in the play Worcester refers to Hotspur as "harebrained" (*1 Henry IV* 5.2.19), which indicates that Hotspur has misunderstood his own nature. *The Oxford English Dictionary* defines "harebrained" as meaning "having or showing no more 'brains' or sense than a hare; heedless, reckless; rash, wild, mad." It's a perfect description of Hotspur's disproportionate and dangerous behavior. In response, his uncle Worcester says to his father, "He apprehends a world of figures here, / But not the form of what he should attend" (*1 Henry IV* 1.3.209–210). Their comments make it clear that Hotspur's tendency to fly off the handle at perceived insults render him incapable of listening to reason or responding with restraint, even when such a response places him in danger with the king.

Another example of Hotspur's excessive and unreasonable anger can be seen just a few lines after this initial exchange. The younger Percy continues with his rant, as though he hadn't said enough to convey his contempt and fury with the king's request. His childish verbal excess results in four repetitions of the name the king has said he does not want to hear ("Mortimer") and the declarations that he'll whisper the name in the king's ear as he sleeps, as well as gifting the king with a bird taught to say nothing but his kinsman's name, to goad him constantly (*1 Henry IV* 1.3.219–225). This time his uncle Worcester scolds him directly with "Why, what a wasp-stung and impatient fool / Art thou to break into this woman's mood / Tying thine ear to no tongue but thine own" (*1 Henry IV* 1.3.235–237). Despite scolding from his elders on his inability to control himself and his temper, Hotspur does not seem to heed their advice, or exhibit even a modicum of self-awareness regarding this weakness in himself.

Bullock's anger makes itself known upon his first meeting with Al Swearengen, who attempts to make a joke about Bullock's role in the shooting of Mason. This sets Bullock on edge, but when Swearengen questions whether Hickok is a silent partner in the purchase of the lot, Bullock snaps. "What business of that is his?" he asks Star ("Deep Water" 1.2). Swearengen replies with a correction to Bullock's question, to which Bullock drops any semblance of polite speech, snarling, "Don't tell me what the fuck I mean" ("Deep Water" 1.2). He feels his honor has been challenged, as he complains to Star, away from the Gem, "I don't like that son-of-a-bitch.... Calls me loose with a gun. Was he there?" ("Deep Water" 1.2). Swearengen even asks Star about it on their second meeting, "What's your partner so mad about all the time?" ("Deep Water" 1.2). Bullock also later loses his temper at the soap-scammer near the corpse of Hickok on display, snapping at him as he takes the scalps away from him, breaks the sticks holding them, and tosses it all into the fire ("The Trial of Jack McCall" 1.5). Later he slips into the tent where Jack McCall is being held, awaiting trial, and threatens him before choking him in response to McCall's taunting ("The Trial of Jack McCall" 1.5).

Bullock's anger, however, is just as often directed at himself as he shows a belated but growing sense of self awareness, especially in relation to his flaws. Bullock tells Star that "What I've done, Sol, and you have to admire me for it, is moved 300 miles to set the same situation up that I left Montana to get away from. Drawing up proposals for refuse disposal," followed by his muttered self-reproach that he "insulted Hostetler out of my own fucking irritability" and that he now has a "wife and child I barely know" ("Mr. Wu" 1.10). Star tries to comfort Bullock by assuring him his brother in heaven probably appreciates it, but Bullock won't have it, astutely countering with "Maybe he sees me borrowing his life so I didn't have to live my own" ("Mr. Wu" 1.10). Bullock confesses to Star that he inadvertently revealed to Swearengen Trixie's unauthorized call to Star in their store. Bullock admits "It might have been me he found out from, Sol. 'Cause I'm sometimes that stupid.... I was hot seeing that tinhorn Stapleton getting installed as sheriff, and I used poor fucking judgment" ("Jewel's Boot is Made for Walking" 1.11). Bullock's temper costs him and those he cares about repeatedly.

Likewise, anger leads Seth Bullock to uncontrollable violence repeatedly. He beats an Indian to death when he is attacked as he tracks McCall out of camp following Hickok's assassination and beats to a bloody, toothless pulp his lover Alma Garret's exploitive and abusive father, Otis Russell, and the ever-annoying but this time blameless gossip E.B. Farnum; he even fights Swearengen. All of these fits of violent anger stem from his protection of Alma Garret and from some unknown element in his past. When he confronts Otis Russell at Alma's request, Russell seems to read something in Bullock, asking him about childhood bullying and a sense of helplessness ("Sold Under Sin" 1.12). From the reactive expression on Bullock's face, Russell has hit a nerve, prompting Bullock to hit him repeatedly. Despite recent glimpses of insight into his own motivations and behaviors, Bullock is unable to control himself.

Returning to *1 Henry IV*, Worcester gives Hotspur a further chiding after he has alienated the Welsh Glendower through insulting him:

> You must needs learn, lord, to amend this fault.
> Though sometimes it show greatness, courage, blood—
> And that's the dearest grace it renders you—
> Yet oftentimes it doth present harsh rage,
> Defect of manners, want of government,
> Pride, haughtiness, opinion, and disdain [*1 Henry IV* 3.1.176–181].

Hotspur's uncle chastises him for his rude behavior with their Welsh ally, Glendower, telling him he must learn to curb his rage, rudeness, lack of self-control, arrogance, and disdain for others. Such behavior does not lend itself to effective collaboration with others, in the military and political context of *1 Henry IV*.

We see a similar chastisement for Bullock from a military leader passing through. When Bullock asks for a safety escort for the abusive Otis Russell, Alma Garret's father, whom he has beaten unconscious and whom he has just suggested to Dority might not make it out of camp, he is told by General Crook, "a man, a former Marshal, who understands the danger of his own temperament, he might consider serving his fellows.... We all have bloody thoughts" ("Sold Under Sin" 1.12). We also see Swearengen offering warnings to Bullock in season three when Bullock sets off to meet Hearst. Swearengen says, "I offer up a fervent 'God-speed,'" then adds, "And hopes for your fucking self-control" ("Tell Your God to Ready for Blood" 3.1). Even Bullock's body language clearly demonstrates his seemingly constantly simmering rage; with a clenched jaw and narrowed eyes, he stalks tightly and angrily through the thoroughfare of the camp repeatedly, on camp business as sheriff, or on personal business to settle a score with someone.

The costuming also contributes to how we view Seth Bullock. His clothing always consists of multiple, pressed, clean, neat layers, buttoned all the way to the top, giving the impression of careful and strict confinement, a cloth veneer of contained civility. When he is agitated, he forgets the order of the layering, as when he is debating going after Jack McCall; Sol Star reminds him of the suspenders he's missed restoring to their original location as he redresses after their construction work on the hardware store. It's the final straw for Bullock, pushing him over the edge to seek justice for his friend's murder elsewhere. Compare Bullock's costuming to that of Al Swearengen, also layered, but often dirty, with either the top buttons of his undershirt undone, or the undershirt missing altogether, revealing his hairy chest. Unlike Bullock, Swearengen's attire doesn't give off the appearance of civility, but a barely contained baseness, constantly straining at its unnatural confines.

Apparent Resistance to Responsibility

In the opening tavern scene of *1 Henry IV* Falstaff and the Prince verbally parry back and forth, trying to outwit one another in jibes about drinking, sleeping half the day away, and robbing others by night. Prince Hal responds to Falstaff's question about the tavern hostess being a sweet wench with agreement and the response, "And is not a buff jerkin a most sweet robe of durance?" (*1 Henry IV* 1.2.42). According to the footnotes, a "buff jerkin" is "a leather jacket worn by officers of the law" and "durance" indicates "(1) imprisonment or (2) durability, a durable cloth."[2] It's a random-seeming reference to bring up here, but it does play off of their earlier conversation about being thieves. Hal's comment suggests that the jacket identifying officers of the law is a form of imprisonment itself for the wearer, connected to his apparent aversion to his responsibilities as heir to the throne. Falstaff says to the prince, "Shall there be gallows standing in England when thou art king?" and "do not thou, when thou art king, hang a thief" (*1 Henry IV* 1.2.57–58, 59–60). Falstaff is ever aware of Prince Hal's future role as keeper and enforcer of the laws of England, even if he contributes to breaking some of those laws at the present time.

Deadwood opens in Montana, where lawman Seth Bullock is in the midst of leaving behind his badge and jail cell, but not before he deals with an angry, drunken, and armed mob demanding his lone prisoner, horse thief Clell Watson. Jacobs notes that Watson realizes "it is Bullock's will, *his choice* to enforce that Law that keeps [the jail cell] locked."[3] He's in transition already. Had this event happened only a few hours later, the mob could have had its way with no restrictions, given that there would be no enforcer of the law in their community. However, Bullock insists on one last enforcement of the law before he departs. Jason Vest claims that "Bullock's determination to carry out Watson's execution by legal means bespeaks his belief that order is necessary to maintaining civil society by quelling the violence that Bullock himself perpetrates when angered."[4] To disperse the angry mob and to adhere to the letter of the law, Bullock rigs up a hangman's noose on the front porch of the jail while he talks to the mob. Acting as judge and executioner, he asks for Watson's last words, messages for his remaining family, and then has him step off the box, jerking the body downward as promised to help him with his fall. Bullock then leaves the marshal's role behind, heading to the lawless Deadwood territory to pursue his fortune as a hardware business owner with his friend Sol Star. Both Prince Hal and Seth Bullock are associated with the responsibility for enforcing the law, in particular public hanging executions of thieves, despite a certain friendliness with the thieves themselves.

Despite the fact that Prince Hal scolds Falstaff at the beginning of the opening scene of *1 Henry IV* for his out-of-place concern for time, by the scene's end we see just how important timing is in Prince Hal's political strategy. His soliloquy reveals his keen awareness of others when he says, "I know you all" (*1 Henry IV* 1.2.189) and that his shirking of responsibility is actually a tactic to gain more approval and support by giving the appearance of growth and maturity when he turns over a new leaf and accepts his duty as heir to Henry IV. It's all political maneuvering, revealing Prince Hal to be a self-directed spin doctor, seeking actively to control the people's perception of him.

Twice in *1 Henry IV*, Prince Hal references what he owes his father in economic language. Early in the play in his first soliloquy he notes "when this loose behavior I throw off / And pay the debt I never promised" (*1 Henry IV* 1.2.202–203). Later in the play, he declares himself to the Douglas in defense of his father, saying that "It is the Prince of Wales that threatens thee, / Who never promiseth but he means to pay" (*1 Henry IV* 5.4.42–43). He speaks twice about paying debts that he never promised, but that he inherited at birth, it seems by virtue of being the king's eldest son.

King Henry scolds Prince Hal for his lack of character in the company he keeps, contrasting the baseness of his chosen environment of the tavern with his elevated status as prince. Most noticeable is the negative language he employs, describing the prince's "inordinate and low desires," noting his "poor," "bare," "lewd," and "mean attempts," his pursuit of "barren pleasures," and the "rude," or low, company he keeps (*1 Henry IV* 3.2.12–17). The term "grafted" suggests, too, that the noble heritage the prince embodies has been removed from the natural garden in which it was planted to be falsely, forcibly joined with that which debases it, reducing its value, its lofty promise (*1 Henry IV* 3.2.15–16). He then goes on to further chastise his eldest son for his public displays of irresponsibility:

> Thy place in Council thou has rudely lost,
> Which by thy younger brother is supplied,
> And art almost an alien to the hearts
> Of all the court and princes of my blood.
> The hope and expectation of thy time
> Is ruined, and the soul of every man
> Prophetically do forethink thy fall [*1 Henry IV* 3.2.32–38].

Clearly, the prince has left some of his political responsibilities to his younger brother, failing to fulfill his duties, being absent and unknown to the court and his brothers, and developing a poor reputation for one who is heir to the throne. The king says that the people predict the prince will make a poor king. The prince promises his father that "I will redeem all this on Percy's head" (*1 Henry IV* 3.2.132). Prince Hal acknowledges the public's contrasting perceptions of them when he references Hotspur as the "child of honour and renown" and "all-prais'ed knight" compared to his own lack of honorable reputation, "your unthought-of Harry" (*1 Henry IV* 3.2.139–140). Surprisingly, he says he wishes Hotspur's honors and his own shames numbered much higher.[5] He declares that he will "make this northern youth exchange / His glorious deeds for my indignities," forcing a switch in public opinion of them (*1 Henry IV* 3.2.145–146). He calls Hotspur his "factor," or benefactor, collecting "glorious deeds" in his behalf, which Hotspur will either present to him, or Prince Hal will boldly and fearlessly take from him, as his father took the crown from Richard II (*1 Henry IV* 3.2.147–148). This makes Prince Hal the heir not only to his father's crown but also to Hotspur's glories and honorable reputation. Interestingly, his reference to Hotspur as "gallant" echoes our introduction to Percy, where this word was used twice in association with him (*1 Henry IV* 3.2.140). It means "gorgeous or showy in appearance," suggesting he's not what he appears, and neither is the prince.[6]

Similar to Prince Hal's seeming rejection of his role as heir to the throne, we see Bullock trying to resist being drawn into a sense of responsibility for the camp, resisting stepping up to take on the role of law-enforcer again, despite the pressure he feels coming from residents such as the Reverend Smith, who preaches during Wild Bill Hickok's funeral from St. Paul, using the metaphor of the body as representative of the community, noting how interdependent all the parts are on one another, each with its own role to play in keeping the body functioning properly ("The Trial of Jack McCall" 1.5). Smith seems to look directly at Bullock during this part of his sermon and Bullock reads into this a call to action to honor his murdered friend. After the funeral, Bullock asks the Reverend for clarification of meaning, and the Reverend Smith says, "What now do you see as your part?" ("The Trial of Jack McCall" 1.5). Frustrated, Bullock asks for silence. His irritation over this questioning of what his role should be carries over to a later conversation with Star, where Bullock, in frustration, exclaims, "I'm not supposed to do anything! Let's agree to that. Not one fucking thing that I don't decide I'm gonna. All right, Sol?" ("The Trial of Jack McCall" 1.5). Cook suggests that "Significantly, Bullock does not understand, or *want* to understand, Smith's words...."[7] Bullock reads into others' comments rebuke[8] for his lack of appropriate action on more than one occasion, but he also acknowledges his desire to avoid serving as law enforcement again.

Another example of his own guilt at this shirking of responsibility occurs when Doc Cochran encourages him to have Mrs. Garret sign over her proxy to Bullock, freeing the widow to leave the camp, and Bullock replies tartly, "Anything else on your schedule I'm behind on?" ("The Trial of Jack McCall"

1.5). We see here evidence of Bullock's guilt and his quick temper, which we have other evidence of as well. Bullock himself acknowledges he volunteered for the position of health supervisor to avoid serving as law enforcement again when he tells Star, "I only raised my hand because I didn't want to be sheriff" ("No Other Sons or Daughters" 1.9). To avoid serving in that capacity, he pre-emptively volunteered for another role.

Association with Pride and Impatience

Hotspur and Bullock also share the weaknesses of pride and impatience, which translate into turning the virtue of honor into an excess or vice for both characters. Although Hotspur displays the positive characteristics of loyalty and bravery, he also demonstrates a "fatal defect," that of arrogance, as well as impatience.[9] We quickly see similar attributes and weaknesses in the character of Seth Bullock. Bevington says of Hotspur, "Like most excessive devotees of chivalry, he divides humanity into two categories: those who are gentlemen, like himself, and those who are beneath contempt."[10] This kind of simplified categorizing is reflected in Bullock's initial exchanges with Hickok and Utter, whom he likes and identifies with, and with Swearengen, Stapleton, and Russell, all of whom he speaks to with open contempt.

Ultimately, Hotspur's honor becomes a weakness that causes his father and uncle to not tell him of Prince Hal's offer of one-on-one combat to prevent all-out war. They know he would take the prince up on the offer and, regardless of the outcome, Hotspur's youth and honor would likely mean forgiveness from the king, but they would not receive such mercy for their part in rebellion. Virtues are usually a mean between excess and absence. Hotspur lacks that balance, "chas[ing] honor excessively and destructively."[11] Some critics claim that while Falstaff lacks a sense of honor and Hotspur is given to an excessive emphasis on honor, Prince Hal eventually "achieves the middle ground,"[12] regarding honor, or he at least *appears* to, anyway. The Douglas, who only sees Hotspur briefly as an opponent and the military leader who holds the Douglas prisoner after battle, refers to him as "the king of honour" (*1 Henry IV* 4.1.10) but Edmondson's description of Hotspur's "life-long enthusiasm for aggressively pursuing honor" seems a more accurate reflection of the young man's relationship with it.[13] Hotspur seems to treat honor as a competition, one that he is determined to win.

There is also a certain level of arrogance in both Hotspur and Bullock's sense of outrage and righteousness, recognized and commented on by others. Hotspur's pride is mentioned early on in the play, recognized by King Henry at Hotspur's refusal to surrender his prisoners of war to the king, allowing that he'll only turn over one of them (*1 Henry IV* 1.1.91, 94). Westmoreland lays the blame at the influence of Hotspur's uncle Worcester, making the young man "prune himself and bristle up / The crest of youth against" the king (*1 Henry IV* 1.1. 97–98), yet we see no other evidence in the play of anyone goading Hotspur on. If anything, we see his elders trying to calm him and dissuade him from continuing to rage against the king.

Swearengen often refers to Bullock as "his holiness," criticizing Bullock's self-righteous stance, beginning in the first season when Bullock threatens him regarding an assayer for Alma Garret's claim ("Bullock Returns to the Camp" 1.7) and again in season two ("A Lie Agreed Upon, Part I" 2.1). Also, in season three, theater leader Jack Langrishe says to Bullock as a group of townsmen attempts to determine what circumstances warrant calling the sheriff back from election speeches in Sturgis, "Surely Sir, you leave in the certain knowledge that you are the camp's irreplaceable man," to which Trixie replies caustically, "He don't need no further encouragement in that way of thinking" ("The Catbird Seat" 3.11). In *1 Henry IV*, we see Prince Hal mocking his rival Hotspur's infamous battlefield prowess and pride in that reputation, with "I am not yet of Percy's mind, the Hotspur of the north, he that kills me some six or seven dozen of Scots at a breakfast, washes his hands, and says to his wife, 'Fie upon this quiet life! I want work'" (*1 Henry IV* 2.4.101–104). That mocking is gentle, though, not vicious. When Prince Hal mortally wounds Hotspur in battle, Hotspur's last lines indicate his focus has been on the wrong things. Hotspur says that Prince Hal has stolen his youth and life, both of which he accepts more readily and less painfully than the "proud titles" his defeat leaves with the prince (*1 Henry IV* 5.4.77–80). Hotspur dies before completing his sentence and Prince Hal finishes it for him, just as he transfers Hotspur's honors to himself by defeating him in defense of the king, his father.

Political Potential

Hotspur possesses a skeptical, cynical perspective of politics and of political, persuasive speech. While "Hotspur is outspoken, courageous, witty, domineering in conversation,"[14] he "has a real distrust of language and its effects, and contempt for politics and compromise."[15] Hotspur admits this himself to Worcester and the Douglas when he says, "By God, I cannot flatter" (*1 Henry IV* 4.1.6). He is also not a motivational public speaker. Compare his speech to his fellow rebels:

> I rather of his absence make this use:
> It lends a luster and more great opinion,
> A larger dare to our great enterprise,
> Than if the Earl were here; for men must think,

> If we without his help can make a head
> To push against a kingdom, with his help
> We shall o'erturn it topsy-turvy down.
> Yet all goes well, yet all our joints are whole [*1 Henry IV* 4.1.76–83].

Essentially, Hotspur is chastising Worcester for complaining that they have fewer soldiers than they thought they would have going into this battle. Yet this speech comes across as very non-dramatic, with a straightforward syntax that makes it easy to follow but not memorable, powerful, or motivational. Instead, it almost sounds as though Hotspur is trying to convince himself that they will be fine without his father's forces in this civil war encounter on the battlefield. He doesn't seem to think about audience and persuasion, winning his listeners over the way that Prince Hal does. Compare it to these excerpts from Henry V's famous St. Crispin's Day speech to his troops, a response to Westmoreland's wish for more soldiers:

> If we are marked to die, we are enough
> To do our country loss; and if to live,
> The fewer men, the greater share of honor.
> God's will, I pray thee, wish not one man more.
>
> *
>
> But if it be a sin to covet honor
> I am the most offending soul alive.
> No, faith, my coz, wish not a man from England.
>
> *
>
> From this day to the ending of the world,
> But we in it shall be remember'd—
> We few, we happy few, we band of brothers [*Henry V* 4.3.20–23; 28–30; 54–56].

In comparison, these excerpts from Prince Harry's speech are much more dramatic, with a more complex syntax. He demands of his listeners agreement when he says, "God's will, I pray thee, wish not one man more" and "No, faith, my coz, wish not a man from England" as he forcefully counters his cousin's worry that they're outnumbered by the French. He uses the conditional "if" three times, recognizing their deaths would prove a meaningful sacrifice to England. He emphasizes their legacy in history and how that honor will be shared with a privileged few and he refers to them as equals to a king, when he uses the first person plural pronoun "we" in "we band of brothers." It's a powerful, highly motivational speech reflecting the providential role of England. While there is much to admire about Hotspur, "he is heroic and idealistic, but he is no politician."[16] He does not lead or motivate other men to follow him.

Similarly, Bullock is not necessarily suited to a career in politics. He often acts before he thinks, or rather, reacts to perceived provocation. He has difficulty envisioning resulting consequences from his actions at times. A brief exchange between Bullock and Swearengen late in season three exemplifies this. Bullock declares, "Tactics and timing ain't the issue," to which Swearengen replies, "The hell you say" ("True Colors" 3.3). Bullock wants to act quickly in response to Hearst's hired murders, but Swearengen considers strategic approaches to the problem, wherein perhaps waiting might better serve their interests. When Bullock acts on his own, out of anger, and arrests Hearst in a public venue, Swearengen notes, "The Sheriff eliminates several of our options" ("A Two-Headed Beast" 3.5). Later, Swearengen shares with Langrishe of Bullock, "Reason ain't his long suit" ("The Catbird Seat" 3.11). These are understatements, identifying impatience and pride as vices that detract from Bullock's virtues.

Hotspur fails to recognize the importance of persuasive rhetoric as a political weapon he could develop and, despite being in the midst of a rebellion, dependent upon clear communication with allies, he dismisses messages he receives immediately before engaging the enemy in battle. Garber notes that, despite his heroic nature, Hotspur "is too impatient either to speak or to listen"; he describes himself as "I, that have not well the gift of tongue" (*1 Henry IV* 5.2.77) and "I profess not talking" (*1 Henry IV* 5.2.91).[17] In short, he doesn't have time for others, but he seems to recognize his own shortcomings when it comes to talking and making speeches. That pose of modesty, though, may be just that, a pose; the humility topos was commonplace in Elizabethan poetry and we find it in many of Shakespeare's plays, often in the mouth of some of his most powerfully persuasive characters.

When it comes to *Deadwood*'s Bullock, he tells Charlie Utter prior to the election speeches that he would rather hang from the speaker's stand than give a speech from it ("I am Not the Fine Man You Take Me For" 3.2). Melody Graulich notes that "In *Deadwood* the relationship between politics and the English language is suspect."[18] Jacobs observes:

> Bullock is alive and attentive to words and their troublesome claims on meaning.... In the first episode of the third season, he asks his wife Martha (Anna Gunn) to assist him in writing his election speech since the words in his draft are "doing the wrong jobs, piling on too heavy, or at odds over meaning."[19]

In addition, he expresses concern to Martha that his language in the election speech not be "showy" ("Tell Your God to Ready for Blood" 3.1). Most of his dialogue is brief and to the point, sometimes just one word responses or questions, in the vein of the laconic cowboy in traditional Westerns. His longest speech is probably when he goes to the Gem to give Dority an angry message for Swearengen regarding Otis Russell's safety ("Sold Under Sin" 1.12). Bullock is an interesting combination of Prince Hal, choosing his words carefully, and Hotspur, in being quick to take action, to enact violence.

It's also worth noting that Bullock, though, is the one to draft the letter of notification and sympathy to the Cornish miners' families after their murder, ordered by Hearst in season three. As such, he takes responsibility for drafting the communal response to this event, but he himself seems puzzled as to why he's done this and why he's sharing it with the town council—or why they end up publishing it. The letter is read aloud by Merrick at the town council meeting, as the camera pans around the table, attentive to attendees' expressions as they listen to it. Bullock adds appeals to pathos through his diction, "my painful duty" and "sad intelligence" that he must convey to the family of the murdered man ("Unauthorized Cinnamon" 3.7). He offers honest praise of the man he hardly knew, noting that those who did know him "all shared the same high opinion of him," and that he himself had observed Pasco's "demonstrat[ion of] grief and deep compassion at the passing of a friend" and heard of his reputation as "an earnest worker and a diligent believer in right and wrong" ("Unauthorized Cinnamon" 3.7). The elements he touches on—especially those last two—could also describe himself, indicating his sympathetic identification with certain aspects of Pasco's life. His condolences are authentic. Bullock has the capacity to see himself in others, despite cultural differences, evident in his empathy for the Cornishman Pasco and the Indian trying to honor his dead friend in season one. As Swearengen points out to Langrishe later, the letter "Never once mention[s] Hearst. Express[es] sympathy to the family, respect for the way the man lived" ("Unauthorized Cinnamon" 3.7). Langrishe responds with "Strategy some may call ingenuous [...] invoking a decency whose scrutiny applies to him as to all his fellows" ("Unauthorized Cinnamon" 3.7). Essentially, Bullock, acting on behalf of the camp, has written the humane letter that was Hearst's responsibility as Pasco's employer; as the one who ordered Pasco's murder, though, and leaving the body in public as a warning to other employees, Hearst can't write that letter. Bullock and Swearengen employ an indirect method to publicly shame Hearst. Yet, Bullock did so intuitively, and uncertainly shares the letter with the town council. He needs Swearengen's support as to what to do with the letter, and Swearengen, in turn, needs interpretation from his old friend as to the wisdom of what they've done. Bullock second-guesses the letter afterwards, leaping without a segue from questions about the Earps with Swearengen to self-criticism: "Letter was a fucking mistake" ("Leviathan Smiles" 3.8). Swearengen reassures him otherwise as they await Hearst's reaction.

Self-Awareness

Hotspur lacks a sense of self-awareness; because of this, he is unable to reflect about himself and learn from his mistakes or the advice that his elders offer him. Garber says that "Hotspur ... is a Marlovian hero; Hal is the Shakespearean protagonist par excellence."[20] Hotspur is passionate and verbose but not necessarily articulate or tactful; he acts and speaks often without thinking through what he's doing or saying. Hal is thoughtful, contemplative, reflective, strategic, more reserved in action, but also capable of calculated, moving public declarations. Consider Hotspur alongside Marlowe's Faust, demanding power without real consideration of the consequences of his actions. Compare Hal with Hamlet, thoughtful, contemplative, patient, and concerned with timing. And yet, Bullock is a combination of both. Witherspoon describes Bullock as "brooding and violent," comparable to Hamlet with the brooding and Hotspur with the violent action; her analysis examines Bullock as "a gothic hero in the mold of *Jane Eyre*'s Rochester (1847), offering both redemption and ruination for the women who love him and the community that needs him."[21] Again, the emphasis in this description is on the great potential Bullock possesses for having a significant impact on those around him, although whether that impact may be constructive or destructive remains to be seen. Bullock himself seems aware of the potentially destructive nature of his personality and behaviors when he asks his friend and business partner, "What kind of man have I become, Sol?" ("Sold Under Sin" 1.12). Sol, however, realizes why that question cannot be answered, when he replies bluntly, "I don't know. The day ain't fucking over yet" ("Sold Under Sin" 1.12). He recognizes that no one is defined by the actions (or lack thereof) they take in any one day; rather, they are still in the process of developing character by each day's, or even each hour's, decisions they make about how they interact with others.

The audience is given insight into a deliberately cultivated distinction between how Prince Hal appears to others and who he claims to be early in the play through his first and most well-known soliloquy (*1 Henry IV* 1.2.189–211). In it, he reveals that the seemingly playboyish, irresponsible, and irresolute prince is playing a part designed to win him greater support and favor with his future subjects than he could inherit by simply showing himself to be the responsible and deserving heir to the throne that he may actually be. He says he understands his audience ("I know you all") and he's only biding his time ("and will awhile uphold / The unyoked humour of your idleness") (*1 Henry IV* 1.2.189–190). He compares himself to the sun, an appropriate comparison for heir to the throne, saying he only "permit[s] the base contagious clouds" to hide the truth of his identity for a while, noting that people don't appreciate the good unless they've been left with its opposite for a period of time (*1 Henry IV* 1.2.191–197). Prince Hal says these base things that hide his true nature only "seem to strangle him" (*1 Henry IV* 1.2.197). It's a calculated performance.

His second analogy in this speech uses the idea of much-desired but rarely occurring holidays. His plan is to give the appearance of reformation, "falsifying men's hopes" (*1 Henry IV* 1.2.205). He goes on to compare his reformed appearance to "bright metal on a sullen ground," all the brighter for its dull environment (*1 Henry IV* 1.2.206). He declares, "I'll so offend to make offense a skill" (*1 Henry IV* 1.2.210). He's following a concept set forth by Machiavelli, that an effective, powerful ruler must give the appearance of virtue, but taking it a step further by adding the appearance of reformation, too. Although he seems out of control in his loose behaviors, they are all part of a bigger political plan of his. Edmondson notes that "such a speech seems less a strategy for a future king and more a subterfuge for a future master criminal."[22] Indeed, Prince Hal is biding his time, playing a long game here, patiently waiting for the right moment to reveal his suitability to lead. But we don't necessarily see him being self-aware or reflective in this. He's simply revealing his plan and goals, as well as his capacity for manipulation, acting, and deceit, which should raise some concerns about his leadership capabilities.

In considering the qualities of a good king or a good leader, self-awareness and the capacity for reflection, self-improvement, and growth are desirable traits. Edmondson says that Hotspur has a "deficit of self-awareness […] which is always a serious moral handicap."[23] By the end of *1 Henry IV*, Edmondson claims that, although Henry appears to change over the course of the play, Hotspur has not; he adds that Hotspur "has learned nothing about himself: he is the same one-dimensional character introduced in Act I."[24] Again, we're shown that while Hotspur's bravery in battle initially evoked envy in King Henry IV, Hotspur is not suited to leadership because of his inability to be self-critical—or even humble at all—and learn from his mistakes. The high standards he applies to others when he criticizes them do not apply to himself.

Seth Bullock sometimes seems puzzled or confused, by others and even by himself. In the pilot episode, we see him writing something in a journal in the jail, at his desk. Jacobs notes that "Bullock's own motives may be obscure to him—his hesitation over the journal entry implies that he is inexpressible to himself."[25] Bullock has obviously chosen to change his life, leaving the badge behind and seeking his fortune through a shared commercial venture in the lawless mining camp. He appears to be choosing chaos over order, or chaos that will require the imposition of order upon it, a different kind of challenge for himself. When he writes the letter in season three to the Cornish miner's family about his death, he also appears uncertain, asking his wife Martha for assistance and then, hesitantly sharing the letter with the town council, an action he admits to being unnerved about afterwards. He demonstrates himself to be a man of both reflection and action, as well as one willing to consult with others and take the time to listen to their advice.

Bullock is aware of his anger-resulting-in-violence flaw and expresses concern about it on more than one occasion. When he speaks to Charlie

Utter shortly after having beaten E.B. Farnum for, he assumes, telling Hearst about his affair with Alma Garret, he acknowledges "I wonder now if I might have mistook," adding "if I tipped Hearst myself is what I'm wondering now," then "And of my temper generally, I'm wondering about, as far as running for office. [...] I'm wondering if I ought to withdraw" ("Tell Your God to Ready for Blood" 3.1). He not only seeks and takes Charlie's advice, he acknowledges that it's likely he made a mistake in his anger and a mistake in accidentally confirming his past relationship with Alma Garret Ellsworth to Hearst. These two realizations lead him to question his ability to control his temper and his propensity for violent action when angered and whether he's suited for running for the office of sheriff. He realizes that if he can't control himself and at least refrain from outright, immediate violence when angered, he has no business attempting to enforce law and order on the citizens of Deadwood. This self-awareness and further attempts to change his behavior as the series progresses distinguish him from Hotspur and make him closer to the more reasonable, calculating Prince Hal.

Compared to *Hamlet*, a "play in which the protagonist is trying [...] to 'find himself,'"[26] Hotspur, as "a man of action,"[27] never seems to engage in self-reflection or self-criticism of any kind. Neither does he heed warnings and advice from his father or uncles. Garber notes that "the play can be understood both as a 'real' set of external individuals and environments (the King, Falstaff, Hotspur and the rebels, the tavern, and so on) and as the projection of these elements *within* Prince Hal upon the stage."[28] Hal's interaction with these other figures as symbolic of competing virtues and vices within himself provides psychological insight into his character. How he resolves these conflicting desires speaks to his maturity and fitness to rule. David Milch, creator of *Deadwood*, has said that Bullock "is a mystery to himself ... a character that comes to know himself very, very slowly."[29] Perhaps the most important aspect of that quote is that Bullock does begin to know himself better as the series progresses.

Unlike Hotspur, Bullock doesn't die during the *Deadwood* series run. Instead he gains an unlikely father figure to whom he listens, learning the value of patience and restraint, despite self-doubt and frustration at choosing inaction. His final exchange with his friend Charlie Utter in the season three finale provides evidence of this when Charlie praises him for his restraint, or doing "nothing" as Bullock describes it ("Tell Him Something Pretty" 3.12). Although Bullock complains in disgust that he did nothing praiseworthy, Utter recognizes otherwise, given the younger man's temperament. Instead of hasty, ill-thought out reaction based on anger, Bullock restrains himself from the violent action he wants to take regarding Hearst's smug assertion of power. Instead he follows Al Swearengen's more calculated lead.

Association with Women

While both Prince Hal as King Henry V and Seth Bullock take wives out of a sense of duty, obligation, and/or political advancement, Hotspur and Bullock are drawn to women who are not their wives. In both the history plays and the television series, Hotspur's and Bullock's association with women and idleness distracts them from their responsibilities with rebellion or governance. Henry V marries Princess Katharine of France as part of his victory over France and the ensuing state negotiations. He presents himself as a persuasive suitor to Katharine, saying he requires her acquiescence, but even she admits that isn't relevant if her father has agreed to the match, which he has. Seth Bullock arrives in Deadwood as a married man, although he doesn't share the details of his marriage and family until the end of season one, with Alma Garret, noting that he has married his older brother's widow, to provide for and protect her and their son. He clearly sets himself apart from them in his admission to Alma.

In a foreign place, Wales, Hotspur expresses his desire for Glendower's daughter, Mortimer's wife. Although Lady Percy is present with Hotspur and Hotspur has criticized the Welsh lady's singing, saying he would rather hear his dog "howl in Irish" (*1 Henry IV* 3.2.233–234), he makes an aside that reveals his attraction to the singer. Lady Percy says, "Now God help thee!" in response to her husband's fidgeting; he replies, "To the Welsh lady's bed" and when his wife asks, "What's that?," he quiets her to hear the singing (*1 Henry IV* 3.1.239–241), before going on to tease his wife about her speech.

In a new place without laws, Deadwood, Seth Bullock finds himself drawn to the widow Alma Garret. He watches her approach her husband's dead body slung over the back of Dan Dority's horse on the thoroughfare early in the morning, something he comments on to Sol Star later. He's then brought into contact with her through Bill Hickok's agreement to locate a trustworthy assayer for her claim. Liberated from both her marriage and her addiction to laudanum, Alma is more open than she might normally be with Bullock, which disconcerts and charms him. His affair with her does distract him from his responsibilities, which he admits to her. He tells her, "I'll intend something, come to myself realizing I've only stood or sat, thinking about you. Just now that your toes are beautiful, when I'd intended to replenish the kindling" ("A Lie Agreed Upon, Part I" 2.1). He finds himself dwelling on beauty and love rather than seeing to practical needs.

For both Hotspur and Bullock, these romantic and sexual attachments to women distract them from responsibilities to other men and the larger community of men to which they belong. Rather than these attachments to women motivating them or inspiring them to lead more effectively, both are idle and somewhat derelict of duty because of the time they spend with women. There is no such distraction associated with either Henry Bolingbroke/Henry IV or Prince Hal/Henry V until the very end of *Henry V*, when the king has a playful scene with Princess Katharine.

Conclusion

Bullock reflects certain characteristics of Henry "Hotspur" Percy in that he is a young man associated with honor, but whose emphasis on honor sometimes reveals a self-righteous arrogance. Bullock is a man of action, stepping up when circumstances call for it, however this quality, combined with his pride, impatience, and volatile temper, often leads to uncontrolled violence. Because of this combination of qualities, he is not suited for the role of politician, something he is keenly aware of. Like Prince Hal, initially Bullock actively avoids serving the community of Deadwood in the most obvious way, as its sheriff, before stepping up to take on a responsible role in the community. Both Prince Hal and Bullock marry out of a sense of duty and obligation, while Hotspur and Bullock are sexually drawn to women other than their wives and that association with women distracts them from their civic responsibilities temporarily.

Seth Bullock can be understood as the character type of the young man with potential, possessing many good traits but also flawed and, at times, obviously lost and in need of more experienced guidance. While Bullock can be read as a combination of Henry "Hotspur" Percy and Prince Hal in several ways, he exhibits a sense of self-awareness and capacity for growth and change that both of those characters lack. This self-awareness and demonstration of growth allow him to develop an improved relationship with his surprising father-figure, Al Swearengen. Chapter 3 interprets Swearengen as a shrewd combination of Henry Bolingbroke/Henry IV and Falstaff, competing mentors for Prince Hal's attention.

3
Al Swearengen as Bolingbroke/Henry IV and Falstaff

> SILAS ADAMS: "When he ain't lyin,' Al's the most honorable man you'll ever meet." ("Tell Him Something Pretty" 3.12)

Clearly the fan favorite on the series, Al Swearengen's popularity with viewers and critics alike can be better understood if we compare him with another beloved fictional character, Shakespeare's Falstaff from the Henry IV plays. Yet, Swearengen also shares several similarities with one of Falstaff's foils, Henry IV. Like Bolingbroke before he became king, Swearengen is ambitious, pragmatic, driven, politically savvy, and sly. These similarities only become clearer once Bolingbroke has become Henry IV: both he and Swearengen are older males in a position of power, astute politicians, corrupt, and defensive. In addition, both seek an admirable protégée that is not initially favorable to having them as mentors. We see, too, that the appearance of honor is important to both men. These qualities balance the characteristics that make Swearengen also similar to Falstaff: he can be charming, witty, and pragmatic; he provides distraction for men of the camp through gambling, women, and liquor, and serves as a substitute father-figure for several of the camp's younger males, who seem drawn to him. Like Falstaff, Swearengen has a physical presence that dominates any scene in which he is present. However, Swearengen appears to grow and develop as a character, adapting to the times as needed, unlike that static nature of Falstaff and Henry IV.

Henry Bolingbroke/Henry IV

Henry Bolingbroke, who will become Henry IV, first appears in *Richard II*, drawing attention by making his first move towards usurping the throne from his cousin. Bolingbroke is the master of the re-directed accusation of treason and villainy. He challenges Thomas Mowbray, another nobleman, on the grounds of treason, accusing him of misuse of pay meant for soldiers and murdering the king's uncle, the Duke of Gloucester. It is a bold move, given that it's likely Richard himself ordered the murder, and therefore Bolingbroke cannot realistically hope for justice by issuing this challenge in front of the king. He challenges Mowbray to a joust on the grounds that "he is a traitor foul and dangerous / To God of heaven, King Richard, and to me" (*Richard II* 1.3.38–39), including himself, but carefully last in that list. His accusation serves as an indirect threat to the king; Bolingbroke displays an astute understanding of Richard's weaknesses and how, carefully and rhetorically, to manipulate his way to the crown while initially avoiding charges of outright treason. Later in the play, he executes two of Richard's favorite followers, also on grounds of treason, claiming that they have willfully misled the monarch.[1] He cleverly manages to eliminate Richard's staunchest supporters by claiming he seeks only to protect king and country from dangerous, deceitful influences. Henry Bolingbroke proves publicly and repeatedly that he is a more fit man to lead England than Richard, but he consistently demonstrates respect for his cousin throughout his steady and deliberate movements ever closer to the throne. He is ambitious but keenly aware of public perceptions of himself and his actions, seeking the favor of the people constantly without swaying from his objective. As Marjorie Garber notes, "Bolingbroke is a realist."[2] Once he is king and must defend his throne against rebels, he utilizes the battle strategy of distraction, dressing many of his noblemen as he is attired. The rebels are never quite sure whether they've killed or captured King Henry IV or one of his followers. Henry's power is obvious, from the beginning of *Richard II* through his final scenes with his son Prince Henry in *2 Henry IV*.

Strategic Political Vision

King Richard recognizes the threat that Bolingbroke presents, in his deliberate attempts at winning the public's favor, evident when Richard tells his cousin Aumerle,

> Ourself and Bushy, Bagot here, and Green
> Observed his courtship to the common people,
> How he did seem to dive into their hearts
> With humble and familiar courtesy,
>
> [...]
>
> With "Thanks, my countrymen, my loving friends,"
> As were our England in reversion his,
> And he our subjects' next degree in hope [*Richard II* 1.4. 23–36].

Richard's description of Bolingbroke's actions insinuates that his cousin has deliberately set out to "court" or "woo" the commoners' support against Richard as a performance, rather than a genuine interest in them, perhaps also a contributing factor in Richard's decision to banish Bolingbroke for six years. He feels threatened by his cousin's garnering of support as a future possible monarch. Richard seems to recognize Bolingbroke's capacity for enacting a long-term political ambition. Bolingbroke has an objective and a strategy for how he might achieve it, beginning with winning the commoners' support and accusing Mowbray of treason, risking banishment. But even banishment cannot stop his progress toward his objective; it only delays his advancement.

Later in the play, when Henry Bolingbroke returns to England, York challenges him as to why he has returned despite having been banished for six years, noting his having come back "before the expiration of thy time / In braving arms against thy sovereign" amounts to treason (*Richard II* 2.3.111–112). Bolingbroke demonstrates his ability to strategize as he defends his early return on a technicality relating to his title when he explains, "As I was banished, I was banished Hereford: / But as I come, I come for Lancaster" (*Richard II* 2.3.113–114). Irving Ribner writes "Honesty and trust mean nothing to Bolingbroke when his own advantage is involved."[3] In the next act, Bolingbroke eliminates two of Richard's closest supporters, Bushy and Green, through a performance of transparency and righteousness, in the name of protecting the king and righting wrongs. He says,

> ... to wash your blood
> From off my hands, here in the view of men
> I will unfold some causes of your deaths.
> You have misled a prince, a royal king [*Richard II* 3.1.5–8].

Bolingbroke recognizes that their execution needs to appear justified. He includes himself in the charges against these two, saying "Myself—a prince by fortune of my birth, / Near to the King in blood, and near in love / Till you did make him misinterpret me—," a reminder of his royal bloodline and claim to the throne through it (*Richard II* 3.1.16–18). His approach to usurping his cousin's crown is subversive.

King Richard refers to his cousin as "this thief, this traitor, Bolingbroke, / Who all this while hath reveled in the night" (*Richard II* 3.2.47–48), associating him with a hidden agenda, the ambition of stealing the throne under cover of darkness and secrecy. Both Bolingbroke and later Falstaff are referred to as thieves; thievery, ambition, and hidden agendas also apply to *Deadwood*'s Al Swearengen, who is often saying one thing while working a contradictory angle for personal gain. In the pilot of the series, Al appears to be advising and supporting Brom Garret's pursuit of a gold claim purchase from Tim Driscoll, with Garret bidding against rival E.B. Farnum; in reality, Swearengen owns the gold claim and Driscoll and Farnum work for him. Swearengen actually arranged the entire situation to profit off Garret's wealth without Garret realizing it. When Tim proves a weak link in the scam, Al orders Dan to kill Tim and make it look like an accident, ordering it almost as an afterthought, "Oh, and don't forget to kill Tim" ("Deadwood" 1.1). Similarly, Bolingbroke insists on his allegiance to Richard but with a just demand:

> provided that my banishment repealed
> and lands restored again be freely granted.
> If not, I'll use the advantage of my power,
> And lay the summer's dust with showers of blood ... [*Richard II* 3.3. 40–43].

It's a clear threat; Bolingbroke demands what he feels he is owed—and then some—or he says he'll start a civil war. He shows no hesitation at threatening bloodshed to achieve his objective.

Bolingbroke's demands seem an excuse for his real ambition of gaining the crown. Richard reminds York, Bolingbroke, Percy, and Northumberland, "For well we know, no hand of blood and bone / Can grip the sacred handle of our scepter, / Unless he do profane, steal, or usurp" (*Richard II* 3.3.79–81). Indeed, Henry Bolingbroke steals the throne from his cousin, usurping Richard's role as England's monarch with the support of some aristocrats and many commoners. By act four of the play bearing Richard's name, he self-deposes himself as king and is replaced by his cousin as King Henry IV. Garber adds, "Identity for Bolingbroke is a matter of ... what he can do rather than (only) who he is by birth",[4] meaning his capacity to present a specific kind of "persona, or role, in malleability and self-creation."[5] Even though Henry neither killed nor ordered the assassination of Richard, he is associated with regicide through the staging that has the final scene dominated by Richard's coffin.[6] It is an association that remains part of his identity, as both he and his supporters remind the audience repeatedly throughout both parts of *Henry IV*. Clearly once we enter the world of *Henry IV*, "Bolingbroke, now King Henry IV, is the villain."[7] Henry's reign stands on a regicidal bloodstain that he can't purify or forget. He demonstrates remorse, but it seems less about Richard, his kinsman, and more about opening the door to regicide, a doorway to disrespect for the position that could ultimately threaten his own reign. Similarly, *Deadwood*'s Al Swearengen is shown repeatedly stepping over literal bloodstains in his establishment. The series ends with him trying to scrub one out of the woodwork, muttering about the demands of others to "clean" harsh reality out of the narrative, evident in the episode's title, "Tell Him Something Pretty" (3.12). He demonstrates no remorse for the murders he has performed or ordered; all of them were pragmatic decisions, done to protect his profit. Witherspoon identifies Swearengen as "the show's principal villain because of his remarkable capacity to contain the world's brutality within his soul" combined with his "unpredictability."[8] His unpredictability is evident in the pilot episode when he asks Jimmy Irons how many people in the bar he told about the Metz family massacre before coming to Al's office. Irons acknowledges a few, and Swearengen punches Johnny Burns, standing slightly behind Irons. Burns works for Swearengen, making it his responsibility to deliver Irons and his news directly and immediately to the boss, but he's failed. It's unexpected, given Swearengen's intense attention on Irons.

Like Henry Bolingbroke, Albert Swearengen creates a place for himself in Deadwood through his foresight of the growth to come in the form of miners seeking their fortune at the site of the latest gold strike and the community that will arise from the wilderness to meet their needs. Speaking to Trixie in season three, Swearengen recalls how he and Dan Dority chopped down trees to build the Gem Saloon before the mining camp even existed. As the camp evolves into a town, he continues to carve an influential space for himself at all levels of society, demonstrating his strength at adapting quickly and efficiently to constantly emerging circumstances. When Michael Hattaway is writing about Shakespeare's history plays he quotes St. Augustine's comments about the "precariousness of what we call the 'state': Remove justice, and what are kingdoms but gangs of criminals on a large scale? What are criminal gangs but petty kingdoms?"[9] Al Swearengen's kingdom is a criminal one that expands significantly and in some surprising ways over the course of *Deadwood*'s three seasons.

In the audience's introduction to the character of Al Swearengen, he is associated with British royalty. Veteran miner Whitney Ellsworth remarks on Swearengen's dialect and asks if he is related to British royalty. Swearengen replies, "I'm related to all those cocksuckers," which tells the audience a great many things about this character ("Deadwood" 1.1). He exhibits a willingness to adapt and play off of a paying customer's amiable but invasive questions, especially if it continues to result in profit for him. And although the question is about some imagined elevated ancestry, Swearengen dismisses the idea of too close an association with foreign authority through his labeling of them as the crude "cocksuckers," a linguistic defensive device to forestall further questioning or encroaching upon his personal history. Walter Hill, director of the pilot episode, comments on Swearengen's costuming, saying "It's the business suit without the shirt underneath. That tells you everything about the character."[10] The black with gray pinstripe three-piece suit, minus a shirt or just with an unbuttoned longjohn shirt, presents a contradiction: it's a fitted, fine suit, practical in its dark shades, fancy in its pinstripes, suggesting perhaps an earlier vanity, but now worn comfortably, adapted to Swearengen and his role at the Gem. His attire suggests a businessman who can present himself civilly, appropriately, but who won't hesitate to act on baser, primal urges for sex, violence, or murder as the need arises. With his dark hair slicked back, mustache, soul patch, and craggy face, Ian McShane's Swearengen appears like a Western version of Satan, dangerous, aware of his own driving ambition and fallen state, but still seeking to take others down with him. McShane has expressed admiration for the character's fearlessness.[11]

Swearengen differs from Henry IV, in that he doesn't occupy a public position of power; he has no official political authority. In some ways this makes him more comparable to Henry Bolingbroke prior to his claiming of the crown. Initially, both men's power is all behind the scenes, making them more modern political animals. In the pilot episode, Swearengen watches the gunfight between Bullock, Hickok, and Ned Mason from behind a window, on the second floor of the Gem, a hidden position of power, observing. This positioning of viewing, above and separate from events occurring at street level, as I noted in Chapter 1, allows Swearengen a certain "visual dominance ... a particularly masculine perspective.... To keep in sight means to keep under control."[12] Jason Jacobs notes that "The balcony is the major space from which Swearengen monitors the Deadwood camp; it represents his distance, his authority, and his purview of power."[13] Swearengen has attained this position through forging his own way into the frontier, building his saloon, and living on the second story. He creates this position for himself and must fight to maintain it. Similarly, Henry Bolingbroke would not likely have become king of England without cleverly and deliberately usurping the crown from his cousin, proving his behind-the-scenes calculated manipulations, backed by the threat of force, extremely effective. Once he has laid claim to it, he finds some of those who once supported him rebelling against him, and he must defend his claim to the throne. Even as he lies ill and fatigued in *2 Henry IV*, he asserts his possession of the crown against his own son, Prince Hal, mistakenly fearing his son's eagerness to see his father dead so that he may inherit the throne.

In the first season of *Deadwood*, even a newcomer like Seth Bullock comes to recognize Swearengen's power. Bullock asks Swearengen why he "let" Stapleton become sheriff, acknowledging that the public positions of authority in the camp are determined by Swearengen ("Jewel's Boot is Made for Walking" 1.11). The saloon owner doesn't deny his behind-the-scenes authority, but defends the choice of Con Stapleton to Bullock, explaining that his sole purpose in that decision was to offer some comfort to Tom Nuttall, who requested it and complained that he was feeling left behind by the camp's rapid development ("Jewel's Boot Is Made for Walking" 1.11). Understanding relationships among others in the camp allows Swearengen to manipulate them to his advantage, but he also makes some surprising decisions not based solely on pragmatics. The decision about Stapleton is a comfort to Tom Nuttall, assuring him of continued friendship with Swearengen.

Henry Bolingbroke understands the most effective means of achieving the throne through issuing righteous and just claims while steadily progressing with a growing army toward Richard. Yet, even though Bolingbroke gains support as a claimant to the throne, he refuses to kill his cousin the king or have Richard killed. When he discovers one of his followers has acted on his own, murdering Richard, he seems genuinely distraught. He declares, "Exton,

I thank thee not, for thou hast wrought / A deed of slander with thy fatal hand / Upon my head and all this famous land," adding that "Lords, I protest my soul is full of woe / That blood should sprinkle me to make me grow. / Come mourn with me for what I do lament" (*Richard II* 5.6.34–36, 45–47). He at least appears publicly to take responsibility for the regicide committed in his name and to demonstrate remorse towards it.

There is no doubt about Al Swearengen's position of power in Deadwood. He is a controller of information, savvy to the underlying meanings of others' actions and the direction of the camp's development; like a feudal lord, he owns much of the land on which the camp is being developed and he controls the road agents in the area, requiring his approval before the robbery of travelers can occur. His intelligence and ability to interpret information make him much more of a threat than his established reputation with a knife does. In the first episode, we see a number of people reporting to, deferring to, or seeking advice from Swearengen: Trixie the abused prostitute, Dan Dority the bartender/bouncer, Johnny Burns, Dority's assistant, E.B. Farnum, the owner of the camp's only hotel, Brom Garret, the moneyed dandy seeking a gold claim, rogue road agents Tom Mason and Persimmon Phil, and apparent gold claim owner Tim Driscoll. Swearengen maintains an elaborate web of information gatherers and pawns in his maneuvers for profit, independence, and control in the camp. According to Shawn McIntosh, "Swearengen's astute use of disinformation, strategic knowledge sharing, and communication networks [make] him the most powerful man in Deadwood."[14] Access to information is one advantage, but understanding the information and knowing what to do with it are others; this capacity sets Swearengen apart from most of the others in the camp and gives him a distinct advantage. Another critic claims that

> Al's status in the camp rests largely on his ability to decode what no one else can; Dan's announcement to his boss in "Complications" (2.5) that "they's developments that need interpretating on every front," and Farnum's insistence in "Amalgamation and Capital" (2.9) that "something strange has happened that I need you to construe," are just two examples among many where Al's authority in the camp rests in large part on his hermeneutic brilliance.[15]

Swearengen serves as an interpreter of meaning or significance for others in the camp, having a keen eye for potential power plays or manipulation. Without him as interpreter, his minions are at a loss to understand one another, much less outsiders, emphasized in the brilliant episodes where a kidney stone removes Swearengen's ability to communicate.

As the television series progresses, the stakes become higher in Deadwood, leading first to a face-to-face confrontation between Swearengen and the outside threat of George Hearst. In a tense exchange with Hearst, Swearengen flexes his muscle, when he warns Hearst, "But bloodletting on my premises that I ain't approved I take as a fucking affront" ("Tell Your God to Ready for Blood" 3.1). Hearst inquires angrily what demonstrations this will result in. Swearengen assures him, "Speeches tonight are cancelled. Unless the insult's cured by tomorrow, there'll be further tearing down. Fuck the fucking elections, and fuck the agreement with Yankton. Let the camp return to its former repute: unstable and unsafe for commerce" ("Tell Your God to Ready for Blood" 3.1). He exerts his ability to alter the reputation of the Deadwood camp to a dangerous, unstable one. Just as he knows the value and necessity of the camp's reputation during this transitional period, so, too, does *2 Henry IV* emphasize the power of rumor, with the play opening on a soliloquy by Rumor personified, spreading misinformation about battles and noblemen's deaths. Hearst demands to know if this threat means Swearengen is dangerous to his interests, to which Swearengen astutely replies, "As capable of inconvenience and of some damage and debt to those that would act against my interests, I cannot fucking argue with dangerous. Different from powerful, though, which speaks to potency longer term" ("Tell Your God to Ready for Blood" 3.1). When Hearst seems to be gunning for the whole town, Farnum turns to Swearengen and plainly pleads with Al to save them to which Swearengen replies, "Have I ever not?" ("A Rich Find" 3.6). And, finally, in the last episode, when it comes down to appeasing Hearst's sense of justice and the camp's response is a lie, Swearengen takes the lead, advising the others, "We show united in the prelude when he's making his entrance and the fucking like. Comes to viewing the body, I stand for virtue alone. The deception failing, I'll make a pass at him with my blade. In the aftermath, play the lie as mine, knowing I speak of you in Heaven" ("Tell Him Something Pretty" 3.12). Swearengen outlines the plan and takes the accountability for the lie upon himself, protecting the others with whom he's allied.

We most clearly see Henry Bolingbroke planning how to approach Richard in *Richard II* 3.3, having steadily advanced, armed and with an army, toward where Richard is; once he reaches the king, he sends Northumberland ahead to declare Bolingbroke's allegiance on the condition that his banishment is repealed and lands restored. When he himself sees Richard appear, his blank verse speech takes a turn for the lyric, rather than the pragmatic. He moves from this:

> Henry Bolingbroke
> On both his knees doth kiss King Richard's hand
> And sends allegiance and true faith of heart
> To his most royal person, hither come
> Even at his feet to lay my arms and power,
> Provided that my banishment repealed
> And lands restored again be freely granted.
> If not, I'll use the advantage of my power ... [*Richard II* 3.3.35–42].

to this

> See, see, King Richard doth himself appear,
> As doth the blushing discontented sun
> From out the fiery portal of the east
> When he perceives the envious clouds are bent
> Of his bright passage to the occident [*Richard II* 3.3.62–67].

The first five lines convey the appropriately submissive loyal tone and language that one would expect from a subject to a monarch, but that turns with the conditional "provided," naming the requirements Bolingbroke makes of Richard before shifting to a threat with "if not." Twenty lines later he describes Richard's kingly appearance as though he is suddenly aware that he is performing in a play. An audience member is in danger of whiplash from this. Bolingbroke seems to be attempting to first perform as a royal subject until his own objectives surface briefly before making a conscious dramatic effort to reinforce the inherent power, not of Richard, but of the position of the king, his true objective with all this verbal and military maneuvering. He still gives himself away with the "envious clouds" that Richard emerges from; those must include Henry Bolingbroke himself. Bolingbroke reveals himself to be clever and adaptable in his approach to usurping his cousin. Irving Ribner notes that "Although Bolingbroke wins little personal sympathy from his audience and his private virtues are questionable, the public virtues which will enable him to remedy the insufficiencies of Richard's reign are evident from his first appearance."[16] Bolingbroke has a keen eye for the importance of appearance in usurping the crown and presenting himself as a viable king.[17]

As King Henry IV, he leads his own forces against rebels in *Henry IV* parts one and two. His heir respects, fears, and loves him, despite the miscommunication between the two men featured throughout their two plays together. Henry IV commands with the sure authority of a monarch, issuing rewards, lectures, and punishment when he determines any form of hesitancy on the part of subordinates to do his bidding swiftly. Although Henry IV does not kill nor order killed his cousin Richard, when his follower commits the murder, the king takes responsibility for it.

The Gem as Swearengen's Court

As Diffrient and Perlman have each noted, the Gem becomes the central location for civic power through the meetings of Deadwood's male business leaders, assembled by Swearengen, to address matters of concern to the entire community.[18] He may not bear a title of authority in the ad hoc government this group creates, but he does act as the king calling his advisors to court to seek counsel for maintaining his power and responding to communal threats.

This has its obvious parallel with King Henry's political court, where his authority is most powerfully demonstrated to his sons, his followers, and even his critics. The first meeting of Swearengen's counsel determines what to do about the trial of Jack McCall for murdering Wild Bill Hickok. The trial is held in the Gem saloon. The second gathering determines the camp's organized response to the plague. The remaining meetings formulate responses to Wolcott's and Hearst's violence. Swearengen initiates and hosts these meetings. Of the plague meeting he says to Cy Tolliver, "Us and several others" should get together to determine what should be done about the plague threat ("Plague" 1.6). Swearengen runs these "town council" meetings, which include the camp's male business leaders. In the plague meeting, he considers image—advising the rest to set up pest tents to treat the sick rather than a building to give the impression of the temporary nature of this crisis, he offers press information to cover the plague spread to assure readers rather than frighten them, he has the cost figured of the tents and vaccines, and the idea of sending riders to retrieve the vaccine ("Plague" 1.6). He takes charge of the meeting entirely.

In "No Other Sons or Daughters" (1.9), in response to Magistrate Clagget's advice for maintaining Deadwood's independence, he tells E.B. Farnum "Be in my joint in two hours. We're forming a fucking government." Swearengen serves as the liaison between the outside government officials and the Deadwood businessmen, yet when they divvy up titles and responsibilities, he doesn't take one. He remains, instead, the most powerful behind-the-scenes conductor of events in Deadwood. Henry also demonstrates a keen consideration of public image when he moves to challenge Richard for the throne, and afterwards, as he seeks to maintain his possession of it against those who helped him achieve it. He scolds Prince Hal for appearing not to consider his own public image in *1 Henry IV*, noting his son's excessive time spent among the commoners, away from court.

Swearengen's pragmatism and capacity for strategic alliances are evident throughout the series. In the first season, he warns against Farnum's proposal to murder both Bullock and Mrs. Garret to regain the gold claim, demonstrating long term thinking by saying that the peace with the Sioux means settlement, annexation, and more profit. He asks Farnum, "How could we fuck this up? By engaging in open fucking bloodletting" when Bullock could be made to serve as "the perfect fucking front man" ("Suffer the Little Children" 1.8). Despite his contempt toward Bullock, he recognizes a larger opportunity to make use of Bullock's honorable appearance and his naïve, judgmental perspective. This is one of many examples of Swearengen serving as a tutor to others in the camp when it comes to strategic alliances. We see further evidence of this in a later exchange with Mr. Wu regarding Wu's request that both dope thieves who stole from him and killed his courier be killed in return. Swearengen counsels Wu otherwise when he says, "you can't cut the throat of every cocksucker whose character it would improve" ("Mr. Wu" 1.10). Swearengen understands that you can't always take the immediate action you desire if you want to maintain your position of strength. Similarly canny when it comes to power, Henry Bolingbroke clearly understands that to achieve the throne, he cannot directly and immediately challenge his cousin Richard. Instead, he wages a progressive campaign against corruption at the king's court, drawing support and followers as he insists he is not seeking to usurp the throne, but to claim only what is rightfully his legacy from his father, taken by the king. Once he has achieved the throne, though, he appears to have forgotten or neglected those who aided him, primarily the Percy family in the north. Henry's allegiances serve his objective and he appears to abandon them when his objective changes from attaining the throne to keeping it against other relatives with a claim to it, too.

Swearengen's strength at understanding others' power plays helps as the ad hoc government tries to maintain control of the camp against the outside interests of George Hearst. Even Calamity Jane, who loathes Swearengen, notes this when she says to Charlie Utter, "Maybe Swearengen's coordinating strategy..." ("Amateur Night" 3.9). She is accurate. Swearengen succinctly analyzes the intentions behind the shots fired at Alma (Garret) Ellsworth to the lady herself in explaining the response he counsels her to present. Swearengen assures her that he has already taken action to prevent Bullock and Ellsworth from reacting with more violence and he adds, "Little in the past commends me to your trust. I'd ask you, accepting the premise that you were bait, not quarry—complete your walk to the bank..." ("Amateur Night" 3.9). He reassures her of the safety of her loved ones, acknowledges the troubled past between them, then asks her—*asks*—to counter Hearst's intimidating move. His methods here reveal an astute knowledge of how best to approach Mrs. Ellsworth to elicit her agreement; he even manages to refrain from using profanity until the very end of this speech, knowing she finds it offensive. As mentioned earlier, we see the clearest parallel between Swearengen's capacity for leadership through calculation, adaptability, and eliciting something like trust from unlikely sources and that of Henry Bolingbroke in his slow but steady campaign to usurp the throne in *Richard II*.

Villainous Behaviors

Despite his capacity to act as a powerful ally and a leader, Swearengen is well known as a violent thief and pimp. He runs the Gem Saloon through a carefully constructed network of spies, enforcers, and his own brute force; he has no aversion to committing murder himself, when necessary to sustain his position in the camp and to reinforce his authority as a figure to be feared. Swearengen even says to Tolliver at one point, "Sometimes I wish we could just hit them over the head, rob them and throw their bodies into the creek" ("The Trial of Jack McCall" 1.5). In Shakespeare's *1 Henry IV*, King Henry's own words about his rise to power are telling: "And then I stole all courtesy from heaven, / And dressed myself in such humility / That I did pluck allegiance from men's hearts" (3.2.50–52). Garber notes that he is using "the language of theft, disguise, and false coining."[19] Henry's language emphasizes his usurpation of the crown from his cousin, Richard II—creating a place for himself where there was none, his employment of a deliberately crafted public pose, and his ability to steal allegiance from other men for himself as king. He acknowledges that he was a master manipulator when it came to achieving the throne and garnering support from other men as he did so.

To some degree both King Henry IV and Sir John Falstaff are corrupt men, thieves on differing social and political levels. Falstaff says to Hal, "I would to God thou and I knew where a commodity of good names were to be bought…" (*1 Henry IV* 1.2.81), which shows the older man's preference for purchasing a good name rather than actually earning one. Hotspur describes Henry Bolingbroke (Henry IV) before he became king as "a poor unminded outlaw sneaking home" (*1 Henry IV* 4.3.60), noting the king's carefully crafted public image, "by this face, / this seeming brow of justice, did he win / the hearts of all that he did angle for" (*1 Henry IV* 4.3.84–86). The veneer of virtue enables the man behind it to gain loyalty, influence, and power. Since the king took the crown and one of his supporters murdered Richard II, Henry is haunted by these corruptions and anxious that he not lose the crown to those who once helped him gain it.

Anxiety About Maintaining Power

Constantly alert for signs of betrayal, Swearengen is highly anxious about maintaining his power. Anthony Easthope notes that "Defensive mastery requires constant vigilance. The masculine ego must be watchful and it will also be anxious, and these effects are worked out very much in terms of sight and vision."[20] Al Swearengen watches the activity of the camp from his second floor balcony; he also relies upon hotelier E. B. Farnum to report to him about all newcomers to the camp, noting to A.W. Merrick that this is Farnum's assignment in the third season. In "Deep Water" (1.2), Swearengen asks Bullock and Star about possible unnamed partners, such as Hickok, in their offer to purchase a piece of property on the main thoroughfare. He wonders about secret alliances intended to compete with the Gem in gambling. Then again, in "Here was a Man" (1.4), Farnum tries to reassure Swearengen's paranoia about overlooking potential threats when he replies, "I think you're a man with so many different responsibilities, you sometimes get to feeling beset.

And in that frame of mind, take things personal" ("Here was a Man" 1.4). Farnum shows an awareness of the difficulties Swearengen faces in trying to maintain control and power over the camp as it grows rapidly, day by day, and newcomers bring a potential threat to Swearengen's empire.

Bolingbroke's emphasis on appearing transparent and just in his actions of claiming the crown is seen when he demands that Richard "in common view / ...may surrender" (*Richard II* 4.1.155–156). Ribner claims "he wants no doubt cast upon the legality of the transaction," leading Bolingbroke to express a second time his concern about the appearance of legality of the transfer of authority to him from his cousin.[21] Similarly, Swearengen orders Adams to remove any record of bribe money and to return the bribe money from Yankton so that documentation of such a transaction won't be used to cast aspersions upon the legality of the town's founding paperwork. Henry Bolingbroke's anxiety about the crown can be summed up with his comment that "Uneasy lies the head that wears a crown" (*2 Henry IV* 3.1.31). When ill in this play, he wakes from a nap to find the crown missing; when he learns Prince Hal has taken it, he mistakenly assumes his heir is ambitiously eager to wear it himself and wield the power that accompanies it (4.5). He demands of the prince, "Dost thou so hunger for mine empty chair / That thou wilt needs invest thee with my honours / Before thy hour be ripe? Oh, foolish youth..." (*2 Henry IV* 4.5.93–95). Here he views his eldest son as he himself was—impatient to claim the crown. But Prince Hal assures him that he walked away with the crown contemplating the burden it created for his father, from his own observations. They are reconciled before Henry's death.

As the threat of George Hearst's ambition to run Deadwood becomes apparent to Swearengen in season three, he criticizes it. He acknowledges a practical similarity between himself and Hearst when he notes, "Running his holdings like a despot, I grant, has a fucking logic. It's the way I fucking run mine" ("Tell Your God to Ready for Blood" 3.1). But that similarity has to do with Hearst's business, that which he possesses. When it comes to Deadwood, Swearengen questions Hearst's scope, saying to Bullock, "There's no practical need for him to run the fucking camp. That's out of scale. It's out of proportion, and it's a warped unnatural impulse..." ("Tell Your God to Ready for Blood" 3.1.). It's not just that Hearst's ambition threatens Swearengen's holdings, but that it threatens the entire existence of the camp that concerns Swearengen. He increasingly moves beyond a mere concern for himself and his own profit over the course of the show's three seasons.

Henry IV expresses concern that the kingdom he leaves his son will regress under Prince Hal's reign, returning to wilderness from the civilizing advances Henry believes he has achieved. He tells Prince Hal,

> For the fifth Harry from curbed license plucks
> The muzzle of restraint, and the wild dog

> Shall flesh his tooth on every innocent.
> O my poor kingdom, sick with civil blows!
> When that my care could not withhold thy riots,
> What wilt thou do when riot is thy care?
> Oh, thou wilt be a wilderness again,
> Peopled with wolves, thy old inhabitants! [*2 Henry IV* 4.5.129–136].

He believes his son wishes for his premature death in order to rule England, and that the seemingly wayward prince will do so badly, causing England to regress from its progress. Once more he uses the word "pluck," twice in this entire section, both times in relation to his eldest son's ambitions. He accuses Hal of having "stol'n" too soon the crown that will ultimately be his (*2 Henry IV* 4.5.100), that Hal will "pluck down" his father's appointed officers (*2 Henry IV* 4.5.116), and, finally, that his heir as king "plucks / the muzzle of restraint" from the "wild dog" ruffians whose company he has kept, to the harm of the innocent, order, and civilization. He worries about England, his family, and what his ultimate legacy will be after his death. Henry must be alert to others like himself, as he once was—young, persuasive, ambitious, unafraid to take what he wants—and the threat they pose.

Falstaff

In other ways as the series progresses, Swearengen may reflect Sir John Falstaff, in that he is witty, verbally adept, corrupt, pragmatic, and through his association with the night, sin, and profit, especially profit gained from the labor of others. Daniel Salerno claims, "The character [of Al Swearengen] is already a legend—beloved by modern audiences and critics—and if there is real justice, he will be as studied and beloved in 400 years as Falstaff and Iago—his closest Shakespearean analogues—are today."[22] At least one source claims that "Milch said he probably modeled [Swearengen] on Shakespeare's nefarious Falstaff from 'Henry IV,' which Milch read before beginning work on 'Deadwood.'"[23] Garber describes Falstaff as the "Lord of Misrule ... a kind of anti-king ... [who] reigned chiefly at night, promoting ... drinking, and his 'misrule' provided a temporary safety valve for pent-up social, sexual, and political energies."[24] Swearengen runs a bar containing gambling and a brothel, appealing to the worst habits of the miners who have come to strike it rich. In *1 Henry IV*, when Falstaff pretends to be Prince Hal and Hal pretends to be King Henry, Hal refers to Falstaff as a negative influence on the prince, describing Falstaff as

> a devil ... that reverend Vice, that gray Iniquity, that father ruffian, that vanity in years ... wherein is he good but to taste sack and drink it?... Wherein cunning but in craft? Wherein crafty but in villainy? Wherein villainous but in all things? Wherein worthy

3. Al Swearengen as Bolingbroke/Henry IV and Falstaff

but in nothing?... That villainous abominable misleader of youth, Falstaff, that old white-bearded Satan [*1 Henry IV* 2.4.442–448].

We may think of Falstaff as a fat, jolly, relatively harmless miscreant, but the charges Hal role-playing as his father lays upon the old man use harsh language: devil, Vice, Iniquity, father ruffian, cunning, crafty, villainous, misleader of youth, Satan. These same terms apply equally to Swearengen's role in the Deadwood camp. Garber notes that Falstaff is known for "his proliferation of disorder; and his facility for lying."[25] The table below draws upon Garber's multilayered comparison of how the characters of Falstaff, King Henry IV, Prince Hal, and Hotspur can be viewed as aligned in pairs but also simultaneously contrasted as foils[26]:

Character	*Alignment*	*Foils*
Falstaff	King Henry IV	*King Henry IV*—"rule," order, law
		Falstaff—"misrule," disorder, crime
	"subversives, rebels, pretenders, elderly examples for Prince Hal"	
	Hotspur	*Hotspur*—driven by honor, "idealist," athletic
	associated with "anarchy and revolt"	*Falstaff*—finds honor pointless, cynical "realist," portly, given to sloth and hedonism
	Prince Hal	*Prince Hal*—young, "vigorous"
	"jokers," cynics, criminals, "wordmongers"	*Falstaff*—old, "dissolute"
King Henry IV	Hotspur	*King Henry IV*—old, "emblem of authority"
	"rivals ... for a crown that belongs to neither of them" (usurpers); the appearance of honor is important to both of them; once viewed as capable soldiers	*Hotspur*—young, "emblem of resistance and rebellion"
Prince Hal	Hotspur	*Hotspur*—driven by anger and honor, acts/reacts recklessly, rashly
	youthful, athletic, ambitious, competitive; eventually held in high esteem by others	*Prince Hal*—driven by reason and calculation

This elaborate character pairing for comparison and contrast purposes in the *Henry IV* plays is a structural device, I would argue, showing Shakespeare experimenting again following his unusual organization of *Richard II*. I address this further in Chapter 4 on father-son relationships and Chapter 6 on structural parallels in these works. In noting the earlier Vice figure's influence on Falstaff, "the personified figure of depravity or corruption," Garber claims, is "established as the contrary of everything virtuous and orderly."[27]

Associations with Unsavory Elements

Both Falstaff and Swearengen are associated with prostitution, lying, and alcohol. When Falstaff is assigned a "charge of foot" in the war in *1 Henry IV*, Falstaff says, "I would it had been of horse" (3.3.188). Garber says, "standard pronunciation in Shakespeare's time would have made this a manifestly bawdy homonym, "horse"/"whores"[28]; this seems to be a foreshadowing of what is to come in the sequel, for in *2 Henry IV*, when the tavern most of his scenes are set in is more clearly a brothel. In the pilot episode of *Deadwood*, we hear successful gold miner Ellsworth tell Swearengen directly and amiably, "Goddamn it, Swearengen, I don't trust you as far as I can throw you, but I enjoy the way you lie," which the saloon owner thanks him for (1.1). Swearengen and Falstaff are associated with brothels, hedonism, lying, and cheating, but provide entertainment to their companions, despite open acknowledgment of these vices they possess.

The company Swearengen keeps also lends itself to comparison with Falstaff. Charged with raising an army, Falstaff recruits the poor, sickly, and elderly, those who cannot bribe him to overlook them and he keeps most of the money intended to pay soldiers for himself, too. Even Falstaff himself recognizes what he has done in the name of profit, saying, "If I am not ashamed of my soldiers, I am a soused gurnet. I have misused the King's press damnably," noting that "my whole charge consists of ancients, corporals, lieutenants, gentlemen of companies—slaves as ragged as Lazarus in the painted cloth, where the glutton's dogs licked his sores, and such as indeed were never soldiers, but discarded unjust servingmen..." (*1 Henry IV* 4.2.11–13, 23–27). In Al Swearengen's case, these ragged fragments of humanity include among the men, Johnny Burns, not the sharpest tool in the shed, Dan Dority, for whom murder is always the answer to whatever the question may be, Silas Adams, perhaps the most refined of Swearengen's henchmen, Jimmy Irons, an opium junkie, and E.B. Farnum, described by numerous characters as "a grotesque," "a rodent-looking fellow," and "coyote-like" ("A Lie Agreed Upon, Part II" 2.2). Jacobs notes that "Al's insight is into the darkness of men's appetites rather than their aspiration for joy" and that "like a catfish in an aquarium, Swearengen is a bottom dweller, who feeds off the labor and detritus of others...."[29] Falstaff lives off of his friends' money, including Prince Hal's, running up bills at the tavern on credit, open to opportunities to rob noblemen on the highway. Critics have also noted that "everyone [in camp] knows Swearengen's game: his superadaptivity is underlined by his winning charm...,"[30] making him sound like a charming but dangerous mob boss. Milch has described him as "a very good man with none of the behaviors of goodness," that "what Al Swearengen thinks he is doing and what he is actually doing are two absolutely opposite things."[31] Again, this suggests a lack of self-awareness on Swearengen's part, although what's most interesting about this is, as Millichap notes, Swearengen's lack of awareness "of his motivations, especially his better ones"[32] toward the more vulnerable in the camp.

Wit and Adaptability with Language

Part of Falstaff's allure for other characters as well as audiences has been his charm and wit. Falstaff's amiability is one of his appealing traits. When Hal accuses him of stealing, Falstaff responds with the pleasant justification of "Why, Hal, 'tis my vocation. 'Tis no sin for a man to labor in his vocation" (*1 Henry IV* 1.2.102–103.) When the Chief Justice critiques Falstaff's financial management and excess, saying, "Your means are very slender, and your waste is great," Falstaff jovially and wittily replies, "I would it were otherwise; I would my means were greater, and my waist even slenderer" (*2 Henry IV* 1.2. 139–142). He generally takes no offense at what could be taken as insults, but which he acknowledges as others speaking the truth about him. Neither does Swearengen take offense at Garret's accusations of his colluding with others against Garret, nor Jewel's teasing critique of Swearengen's physical infirmities following his stroke. When Bullock replies that one of the first things he knew about Swearengen was that he was "a killer," Swearengen acknowledges, "Certain facts show in the mug" ("Childish Things" 2.8). Some truths about himself, he readily acknowledges.

When Poins and Prince Hal secretly rob Falstaff, Bardolph, and Peto of the money they have just robbed the travelers of, they anticipate Falstaff lying about how many men attacked them. He does not disappoint. The numbers rocket, up to 100 in Falstaff's first recounting of the incident, claiming he fought hand-to-hand with a dozen of them (*1 Henry IV* 2.4.159–160, 163). By the time the prince calls him out on his lying about the numbers and the fact that he ran away rather than fight their assailants and asks him to explain his apparent cowardice, Falstaff is ready with a clever response, claiming amiably, "By the Lord, I knew ye as well as he that made ye. Why, hear you, my masters, was it for me to kill the heir apparent? Should I turn upon the true prince?"

(*1 Henry IV* 2.4.264–266). Part of Poins, Prince Hal, and the audience's entertainment comes from seeing how Falstaff will manipulate the truth to show himself in the best possible light.

We also see Falstaff imitating others, including Prince Hal and Henry IV in the tavern, allegedly to help the prince practice his answer to his father's chiding over the company he keeps in Eastcheap. Falstaff shifts from speaking in prose as himself, a more informal, slang-filled form of speech appropriate to the tavern setting, to speaking in iambic pentameter, imitating at first common theatrical performances of kings. He says, "I must speak in passion, and I will do it in King Cambyses' vein" and starting with the iambic pentameter line, "Weep not, sweet queen, for trickling tears are in vain" (*1 Henry IV* 2.4. 382–384, 388), but finds this has a formality he cannot or does not wish to attempt to sustain.

Swearengen's capacity for wordplay, mixing high and low language frequently, is evident throughout the series. In response to Brom Garret's accusations, Swearengen denies them using Garret's own phrasing, mocking it, when he says, "I don't *collude*. I don't *cahoot*" ("Reconnoitering the Rim" 1.3). After Bullock and Swearengen fight in season two, as an attendant wraps Swearengen's torso with a bandage, saying, "It wants to be tight, Al," Swearengen replies sharply, "Does it?" ("A Lie Agreed Upon, Part I" 2.1). Farnum suggests to a bloody Al that he serve as messenger, returning Bullock's gun and badge while assessing his intentions for further violence. Swearengen asks tartly, "And how would that chat start, E.B., huh? [*he imitates E.B.*] 'Here's your hardware, and as he looks a cunt anyway, Al would like you to have this rose'" ("A Lie Agreed Upon, Part I" 2.1). In a later season, Swearengen warns Bullock, "We who will be the object of his wrath ought to stay close and confide," an articulate and complicated syntax ("A Rich Find" 3.6). As the series progresses, Swearengen's sharp wit and wordplay are on display more frequently.

Matt Feeney notes "as the camp's chaos subsides, Swearengen uses his Machiavellian acuity to civically useful ends (if for selfish reasons), and his aggression is increasingly expressed not in physical violence but in high-wire verbal gamesmanship and hilarious insults."[33] In season three, after Captain Turner knocks Swearengen to the ground and then holds him while Hearst, brandishing a pick, demands Swearengen's assistance in persuading Mrs. Ellsworth to sell her mine claim to him, Swearengen still manages a witty retort with, "As far as making your way into her … act averse to nasty language and partial to fruity tea" ("I am Not the Fine Man You Mistake Me For" 3.2). When Bullock can't contain himself and asks Hearst how his ear is doing after having led him through town by it while arresting him, Swearengen sarcastically quips, "Good, Bullock, good. By dissembling our feelings we keep the strategic edge" ("A Rich Find" 3.6). But it is not only his dry wit and acerbic commentary that make Al Swearengen an unexpectedly humorous and entertaining figure. While he does not attend or perform at the amateur night the theatre company holds, he sings a ditty during clean-up alone at the bar. This is a multifaceted, energetic, and entertaining character whose charisma and authority draw others—both characters and the audience—to him repeatedly.

Bolingbroke, Falstaff, and Swearengen use language to manipulate others. Garber notes, "For Bolingbroke, language is a tool and performance second nature."[34] We note this particularly when Henry IV is speaking to his wayward son in his use of guilt, shame, and frustration to chide his heir. Falstaff invites Prince Hal to role-play the parts of the king and his heir in the tavern, using the speech of the king to try to persuade his young friend to guarantee Falstaff's debauchery once Hal takes the throne. Salerno notes of Swearengen that "Al ... is expert of all of Deadwood's discursive registers: high, low, verbal, and non-verbal[, and his] highly versatile linguistic competence leaves him never at a disadvantage...."[35] Swearengen can clean up his language, momentarily, when speaking with the upper crust, such as Alma Garret; his dialogue about political maneuverings occurring within and outside the camp reveals an astute mind and clear articulation about what he observes or suspects in these machinations. He is flummoxed in his ability to communicate only when it comes to Johnny Burns, one of his staff whose critical thinking skills leave something to be desired. Graulich notes, too, that for all that Swearengen's "loquaciousness, exaggeration, and wordplay might exert power and control, but his insults to characters for whom we know he has affection (Trixie, Dan, Jewel, Doc, Silas, Wu, Bullock, even "the Jew") are a defensive way of sustaining relationships."[36] His insults often convey affection towards these characters, similar to the way that Falstaff often speaks to Prince Hal. Falstaff calls Prince Hal, to his face, "'Sblood, you starveling, you eel-skin, you dried neat's tongue, you bull's pizzle, you stockfish!" He also tells Hal to "Go hang thyself in thine own heir-apparent garters!" (2.2.42–43). Swearengen refers to Trixie as a "loopy cunt," with the intent to insult in the pilot, but in an obviously affectionate way in the third season finale. He complains about Jewel, "always dragging that leg around" ("Deep Water" 1.2), as though her disability is a just a sign of laziness on her part; what's surprising is when she describes him the same way after his stroke—and he allows her to ("E.B. was Left Out" 2.7).

Relationship to Honor

Given the deceptive manipulation carried out on a serious level by Henry Bolingbroke and on a comic level by Sir John Falstaff, audiences don't necessarily associate honor with either of them; in fact, Falstaff rails against honor in *1 Henry IV*, positing himself as the antithesis of Hotspur, who claims to actively pursue honor. Falstaff says to himself,

> What is honour? A word. What is in that word "honour"? What is that "honour"? Air. A trim reckoning! Who hath it? He that died o'Wednesday. Doth he feel it? No. Doth he hear it? No. 'Tis insensible, then? Yea, to the dead. But will it not live with the living? No. Why? Detraction will not suffer it. Therefore I'll none of it. Honour is a mere scutcheon [*1 Henry IV* 5.1.133–140].

Falstaff's pragmatic perspective declares that honor accompanies the dead; it has no measurable merit and so, he has no interest in it. He even claims to have killed Hotspur, knowing full well Prince Hal did so. In contrast, though, King Henry's guilt over both usurping the crown and the murder of Richard is emphasized in that "The language that pursues him throughout the play is the language of costume and counterfeiting...."[37] Garber goes on to compare King Henry's insomnia and "the language in which he describes it" with that of Richard III or Macbeth—"both, like Henry IV, kings with murder on their conscience, who have in effect 'murdered sleep' (*Macbeth* 2.2.40)."[38] Henry is troubled by Richard's murder until the day he himself dies. This remorse, however, doesn't prevent him from achieving and maintaining his ambition.

Differing somewhat from Henry IV and especially from Falstaff—and despite his criminal behavior—Swearengen does claim a code of ethics. As Swearengen himself tells Cy Tolliver, a competing saloon owner, that he while he may be a liquor and drug dealer and even a thief at times, at least he "ain't no fucking hypocrite" ("Mr. Wu" 1.10). We see evidence of his honor in his oath to Bullock to leave Mrs. Garret alone in the first season, despite his annoyance that she isn't leaving Deadwood, in his loyalty to Mr. Wu against outside threats and insiders who fail to understand him, and his protection of other vulnerable individuals in the camp, including the disabled Jewel, the infirm Reverend Smith, and a panicked Trixie.

As Silas Adams says, "When he ain't lyin,' Al's the most honorable man you'll ever meet" ("Tell Him Something Pretty" 3.12). This seemingly contradictory description fits Swearengen. In season two, as Swearengen dictates to Adams terms for the Yankton agreement, he says to Adams, "Take out the fucking 50 from Yankton to us. [...] I don't want the founding document recording a fucking bribe" ("Boy-the-Earth-Talks-To" 2.12). He thinks about the future of the camp and how such recorded corruption might endanger its stability, deciding to forego his immediate profit for, he alleges, longer term thievery. In the third season, when Al expresses that he is mystified as to why he supported publishing Bullock's letter about the murdered Cornish mine worker, Langrishe offers an admirable interpretation based on his knowledge of Swearengen ("Unauthorized Cinnamon" 3.7). Al's friendship with Langrishe is a surprise as well, suggesting still-hidden facets of his personality and past. Mittell notes that "elaborating more about a character's backstory can make a static figure seem more dynamic, so that our own shifting knowledge and attitudes create the illusion of character change."[39] It's not clear how much Swearengen grows and changes over the course of the series, but as the audience learns new information about his character, it at least appears as though he is developing.

Self-Awareness

Swearengen, like Bullock, sometimes appears not to understand himself or his motivations, but he rarely shares such self-doubt with anyone who might actually answer his questions. Neither does Henry IV; men in powerful positions cannot afford that luxury, given how such vulnerability might be used against them. Langrishe's answer reinforces Swearengen's rhetorical and political savvy at proposing the letter be published as witness against Hearst, who ordered the murder of his own workers and does not notify their families of their deaths afterward, publicly countering Hearst's lack of respect for human life.

At the final town council meeting in the camp, Al turns to his peers for advice on how they might best proceed with the least damage, admitting his own limited thinking. Al comments, "My instinct's to act alone, chart the course for fucking carnage. [...] the fucking innocents is what give me fucking pause. I invite the suggestions of others against my instinct to send for the guns" ("Unauthorized Cinnamon" 3.7). His concern for the children of the camp prevents him from acting alone and initiating all-out war on Hearst and his men. A man with no conscience would not take that collateral damage into consideration, as we soon see from Hearst.

In the final episode of the series, when Hearst demands Trixie's death for taking a shot at him and the camp alliance meets to determine how to avoid a Hearst-initiated bloodbath, Al refuses to carry out Hearst's demand, asserting a loyalty and debt to Trixie that outweighs any threat from Hearst ("Tell Him Something Pretty" 3.36). He publicly acknowledges that he owes Trixie, adamantly refusing to take her life, ironic given that the series began with him beating and threatening her. His sense of loyalty to Trixie is stronger than his self-preservation in this case.

Popularity

As Phyllis Rackin writes about Shakespeare's Falstaff, for many critics, he becomes "far more than a character in a play"; he pulsate[s] with vivid life, [and] seemed to transcend the historical moment of his creation and the historical world in which Shakespeare originally installed him [...] His irrepressible, transgressive eloquence enabled him to debunk the conventional pieties that defined the limits of historical representation. He seemed to break through the frame of the represented action to join the audience in an eternal theatrical present.[40]

Rackin's description of the impact the larger-than-life character of Falstaff has had and continues to have on readers and viewers in many ways also applies to how many viewers come to see Al Swearengen, who also possesses an "irrepressible, transgressive eloquence" when the situation deems it necessary. The writers, too, seem to fall for such characters, providing more and more dialogue and/or stage/screen time for such unusually complex and rich characters. Typically, in Shakespeare's history plays, the monarch in the title of the play has the most lines. In *Richard II*, Richard has 785 lines, followed by Bolingbroke at 413.[41] But in the Henry IV plays, this is not the case; Falstaff dominates these plays, with 616 lines in *1 Henry IV* and 637 in *2 Henry IV*.[42] Swearengen also comes to dominate the *Deadwood* series; take a look at the two episodes where he is silenced and removed from the action in season two to see the impact that has on the show and its characters' reliance upon him.[43]

Conclusion

Henry Bolingbroke, Sir John Falstaff, and Al Swearengen embody power, corruption, political vision and ambition, wisdom, and, more often than not, an utterly self-serving perspective. Yet all lack some degree of self-awareness about their own character, motivation, and desires, a characteristic they share with the young men they mentor. In contrast to Bolingbroke and Falstaff, however, Swearengen does exhibit a sense of honor and loyalty, and he at least has the appearance of a character that has grown and changed over the course of the series. Henry IV, Falstaff, and Swearengen possess a strong influence over the young men whose company they keep, acting as fathers to several, advising, scolding, and teaching these followers from their own experience how to succeed in the transitional and unstable environment. Swearengen takes in Bullock as another potential substitute son, mentoring him in the ways of politics at the edge of the frontier. A loyal and an astute reader of others, knowing just how to manipulate them to elicit the response he wants, Swearengen is a consummate politician in many ways, persuasive and clever with speech, exactly the skill(s) that the plainspoken Bullock lacks.

4
Father-Son Relationships

> AL SWEARENGEN: *"I get back on my fucking feet, I'll carry my share of the water."*
> SETH BULLOCK: *"My money's on you."* (*"Complications"* 2.5)
>
> "[J]ustice must be dispensed by men who are just as strong and just as daring as the criminals.... There is often little moral difference between the outlaw and the man who operates within the law."[1]

Seth Bullock and Al Swearengen are clearly set up as framing devices in the *Deadwood* series, beginning and ending the first episode. Although initially introduced as young hero and older villain, these two men's relationship evolves from one of conflict to a more familial one, with Swearengen taking on a father-figure role, mentoring Bullock as one of several son figures he acquires. As the quote above from Bazin regarding Western films indicates, the men facing off with one another must exhibit an equal measure of strength and daring, emphasizing parallels emerging between characters initially introduced as seeming opposites. Complicated father-son relationships are the core of the storytelling found in Shakespeare's history plays, the conventional Western genre, and Milch's *Deadwood*. As Phyllis Rackin notes,

> In a very important sense, chronicle history was not simply written without women: it was also written *against* them. Patriarchal history is designed to construct a verbal substitute for the visible physical connection between a mother and her children, to authenticate the relationships between fathers and sons and to suppress and supplant the role of the mother.[2]

All four of the Henriad plays present at least references to Bolingbroke/Henry IV and Prince Hal as his son, but there is no mention made of Bolingbroke/Henry IV's wife or Prince Hal's mother. The conflict between the father and son must be directly negotiated between the two of them without a female intermediary, such as the Duchess of York who pleads on her son

Aumerle's behalf to first his father, the Duke of York, and then the king in *Richard II*. References to men's familial relationships proliferate in both the Henriad and *Deadwood*, which reveal a preoccupation with fathers, sons, and brothers.

Father-Son Relationships as Confrontational

The notion of father-son relationships as consistently confrontational is reflected in Shakespeare's *Richard II* and *Henry IV* and Milch's *Deadwood*. Geoffrey Gorer observes that the rite of passage for boys into manhood in 1940s U.S. culture called for him to "reject his father."[3] Robert Bly asserts that "Young men in Europe ... traditionally imagined the father [as] a demonic being whom they must wrestle with."[4] Along these same lines, Anthony Easthope says that the Western film "*Red River* perfectly illustrates a main feature of the masculine myth, a social order relying on the endless negotiation of conflict."[5] We see in the father-son relationships presented in *Henry IV* parts one and two and *Deadwood* that "endless negotiation of conflict" that allows each to establish the boundaries of his identity separate from yet connected to the other man. Bly also addresses fairy tale references to fathers and sons, in that some such fairy tales contain two kings, beginning with the son's conflict with his biological father, the first King, whose castle he must then leave; "After some time of suffering and isolation, a second King somehow appears, adopts [the son] and sets a task. Then a complicated dance begins as the adventurer tries to establish a fruitful connection with the new King."[6] At the end of season one of *Deadwood*, we learn that Bullock's father served in the British Royal Army and his distant older brother served in the U.S. Cavalry ("Sold Under Sin" 1.12), setting a male legacy of military service that Bullock inherits. Milch has written of Bullock's father, he "was an alcoholic sergeant major who beat his son."[7] In Deadwood, Bullock initially identifies a potential father figure in Wild Bill Hickok. The men share the skill of being expert shots and former U.S. Marshals, as well as a sense of irony about human nature and a desire to protect the vulnerable while also punishing the malevolent. The men strike up a quick and easy friendship, riding out to check on the Metz family massacre, facing off with Ned Mason in the street, and facing the threat of Tom Mason in the No. 10 Saloon.

The *Deadwood* episode from season one in which Seth Bullock loses his first father figure in the community, Wild Bill Hickok, is titled "This was a Man," borrowed from what Antony says of Brutus in *Julius Caesar* (5.5.68–74) offering direct and explicit evidence of Milch and the writing staff drawing upon Shakespearean themes regarding masculinity. Antony says of the death of his friend/enemy Brutus:

4. Father-Son Relationships

> This was the noblest Roman of them all. [...]
> He only in a general honest thought
> And common good to all made one of them. [the assassins]
> His life was gentle, and the elements
> So mixed in him that Nature might stand up
> And say to all the world, "This was a man!" [*Julius Caesar* 5.5.68; 71–74].

Here Antony speaks in superlatives of Brutus, as the most admirable Roman, honest, seeking the common good above personal gain, exhibiting a kindness to others, an exemplar of man, such that even Nature herself would proclaim him a model for others. In some ways this, of course, applies so clearly to Hickok, seen from Bullock's perspective as a father-figure model, coming from a similar law enforcement background and being a quick draw with a conscience. Bullock even accepts the nickname Hickok gives him of "Montana," referencing where the younger man served as U.S. Marshal and moves from calling his new friend "Mr. Hickok" to "Bill" at his request. Charlie Utter, Hickok's manager/friend, recognizes, too, similarities and differences between the two men, asking Bullock to share his secret for getting along, as it's something Hickok lacks. Antony's praise of Brutus comes after he faced off with Brutus in a public forum with a speech designed to raise doubts about Brutus's claims of honorable intentions; Antony's posthumous praise of Brutus seeks to excuse his faults. Hickok, too has flaws, evident in his own problems, with a new wife and responsibilities, the fading of the West he established his reputation in, and his addiction to gambling to the point of poverty and charges of vagrancy that he has attempted to outrun.

While the initial relationship between Bullock and Hickok is an easy, supportive one that both parties seem to desire, the relationship between Bullock and Swearengen begins in conflict, insults, and tension. In the first episode, Bullock and Star go to Swearengen to make an offer on the lot they're renting from him. Swearengen makes a joke about the gunfight he observed, saying "Well, I hear you're not a man I'd want mistaking my intentions," which agitates Bullock into testily responding with, "Who said that? I'd like to ask him what he meant" ("Deadwood" 1.1). Swearengen apologizes to Bullock, but then asks about possible unnamed partners, like Hickok, in the purchase offer. He wonders aloud about secret alliances intended to compete with the Gem in gambling which angers Bullock again. *Then* Swearengen corrects Bullock's grammar:

> BULLOCK says to Star: "What business of that is his?"
> SWEARENGEN to Bullock: "You mean what business of *mine* is *that*."
> BULLOCK, furiously, to Swearengen: "Don't tell me what the fuck I mean."
> SWEARENGEN: "Not a tone to get a deal done in" ["Deadwood" 1.1].

Swearengen seems to be intentionally testing the younger man's limits, calling off the business negotiations once it's clear that Bullock's anger is only escalating. David Milch, in *Deadwood: Stories of the Black Hills*, says, "When Bullock arrives in Deadwood, Swearengen takes one look at him, and they go at it. Both recognize how similar they are. They are personally and professionally cut from the same cloth."[8] Milch also states, "they're two parts of the same personality. They both, I think, are more dependent on each other than either would be [willing] to admit."[9] Seth Bullock and Al Swearengen are clearly set up as framing devices in the *Deadwood* series, beginning and ending the first episode. Both check on Sofia, the child rescued, personally, albeit with differing motives. Doc Cochran doesn't trust either Bullock or Swearengen—he comments to Jane Canary about the two men's similiarities that "I see as much misery out of them moving to justify theirselves as them that set out to do harm" ("Deep Water" 1.2). Both are kind to the Reverend Smith. Both have violent impulses and act on them. McGee's analysis of classic Western films *Red River* and *The Searchers* notes that "the founding father must once again come to terms with the son who opposes not only the father's authority but the origin of the social system the son inherits from the father."[10] We can see something similar occurring in both *Richard II*, between Aumerle and his father the Duke of York toward the end of the play, and *1 Henry IV*, between the king and Henry "Hotspur" Percy.

In *Richard II*, Aumerle's loyalty remains with his cousin Richard throughout the play, even to the point of his participating in the planning of a plot to assassinate the new king Henry IV. Aumerle's father, the Duke of York, has switched loyalties from Richard to Henry as the play progresses and Henry gains power and the throne. When York discovers that his son is involved with these plots, he declares, "Now, by mine honor, by my life, my troth, / I will appeach the villain" (*Richard II* 5.2.78–79), meaning he will publicly accuse his own son of treason in front of the king. When the Duchess of York attempts to dissuade him, reminding him they aren't likely to have more sons at this age, York replies, "Were he twenty times my son / I would appeach him" (*Richard II* 5.2.101–102). York's loyalties lie with the king, and with his need to maintain his honor and reputation with Henry IV, rather than his own family and his only son. York does accuse Aumerle of treason in front of the king, adding that "he shall spend mine honor with his shame. / As thriftless sons their scraping fathers' gold" (*Richard II* 5.3.68–69). The imagery he uses here, of careless, reckless sons spending all of the gold their fathers have attempted to store up for them, is echoed in a speech by Henry IV in *2 Henry IV* 4.5.64–78, when he complains about his own son's behaviors, which I analyze in Chapter 6. York ends up competing with his son and his wife in pleading for the King's ruling as to either condemn Aumerle or pardon him. The scene quickly takes on a comic tone, despite the seriousness of the charges and the division in the family; ultimately, Henry IV pardons Aumerle, blaming his fierce loyalty on his youth, but York and Aumerle have not reconciled by the end of the play.

Early in *1 Henry IV*, the King asks an advisor what he thinks of "this young Percy's pride" (1.1.91), with Hotspur having kept prisoners of war from the King, who demanded them. Despite Hotspur's audacity, or perhaps because of it, King Henry seems to recognize something of his own past behavior and, rather than becoming angry with the young man, he confesses an admiration of him and a longing that this Henry was his son, instead of Prince Hal. Bevington notes that, despite his opposition to them, King Henry IV and Owen Glendower express admiration for Hotspur, mainly because his rebelliousness "promise[s] manliness and fame"; Prince Hal's apparent rebelliousness provokes fear and loathing from his father since his behaviors "seem to reject the values of duty and leadership" so dear to King Henry.[11] If we view this play as a rite of passage into adulthood for Prince Hal, then these issues must be resolved; Hal must demonstrate publicly an acceptance of his familial and political responsibilities as well as prove his capabilities to his father and his subjects. Bevington says that "Hal must find his adult self—a self that differs greatly from that of King Henry—but must do so in a way that preserves the integrity of their relationship and the real debt he owes his father."[12] The play deliberately pairs older men with younger men repeatedly, offering assessments of the younger men's developing character and leadership potential, and the edge of conflict between the generations emerging again and again. Both Henry IV and Glendower respect Hotspur for standing up to them, his elders, demonstrating his strength of character and willingness to test established authority. Prince Hal proves more problematic as he seems to be indifferent altogether to his elders, gaining their respect, or even recognizing authority, the very authority he himself is expected to inherit. His avoidance of aiding in defending his father's claim to the throne or even appearing at court removes him from any possible positive assessment by his elders in positions of authority.

Dishonorable Elders and Honorable Youths

Early in the play bearing his name, Henry IV describes Hotspur with longing, calling him

> A son who is the theme of honour's tongue,
> Amongst a grove the very straightest plant,
> Who is sweet Fortune's minion and her pride....
> O, that it could be proved

> That some night-tripping fairy had exchanged
> In cradle clothes our children where they lay,
> And called mine Percy, his Plantagenet!
> Then would I have his Harry and he mine [1.1.80–82; 85–89].

King Henry praises Henry "Hotspur" Percy for his reputation of honorable behavior, describing him as "the theme of honour's tongue," a young nobleman who "amongst a grove [is] the very straightest plant"—implying that no other young men hold the virtuous, non-crooked or corrupt, promise that Hotspur does, including his own son, Prince Henry. He goes so far as to call Hotspur "sweet Fortune's minion and her pride" and then directly admits his envy towards Northumberland over his son. What King Henry admires in Hotspur in part is that which he deems that he himself lacks and which his errant son is not supplying: honor and virtue. As the *Henry IV* plays progress, we see consistent signs of King Henry's growing guilt over how he took the throne from Richard II. When he speaks to Prince Hal, he lays the prince's errant behavior to God's judgment against himself, saying "I know not whether God will have it so / For some displeasing service I have done," that God might "breed revengement and a scourge for me" out of the king's own bloodline (*1 Henry IV* 3.2.4–5, 7). He mentions Richard again in *2 Henry IV* 3.1 and 4.5, where he tells Prince Hal, "God knows, my son, / By what bypaths and indirect, crook'd ways/ I met this crown" (*1 Henry IV* 4.5.182–184). E.A. Rauchut claims that "Hotspur's code of chivalric honour serves as a dramatic foil to Henry IV's *realpolitik*."[13] They complement one another. This relationship is characterized by hostility and conflict, but also admiration, respect, and longing, too, ultimately, for connection, at least from the older male authority figure towards the younger man. Hotspur wants a demonstration of respect from Henry IV. Similarly, whereas a code of honor seems to motivate Bullock, pragmatics drive Swearengen.

Declarations of honor and justice often take the form of anger from Bullock. A few lines later in the same pilot episode of *Deadwood*, Bullock fumes over Swearengen's perceived insult to Star. "I don't like that son of a bitch," he declares ("Deep Water" 1.2). Bullock remains incensed at Swearengen's new counter-offer, which is to pay half, then wait an extended period before finalizing their deal. "I won't be partners with him," declares Bullock ("Deep Water" 1.2). But this tension is somewhat diffused by a surprising shift in Bullock's tone and physical stance that foreshadows the father-son relationship that later develops between these two. Swearengen demands of him, "You come into my camp, rent my lot, within six hours you blow in a guy's eye with Wild Bill Hickok backing your play. Next day I'm supposed to sell you the lot, put you in business without asking who the fuck you are or what the fuck you're doing here?" ("Deep Water" 1.2). Bullock sees the reasoning in Swearengen's demand. His gaze drops to the floor and his stance indicates awkward discomfort. His almost mumbled answer is that of a boy called to account for his questionable actions by his father and doing so poorly.

> BULLOCK: Far as what happened in the street, with Bill Hickok being involved, that was a turn of events.
> SWEARENGEN: A *what?*
> BULLOCK: It was a turn of events.
> SWEARENGEN: *Oh*, "a turn of events" ... ["Deep Water" 1.2].

This is the first sign of Bullock's acceptance of Swearengen as a potential father-figure, but they aren't finished with conflict between them verging on violence yet. In the same episode when Swearengen makes an anti-Semitic comment to Star, Bullock warns him, "You don't want to be talking that way" ("Deep Water" 1.2). Swearengen's reply is "What makes you talk to *me* in that tone of voice?," which leads to a stare-down between Bullock and Swearengen broken only by Trixie's whispering erotic offers to Bullock, in response to her boss's terse order to get Bullock out of his establishment ("Deep Water" 1.2). The tension between the two men is palpable. After another round of conflict on this topic, the men do finalize the deal for Bullock and Star to purchase the land for their hardware store.

Similar to the initial Bullock and Swearengen clashes, Hotspur and Falstaff represent differing extremes on the spectrum of honorable behaviors, allowing Prince Hal to occupy a middle range between them, a balance, albeit with one as a peer-competitor figure and the other as a father-figure. As I mentioned in the previous chapter, a number of critics have recognized the father-son relationships in *1 Henry IV* as contributing significantly to the structure of the play's complicated mix of aligned characters and foils.[14] Falstaff presents an alternative father-figure for Prince Hal, rejecting the more self-controlled and responsible behavior expected of an older knight. In his failure to appear at court or to take part in the battles defending his father's claim to the throne initially, Prince Hal appears to be modeling his behavior after that of Falstaff. In addition, Falstaff's and Hotspur's distinctly opposing perspectives of honor make them "dramatic foils for each other, representing extremes between which Hal must choose."[15] Given that Prince Hal provides the audience with a soliloquy regarding his behavior early in the play, it's clear that the prince has already chosen his path, and it's not following Falstaff's model, although it appears otherwise. While Hotspur strives to achieve honor for himself, Falstaff sees no point in it, reasoning that most who have achieved it have done so through death. While "Falstaff's vices are Hotspur's virtues, and the reverse,"[16] Prince Hal never reaches the extremes of either of these potential models. Some critics claim that "Hotspur is easy to parody, because he, too, is a figure of excess."[17] Both Swearengen and Bullock can be given to excess. If we view Hal as influenced by both Falstaff and Hotspur, as well as by his own biological father, Henry IV, then "in a sense the whole play is the working out of this inner conflict, the acknowledgement—rather than the suppression or elimination—of the various aspects of his persona that reflect upon, and learn from, the models ... around him."[18] Bullock contains elements of both Hickok and Swearengen and must negotiate his own identity between the two.

Parallels Between Elders and Youths

King Henry IV and Hotspur are initially aligned politically through Hotspur's service in defending the throne against the Scots and rebels, and through their use of some of the same significant language in regard to themselves. From the *OED*, to *pluck* means "to steal, to pull a thing out of the place where it's planted or where it grows, to gather, to snatch, to sound or play." Garber points out that "pluck" as a verb is used by both King Henry and Hotspur.[19] Henry is reflecting on his ability to pull from men their loyalty, to draw it to himself, to benefit himself. Hotspur uses it to talk about his desire to rescue honor from the depths to which it has sunk, to enhance his own image alone, "without corrivals." Through the deliberate parallels in their language, Hotspur and Henry IV are shown to share some similarities in ambition and image, but they seem to possess different agendas or aims. For example, it's difficult to take Hotspur seriously as a threat to Henry IV's sovereignty without the support of Northumberland and other older, more experienced courtiers and soldiers.

First impressions of both Bolingbroke and Bullock are positive. Bevington says that "our first impression of Bolingbroke is of forthrightness, moral indignation, and patriotic zeal."[20] Sounds a lot like our first impressions of Bullock, in his role of injured sheriff, determined to follow the letter of the law even when confronted by a drunken, armed mob demanding his sole prisoner. Shakespeare does not provide any insight into Bolingbroke's motives, thoughts, or his plans, since, unlike Richard, he has no soliloquies. Too, Bevington notes that "As a man of action, [Bolingbroke] lives in the present."[21] We're given very little insight into Bullock's thoughts and motivations, although we see him writing in a journal in the pilot. Swearengen provides long monologues or soliloquies that allow audience members to understand his background or current thinking, but we hear nothing comparable from Bullock, aside from a couple of needling comments from others (Otis Russell and George Hearst) speculating on Bullock's history with bullies that elicit strong responses from their target, seeming to confirm their accuracy.

A second round of conflict between Bullock and Swearengen emerges over Alma Garret's gold mine claim after Hickok's death. Acting on behalf of Garret, and at Hickok's request, Bullock demands that Swearengen name an honest assayer for Garret's claim, noting bluntly that he plans to hold Swearengen accountable if the assayer lies or is mistaken. Swearengen tries to bluff his way out of any involvement with the claim, but Bullock won't let up. His threats to Swearengen are brief and direct: "I know what you been trying to do to her," "You and I know how it is, Mr. Swearengen," and, finally, the unambiguous, "She gets a square shake, or I come for you" ("Bullock Returns to the Camp" 1.7). Swearengen responds with a counter-complaint when he says, "So here you come, in all nobility, threatening me with a dire result, if the property that widow's husband thought worthless and wanted sold, turns out not to be pinched out," followed by a threat against Bullock ("Bullock Returns to the Camp" 1.7). The younger man calls Swearengen out over his intimidation tactics at trying to pressure Mrs. Garret into selling the claim back to him; he says outright, but in an amused way rather than a challenging one as in their previous encounters, that "Farnum is your waterboy" ("Bullock Returns to the Camp" 1.7). In response, Swearengen nicknames Bullock with "his Holiness," a critique of the younger man's arrogant disdain and his sense of righteousness. It seems as though they have drawn sides again in a new conflict and there can be no easy reconciliation between the two adversaries. However, another surprising turn occurs when Bullock reports back to Swearengen after the claim has been assayed by Ellsworth, with help from Dority as a guide, and it hinges on Swearengen's declaration of honor towards Bullock.

Alliances

Swearengen displays a form of the same amused amiability that Bullock had in their previous encounter. On the news of Alma Garret's having struck it rich with her gold mine, the older man invites the younger one to sit with him, saying "Come here, Bullock. Come drink with your vanquished foe" ("Suffer the Little Children" 1.8). We see a similar amiability from Falstaff when Prince Hal catches him in a lie about the number of thieves that attacked him and calls him a coward for running away from the scene of the robbery. Falstaff isn't offended by these challenges to his honor and masculinity; instead he cleverly sidesteps them, by saying he recognized the prince in disguise and therefore chose not to fight back. Swearengen commends Bullock and Star for their civic-minded action of offering their store as a location for the smallpox vaccine distribution and then moves on to seek a detente with Bullock in regard to the widow Garret and her charge, Sofia Metz. This is one of the first examples we see of Swearengen as civic-minded, showing a genuine concern for the bigger picture of community building in Deadwood, rather than focused solely on his own profit. In thinking ahead of that community development, Swearengen proposes a surprising collaboration with Bullock, which the younger man takes quick advantage of for his own interests—a reversal of roles for the two men. Swearengen offers to "show [Bullock his] bona fides for cooperation," noting that if official peace with the Sioux comes about, it would "be wise for you and me to paddle in the same directions. Tics or habits of behavior either finds dislikable in the other gotta be overlooked or taken with a grain of salt" ("Suffer the Little Children" 1.8). Swearengen is already beginning to act as a mentor to the younger man with this advice. Bullock asks if the saloon owner's guarantees could extend to Mrs. Garret's safety, which Swearengen readily agrees to, referencing his assumption that she is leaving camp to return to New York. Then Bullock breaks the news that she's remaining in camp. Swearengen pauses before graciously and respectfully confirming that "The oath stands as a gesture to you" ("Suffer the Little Children" 1.8) In this exchange, we see Swearengen proposing an alliance against outside threats, considering their collective future in Deadwood.

He also takes on a mentoring role in explaining how they need to respond to one another in the future, overlooking habits that one another finds dislikeable. His oath to leave Mrs. Garret alone is one he makes under the mistaken impression that she is leaving. Learning otherwise, he reiterates it, he says, out of respect for Bullock. In response to this overture of respect and collaboration, Bullock offers two things in return: a limited trust and information. He asks permission for a shave in the Gem, a gesture of trust since it means allowing an employee of Swearengen's to place a blade at his throat in Swearengen's establishment, a gesture that doesn't go unremarked upon by the saloon owner himself. Then he reveals Farnum's attempt to profit on the offer to Garret ("Suffer the Little Children" 1.8). Bullock not only demonstrates a level of trust toward Swearengen, he now shares information with him, warning him that those acting on his behalf (Farnum) were attempting to cheat him by withholding the full offer he had approved for Garret's gold mine claim, a minor betrayal. In this way, we see Bullock becoming another agent for Swearengen's information gathering machine.

Bullock's sense of justice leads him to critique the naming of Con Stapleton as sheriff in the ad hoc government for Deadwood, but it's still a job he no longer wants to take on himself. Even Swearengen recognizes that Bullock is the man best suited for that responsibility. Swearengen says, consideringly, "Now, if you were fucking sheriff and you said 'Do this, do that,' I'd consider it 'cause you're not a fucking whore. I'd go downstairs for that fucking swearing in. And I'd follow your career, 'cause you're one of those pains in the balls who think the law can be honest" ("Jewel's Boot is Made for Walking"

1.11). Bullock rejects the idea with the vague excuse of "I have personal responsibilities" followed by the more direct "I don't want it" ("Jewel's Boot is Made for Walking" 1.11). Swearengen responds with "Well, I do lots of things I don't want to do," suggesting that is what adult men do, and Bullock defensively agrees with "You think you're the only one?" ("Jewel's Boot is Made for Walking" 1.11). Swearengen and Bullock acknowledge here the larger responsibilities of men upon whom others depend and the tasks that no one wants to do, but that have to be done anyway. They share some common ground for the second time. Bullock also learns that Swearengen would approve of him, even encourage him, to take on the role of law enforcer in Deadwood. That opens the door to his eventual acceptance of this responsibility.

Finally, we see Bullock stepping up to take the role he has sought to avoid, that of law enforcer for the camp, comparable perhaps to Prince Hal defending his father's right to the throne by defending his life in battle in *1 Henry IV* act five scene four. Henry tells his eldest son, "Thou hast redeemed thy lost opinion, / And showed thou mak'st some tender of my life / In this fair rescue thou hast brought me" (*1 Henry IV* 5.4.48–50). Bullock warns Swearengen away from Otis Russell as he reluctantly agrees to serve as the camp's public enforcer of order when he says, "I'll be the fucking Sheriff" ("Sold Under Sin" 1.12). Then they engage in a brief back and forth exchange that determines when Bullock will begin in this role—immediately—and display the badge that identifies him as the keeper of communal order; it almost comes across as a catechism quiz, with Swearengen asking questions and prompting answers from the younger man, down to Swearengen insisting Bullock wear the badge in the appropriate place at once, with Bullock sullenly retorting, "I know where it goes" ("Sold Under Sin" 1.12). Here they are just beginning to fall into the more amiable but honest exchange that defines the growing closeness of their relationship. In *1 Henry IV*, the father-son conflict seems to have been resolved by the play's end, as father and son go into the next battle together to face Glendower and Mortimer, however, in *2 Henry IV*, Henry is once again asking if anyone has seen the prince and conflict arises again when he believes Hal has taken the crown from him out of ambition.

Re-Emergence of Conflict

Season two of *Deadwood* opens with renewed focus on the relationship between Swearengen and Bullock, with the saloon owner feeling ignored and insulted by the Sheriff's preoccupation with Alma Garret. Swearengen tells Dority, "Self-deceiving cocksucker I am, I thought when America took us in, Bullock would prove a fucking resource ... look at him, striding out like some randy maniac bishop" ("A Lie Agreed Upon, Part I" 2.1). Alexandra Shepard notes that in the early modern period in England, advice literature about masculinity was overlaid with anxieties stemming from "male fears about both attaining manliness and sustaining the patriarchal order, particularly through controlling women."[22] Despite a four-hundred-year gap between the settings of *Henry IV* and *Deadwood*, the same rules prevail when it comes to patriarchal control of femininity. From Swearengen's perspective, Bullock has allowed Garret to distract him from other business at hand, civic business that concerns Swearengen and, he thinks, should concern Bullock.

In *1 Henry IV*, Shakespeare gives us scenes of Hotspur with his wife demanding to accompany him to Wales to discuss strategy for attacking King Henry's forces; Hotspur at first denies her but then gives in to her requests (2.3). We later see him in Wales, idle with his wife at the end of the day (3.1). We're given no such feminine associations for Prince Hal. As a result, we may come to see Hotspur's connection with his wife as an area of dependence, of weakness, on his part. Prince Hal has no such distractions from politics; instead, he follows a set path to inherit the crown and win esteem from his subjects by appearing reformed. This deliberate manipulation on Prince Hal's part is revealed to the audience through a soliloquy in the first act of the play. He has allowed himself to appear distracted and corrupted by spending his time at a tavern with Falstaff, drinking, cavorting with prostitutes and thieves, disregarding his responsibility to the kingdom and to his own father, and avoiding court for long periods of time.

In *2 Henry IV*, the King scolds his son for his absences from court while also admitting his longing for his son's presence, saying, "Not an eye / But is aweary of thy common sight, / Save mine, which hath desired to see thee more..." (3.2.87–89). Henry says that it seems as though everyone else gets to see Prince Hal except him, the father who longs for his son and assurances that his son will step up to the task of defending the crown against rebellion. He suggests that his son has been deliberately avoiding him and his responsibilities as heir.

Similarly, the new, fragile alliance between the sheriff and the saloon owner seems in danger at the opening of season two of *Deadwood*, as Bullock seems to be avoiding consulting with Swearengen. From the balcony of the Gem, Swearengen provokes a fight with Bullock, after which he comments on his intent, "You want a donkey's attention ... bring a fucking pole down between his ears" ("A Lie Agreed Upon, Part I" 2.1). Commenting on Bullock's stubborn distracted state, Swearengen's deliberate provocation of Bullock is intended as discipline for misbehavior. Swearengen is feeling ignored and neglected by his new protégé. When Bullock shows up to fight with Swearengen, he receives a scolding about how he has been spending his time, "instead of doing [his] civic duty" ("A Lie Agreed Upon, Part I" 2.1). Swearengen chides him, saying of the widow, "And it's time for her and some others to quit their fucking shirking.... Now I can handle my areas, but there's dimensions and fucking angles I'm not expert at. You would be if you'd sheathe your prick long enough ... and resume being the upright pain in the balls that graced us all last summer" ("A Lie Agreed Upon, Part I" 2.1). Swearengen clearly scolds Bullock as "some others" for "shirking" his civic responsibilities, acknowledging his need of Bullock's strengths, areas that Swearengen himself is lacking in, those "dimensions and fucking angles I'm not expert at. You would be...." In response, Bullock looks dumbfounded before removing his badge and gun to fight over Swearengen's insult to him and to Mrs. Garret.

In season three, Swearengen again accuses Bullock of avoiding him intentionally, out of a desire not to be called into accountability. The night before, Bullock's anger at Hearst leads him to arrest Hearst, marching him through the thoroughfare by the ear, which Swearengen observes from his balcony. The next day he confronts Bullock over taking a route home that avoided Swearengen altogether. Bullock replies bluntly, "It bespoke I didn't feel like talking to you" ("A Rich Find" 3.6). Swearengen offers two brief "I-don't-want-to-talk" alternatives Bullock could have given him before acknowledging, "I, too, Bullock, when suspecting I've fucked the dog, keenly seek some solitude" ("A Rich Find" 3.6) then offering the options he sees as viable for their next action together in response to Hearst. Swearengen visits Bullock at home to have this confrontation over Bullock's independent action that has intensified the tensions in the camp regarding Hearst. He scolds Bullock for avoiding reporting to him after the deed had been done, reminding him of the necessity of their remaining in close communication with one another, despite any shame or self-recrimination over mistaken action already taken. It is rare that Swearengen himself ventures out from the Gem to seek out Bullock directly. When he does so, it's usually connected to his level of disturbance and/or a demonstration of respect towards Bullock. And Bullock's responses to these overtures usually include apology and contrition, in recognition that he neglected his responsibility of communicating with Swearengen, forcing the older man to seek him out.

Father Figure Mentoring Sons

During season two, Swearengen seems more overtly to take on Bullock as another substitute son. He shows he understands something about the younger man's nature when Bullock shows up outside the Gem's balcony the night after their fight, demanding Swearengen step outside in five minutes. Swearengen says, more to himself than to Dolly who is with him, "That Bullock's a fucking strategist, ain't he? Sets terms to publicly humiliate me, and my penalty if I don't comply is he walks into the bar downstairs and takes 15 bullets in the chest" before he adds thoughtfully, "I suppose I do fucking understand. So fucking confused and disgusted and wanting it to end and looking for the blessing of a quick way out. Sets himself to a higher fucking standard than our natures, and he wants execution 'cause he's failed" ("A Lie Agreed Upon, Part II" 2.2). Astutely, he recognizes Bullock's frustration and desperation with being assigned the task of maintaining order and control in Deadwood, when he cannot control or order his own life, which manifests itself in anger and violence. Once Swearengen believes he has some insight into Bullock's state of mind, he goes on to give the sheriff some advice, which is so clearly attuned to Bullock's thoughts that the younger man looks stunned in response. Swearengen returns his gun and badge to him, saying, "I hope [you'll] reside with us and improve our general fucking atmosphere for a good long fucking time, even with all the personal complications and fucking disasters that we all fucking have, and where, running away solves absolutely fucking nothing" ("A Lie Agreed Upon, Part II" 2.2). Swearengen does not have knowledge of the fact that Bullock's new wife and adopted child arriving in Deadwood have resulted in Bullock's offering to leave Deadwood with his lover Garret, to preserve their newfound love while not openly, daily shaming his spouse and child. Bullock is in a holding pattern, leaving the choice of flight or remaining in Deadwood, breaking off their relationship, up to Alma Garret. Honorable as he claims to be, Bullock cannot trust himself to determine which relationship to dishonor. He is obviously startled by Swearengen's insight into his predicament and options. Series creator David Milch says, "To me, they're part of the same personality."[23]

Perhaps, then, not surprisingly, we begin to see a change in Bullock's attitude toward Swearengen after this exchange between them. In "New Money," Bullock reports Swearengen's political news concerning the lack of Deadwood representation in the county commissioner appointments to Star. Star asks when Swearengen informed him of this, and Bullock smiles, fondly, as he replies, "Just before we hit the mud" ("New Money" 2.3). The fight itself seems to have forged some kind of bond between the two adversaries. In *2 Henry IV*, the newly crowned Henry V publicly rejects Falstaff, embracing his new responsibilities and legacy from his late father. After Swearengen's near fatal illness with kidney stones, he requests Bullock be summoned and when the sheriff arrives, they greet one another with some affection before resuming their conversation about political power plays for Deadwood, in which Swearengen schools Bullock. Swearengen chuckles, saying "You got gall—coming before me prettier than ever" to his former adversary; Bullock responds with an expression of concern, asking "Are you all right?" which Swearengen dismisses with "On the fucking mend, that's all to say on that" ("Complications" 2.5). Then the older man changes the topic to political issues in the camp, primarily Commissioner Jarry's notice on gold claims provoking anger among claim holders. Swearengen says he wouldn't want to see Jarry harmed, which Bullock responds to defensively, as if Swearengen has accused him of plotting against the man ("Complications" 2.5). Then he does scold the younger man, followed by a series of questions to which Bullock gives one-word answers.

> SWEARENGEN: Don't be fucking clever with me. He's allied with Tolliver. Are you aware of that?
>
> BULLOCK: No.
>
> SWEARENGEN: Bedridden, I know more than you. The point is, if their man's allied with Tolliver and fucking harm comes to him, between the hoopleheads and me, who will Yankton put it on?
>
> BULLOCK: You.
>
> SWEARENGEN: Yeah. Do they understand how most of what happens is people being drunk and stupid and trying to find something else to blame besides that-that makes their lives totally fucked? No, they don't.
>
> BULLOCK: Yankton.
>
> SWEARENGEN: Yankton, exactly. They're too busy stealing to study human nature.... And both of you being government officials ... you ought to fucking look out for each other ... *(lifts his teacup in a mock toast)* Sheriff ["Complications (Formerly 'Difficulties')" 2.5].

Swearengen scolds him for his quick defensive response, pointing out that Commissioner Jarry has already formed an alliance with Cy Tolliver, an alliance that Bullock is unaware of. Possessing this knowledge is a point of pride on Swearengen's part, as he states. He is resuming the lesson he began with Bullock in his office just prior to their fight; note that he has more lines here and those lines bear significant content revealing his insight into how the outside threat of Yankton will likely play out with the people of Deadwood. Bullock responds briefly and only to the prompts Swearengen gives him. From this point on, he not only follows Al's advice, but returns to report an update to him.

Masculine Identity Comes from Other Men

Bruce R. Smith observes that "masculine identity ... is something men give to each other. It is not achieved in isolation."[24] Smith notes that in *1 Henry IV*:

> Harry illustrates another conflict involved in the achievement of masculine ideals as he negotiates a tension between affiliation and aggression. If masculine identity is something that men give each other, they do so under a complicated system of rules whereby they alternately abet and oppose one another. Harry's relationship with Hotspur is a

case in point. In terms of body chemistry, what we witness in the rivalry between Harry and Hotspur is a contest between Hotspur's choler-driven anger and Harry's calculated reasonableness. In terms of ethical ideals, it is an act of collaboration, an achievement of masculinity in terms of one another's identity.[25]

This "negotiation of a tension between affiliation and aggression" we see played out in *Deadwood* through the relationship between Swearengen and Bullock. They "alternately abet and oppose one another," ultimately collaborating to achieve a shared goal. Berrettini claims that "Bullock and Swearengen's shared anticipatory fears focus on how the arrival of the law—or more precisely, the State in the form of the United States—will impact their personal economic interests."[26] If the tentative partnership they form originates in shared economic interests, it doesn't remain restricted to that impersonal realm for long.

Later, after having checked in with the commissioner and prevented his beating at the hands of an angry crowd, Bullock reports back to Swearengen on his perceptions of the political maneuvering Yankton is doing via the commissioner's actions ("Complications" 2.5). Swearengen takes a drink from the bottle of whiskey at his bedside, then offers it to Bullock, who steps forward to take it. He teasingly threatens to punch Bullock if he wipes the lip of the bottle before drinking from it, prompting a grin from the sheriff as he takes the bottle, lifts it in a toast to the saloon owner, then drinks from it. They take turns speculating about the political and economic forces at work behind the scenes, seeking to cut out local political representation from the Deadwood camp. As they wrap up their meeting, Swearengen promises, "I get back on my fucking feet, I'll carry my share of the water," to which Bullock replies confidently, "My money's on you" ("Complications" 2.5). This scene of political analysis and speculation together is bookended by the reciprocal performance of personal affiliation between the two men. This scene opens with Bullock assuring Swearengen that the commissioner is safe, having carried out what amounts to Swearengen's orders. In response, Swearengen again invites Bullock to a sort of communion with him, this time not only sharing a drink, but drinking directly from the same bottle, threatening him if he dares to wipe the rim off first. Together, they speculate on the power behind the political movements threatening the independence of Deadwood as they pass the bottle back and forth. The scene comes to a close with Swearengen's assurance of shared responsibility for the camp's continued independence, once he has fully recovered from his illness. It is significant that Bullock pledges confidence in Al with the exact same phrase he offered to Hickok after they faced off with Mason, as to whose shot had killed the man: "My money's on you" ("Deadwood" 1.1). Whether Bullock fully acknowledges it or not, Swearengen has just replaced Hickok as Bullock's father-figure in the camp.

After the meeting with the camp leaders once again, this time to discuss the violence associated with Hearst's representative Wolcott, Swearengen has praise for Bullock, telling his minions, "Who impressed me at that meeting was Bullock, that avoided putting his pet interests—innocence, so forth, guilt, fucking who did what to fucking who—before the needs of the fucking camp. It shows fucking progress. It shows growing maturity to what makes the world's fucking tail wag" ("E.B. was Left Out" 2.7). Swearengen recognizes some growth on Bullock's part when it comes to the bigger political picture of Deadwood, as though the tutelage of the older man is having an observable effect on his newest protégé. Swearengen is proud of Bullock's restraint and focus on the larger issues at play.

We see Swearengen and Bullock moving closer to an alliance of sorts in the next episode, "Childish Things" (2.8), which opens with morning at the Gem, Swearengen and Bullock seated together at a table in the saloon. Swearengen amiably asks Bullock about the first impression the younger man formed of him, to which Bullock replies casually, "That you were a killer" ("Childish Things" 2.8). Swearengen acknowledges, "Certain facts show in the mug…" but notes, there's an absence of such identifying features in Bullock's face, making it difficult, if not impossible, for others to interpret what motivates the younger man more, lust/love madness or reasoned, moral principles; Swearengen clarifies the advantage of this, saying "The many cannot tell, for you yourself are so fucking confused. But you do make a good appearance, so they're prone to grant you their trust, which we will use as an asset in the coming campaign" ("Childish Things" 2.8). Bullock notices the plural pronoun "we" in Swearengen's statement and asks about the campaign. The older man quizzes the younger one about his parting with a judge in Montana without offering explanation, leading Bullock to amused speculation about Swearengen, saying his cagey responses may be why people don't fully trust him more than his appearance as a killer ("Childish Things" 2.8). Swearengen relents, offering the possibility of spreading rumors of Deadwood's annexation to Montana instead of Dakota to resist being controlled by Yankton or Hearst. Bullock seems surprised at Swearengen's strategy, asking, "No dictatorship?" ("Childish Things" 2.8). Swearengen retorts, "What the fuck do we need a dictatorship for, that silences the public voice, that eases the enemy's way? Noise made, overtures to outside interests and enlistment of the hooples' participation is what this situation demands" ("Childish Things" 2.8).

Bullock continues to be surprised, and maybe a little impressed, by Swearengen's forward-thinking on behalf of the camp's best interests, rather than just his own. However, he flatly declares his disinterest in serving as what Swearengen described as a "trustworthy mug with a vague motive," or being the figurehead for these rumors ("Childish Things" 2.8). Swearengen then asks the younger man if he agrees to proceed in an alliance against outside interests; he answers in the affirmative. Despite Bullock's disinterest in serving as a figurehead espousing annexation to Montana, Swearengen pushes to move forward with his plan to facilitate rumors to that effect, getting Bullock to acquiesce by body language ("As you see," Bullock responds) alone ("Childish Things" 2.8).

Near the conclusion of season two, when Commissioner Jarry checks in to see if Swearengen speaks for Bullock regarding the coming elections on the day of Bullock's son's funeral, Swearengen takes their collaboration a step further by declaring to Jarry, "And as his proxy, I don't do business on the day *(turning back)* of my godson's passing" ("The Whores can Come" 2.11). Beyond serving as the grieving father's political proxy, Swearengen exaggerates a familial closeness through his role as godfather to Bullock's son.

At the close of season two, Swearengen is openly advising Bullock, even on personal matters. During the festivities celebrating Alma Garret's wedding to Whitney Ellsworth, when Swearengen sees Bullock drinking alone at the Gem, he demands, "Don't you have a fucking home to get to?" which prompts the sheriff to leave ("Boy-the-Earth-Talks-To" 2.12).

By season three, their relationship has clearly moved into that of a substitute father-son status. Swearengen coaches the younger man politically, advising him regarding his first meeting with Hearst to "Speak as a candidate of your hopes for the camp and its future. Confine yourself to generalities" ("Tell Your God to Ready for Blood" 3.1) before articulating a theory as to why two murdered Cornish miners have been killed, likely ordered by Hearst. Swearengen posits that perhaps it was a message to him that Hearst views his power extending into Swearengen's territory (the Gem) and a test of Sheriff Bullock's flexibility going into the elections. The astute saloon owner adds, "What we know, fucking Bullock, is if when you two meet, Hearst does ask you to go easy, and you, for love of his type, say 'Fuck yourself,' no more illumination can come to us, because you will have muddied the fucking waters. Is why I'd hoped you'd skirt the topic" ("Tell Your God to Ready for Blood" 3.1). Accurately interpreting why those bodies were left out in the open, Swearengen demonstrates why he remains a powerful figure in Deadwood, despite Hearst's threats. He also accurately predicts Bullock's likely response to any requests from Hearst on the basis of his powerful status, offering that as a rationale for his advice about general comments during the speeches, rather than something that is apt to ignite the sheriff's notoriously short fuse.

When it appears that alliances in the camp will hold despite pressure, Hearst attacks his opposition's leadership in the form of Swearengen, privately, within the confines of his own rooms. Hearst and Turner attack Swearengen, beating him and cutting off his middle finger, but Swearengen makes his own way out to the street, albeit slowly. It's obvious to an alert Bullock that something is wrong with Al, prompting him to ask quietly, "What happened?";

4. Father-Son Relationships 99

Swearengen makes an innocuous response to the speeches then equally quietly admits he needs physical assistance, but also ordering the younger, easily-angered man how to respond when he says, "I need to lean on you, but don't you fuckin' look up" ("I am Not the Fine Man You Mistake Me For" 3.2). Bullock asks for further orders from Swearengen and offers a suggestion, which the older man refuses by saying, "Stay the fuck away from him. Hmmm? I'm having mine served cold"; he adds to his other minions, "First one to touch me I kill" ("I am Not the Fine Man You Mistake Me For" 3.2). He won't allow Dan or Johnny to provide physical support for him, but he did acknowledge his vulnerability and permit assistance from Seth. Despite pain, anger, and pride, Swearengen focuses on the performance of normality in this scene. The two men rely directly on one another, with Swearengen asking for Bullock's physical assistance to make it across the street and Bullock asking for direction in how to respond to this unexpected situation. Swearengen warns Bullock to demonstrate some self-restraint against his tendency to react violently and immediately when he is angered. Bullock is furious about the damage done to Swearengen by Hearst, but abides by the saloonkeeper's orders, for the moment. The two men's dependency on one another is evident in this scene. Even though Swearengen's minions have been watching Hearst's building since their boss entered it, it is Bullock who observes a problem with Swearengen first and who first reaches him to offer support and vengeance, the first of which he accepts.

Likewise, Bullock turns to Swearengen for reassurance when he is in doubt about the effectiveness of publishing his letter as a strategic move countering Hearst's actions. He storms over to the Gem, first demanding of Swearengen, "Are those assholes working for you?" about the Earp brothers, as if to renew conflict between the two men ("Leviathan Smiles" 3.8). Swearengen denies it calmly, diffusing the misdirection of Bullock's ire, and then Bullock gets to the real issue, a question of their collaborative action in publishing the letter Bullock wrote to the family of one of the Cornishmen killed by Hearst's men. Bullock glumly says, "Letter was a fucking mistake" ("Leviathan Smiles" 3.8). Swearengen, the more experienced strategist, says no, it wasn't. After reassurance from Swearengen, Bullock returns to the hardware store with a more reasoned response to the Earps' mess. He says to Wyatt that he realizes some former lawmen turn to lawless work because they can, adding an emphatic qualifier and an admission of his own tendencies when he notes, "Some do that. I took the badge off myself once ... without losing my impulse to beat on certain types" ("Leviathan Smiles" 3.8). Bullock acknowledges his potentially dual nature, his own capacity to work for the law or against it. Perhaps, too, he recognizes that others, including Swearengen, also possess that capacity.

Despite being posited as enemies initially, Hotspur and Henry IV are much alike, as are Bullock and Swearengen. Mitchell and Wright note that "Bolingbroke himself sees significant similarities between Hotspur and himself as he was when prepared to depose Richard II. As he says to Prince Hal, '...even as I was then is Percy now'" (3.2.96).[27] Mitchell and Wright also suggest that Hotspur's anger with Bolingbroke stems from what he perceives as the king having lied to and therefore dishonored Northumberland and Worcester once they helped him to the throne; yet, Hotspur, as they point out, may have "sensed the capacity in himself to resort to dishonourable deceit ... he may have sensed that his hatred of Bolingbroke ... is greater than his sense of honour, [thus he] has a deeply conflicted sense of honour."[28] When it comes to *Deadwood*'s Bullock and Swearengen, series creator David Milch says that they recognize their similarities right away and "it's no accident that they eventually become friends."[29]

In "Amateur Night" (3.9), when Johnny Burns shows up to summon Bullock to Swearengen's office, Bullock doesn't even need to be told before he refuses, sounding very much like a boy talking about his father's disapproval. Bullock responds to Burns' simple, "Sheriff?" with "Tell him I ain't coming for his lecture. Tell him I don't need it. Tell him if my temper was gonna get the best of me, this cocksucker's brains would be on the floor. Tell him *I got it*. All right? Tell him I'm on top of it" ("Amateur Night" 3.9). Bullock uses five repetitions of "tell him" referencing Swearengen, like a defensive, frustrated boy assuring his father that he doesn't need supervision or assistance with the task at hand. Later in the same season, Swearengen worries about divisions in their alliance when he observes a gathering he has no information about. He says, "What the fuck is afoot in that hardware store? Facing the dawn united, we're even odds for disaster, let alone fucking factions. Knowing him for an errant maniac, I'll still not believe Bullock doubts me" ("The Catbird Seat" 3.11). His reference to anxiety about "factions" or divisions in loyalty has its parallel with Henry IV's fear of the Percy family also splintering off into a rebellious political faction. He goes to the store, uninvited, noting as he enters, "A meeting, I gather, of the upper fucking crust exclusively. No hoi polloi need apply" ("The Catbird Seat" 3.11). His wording indicates his awareness of how Bullock has judged and condemned him in the past, but now Bullock apologizes at once, saying, "I ought to have called you. What events argue I be called back from Sturgis is what we are trying to decide" ("The Catbird Seat" 3.11). When Al leaves, he offers a small criticism, "My meetings—I provide refreshments," that also suggests his forgiveness at being excluded ("The Catbird Seat" 3.11).

And in the final episode of the series, "Tell Him Something Pretty" (3.12), Swearengen instructs the others present in the Gem awaiting Hearst's arrival that while they should present a united front, if Hearst calls them on the substitution of Jen for Trixie in the casket, Swearengen alone will take responsibility.

But he looks directly at Bullock, a gesture not lost on the younger man, when he advises that, "Others owe thought to the future—that thinking straightforward don't come that naturally to" ("Tell Him Something Pretty" 3.12). The suggestion is that if Swearengen is removed by Hearst, the task of planning ahead for next steps for Deadwood will be in the hands of the survivors, lead by Swearengen's implied heir as leader of the Deadwood community, Bullock.

By the close of *2 Henry IV*, King Henry V has taken the throne after his father's death and has himself named who shall serve as a new substitute father for him, a symbolic choice considering it's the Chief Justice. Henry V says,

> You shall be as a father to my youth.
> My voice shall sound as you do prompt mine ear,
> And I will stoop and humble my intents
> To your well-practiced wise directions [*2 Henry IV* 5.2.118–121].

Henry acknowledges his need of experienced guidance in this new role as monarch, and that he shall consult with the Chief Justice before issuing edicts or even establishing goals to strategize towards achieving. He goes on to claim that his heretofore pride dominated his actions, but from henceforth he will temper that with wise, experienced advice. He closes this speech by saying to the Chief Justice, "you, father, shall have foremost hand" in determining England's future, "whether it be for peace or war" (*2 Henry IV* 5.2.140). This is a deliberate choice on Henry's part, naming the lead figure of justice, law, and fairness as his new father-figure. In two more scenes he will publicly disavow even knowing Sir John Falstaff, another necessary step in establishing the tone of his monarchy as a serious, sober, and just one, just as his own father wished.

Conclusion

Despite repeated conflict between older men who are father figures to younger men, the two parties come to trust and depend upon one another. Father figures mentor son figures, using their own experience in business management and political maneuvering to teach the less experienced men how to advance their agendas and gain or maintain their power. The father figures also attempt to aid the son figures in looking beyond personal considerations to focus on the longer-term community stability and how they might positively contribute to achieving that goal. Swearengen, Falstaff, and Henry IV, seemingly less honorable older men in positions of power, seek younger and more honorable men in the form of Bullock, Prince Hal, and

Hotspur, to act as father figures for, mentoring how and when to respond in difficult situations.

The emphasis on men's relationships with one another in the history plays and the television series raise questions about the few female characters and their restricted juxtapositioning in relation to the prominent male characters and themes of the works. In addition, men's treatment of, and association with, women aids in defining men's characters in often contradictory ways, in the eyes of other characters and the audience.

5
Women's Marginalization

> ALMA GARRET: *"If we had a kitchen, Sofia, after supper we would retire to it, to chores and gossip and the most minute domestic matters, while the men walked and smoked and argued more important matters. And, incidentally, decided our fates." ("Jewel's Boot Was Made for Walking" 1.11)*

There are few women in Shakespeare's Henriad and in Milch's *Deadwood* and all of them are primarily positioned in relation to men, serving men's needs. Women are at least initially restricted to the domestic, private sphere in both works. The history plays and the television series share in common the repeated association of the few privileged women with loss, grief, helplessness, and passivity, the treatment of and association with women used to define men's character, and the use of female prostitutes as a background prop. Distinctions between women's roles in the two sets of work are primarily due to how each reflects the culture and time period that produced it.

Few and Marginalized Women's Roles

The second tetralogy, consisting of *Richard II*, *1 Henry IV*, *2 Henry IV*, and *Henry V*, features fewer women's roles, with fewer lines as well, than the first tetralogy. Rackin notes that "In the most highly esteemed of Shakespeare's history plays—*Richard II*, the two parts of *Henry IV*, and *Henry V*—the percentage of words assigned to female characters never reaches 10 per cent of the script."[1] The history play that is most often taught, *1 Henry IV*, "is also the one in which female characters are most marginalized, speaking less than 3.5 per cent of the words in the script."[2] *1 Henry IV*'s two speaking women, Lady Percy and Mistress Quickly, who have no scenes together, have 106 lines combined, compared to Hotspur's 562.[3] The most surprising aspect of Rackin's analysis is documentation from the early modern period that indicates larger attendance for longer periods of time for the first tetralogy, leading her to conclude that perhaps the frequent teaching of and performance of the second tetralogy in modern times tells us more about our own preferences—keeping women out of the political and public spheres, while featuring a larger-than-life amusing male character, in Falstaff.

In *Deadwood*'s first season, the audience is introduced to only four significant women: Trixie, a tough prostitute at the Gem, Jane Canary, a rough, cross-dressing companion of Wild Bill Hickok's, Alma Garret, the laudanum-addicted wife of dandy Brom Garret, and Joanie Stubbs, who, although dressed as the social equal of Mrs. Garret, is a prostitute/madam at the Bella Union. The limited interaction these four have with one another in any combination is initially bound to their concern over the orphaned girl, Sofia Metz. Most of the time they are separated and interacting with one or more men. The pilot episode contains twenty named men with speaking parts to three named women with speaking parts of more than one line. The two lead male characters, Seth Bullock and Al Swearengen, have approximately 140 lines total. The three named women, Jane Canary, Trixie, and Alma Garret, have roughly 38 lines combined. These women have no scenes together in the pilot.

Domestic vs. Public Spheres

One reason for the few female characters of name in either the history plays or the television series is the separate historical and cultural sphere of influence occupied by men and women, with men of a certain status or influence participating in public life in both the English Early Modern period and in the American frontier of a mining camp. In Shakespeare's history plays, this negotiation of "public life," or political and state affairs, takes place at court or on the battlefield, sites for male interaction.[4] Women in both of those historic settings were often relegated to the domestic sphere, the private life. As Meghan C. Andrews has noted, "Generally, critics have located [the play's] feminine power in the private realm."[5] Female characters in both dramas are presented as mothers, wives, or daughters of upper or middle class socio-economic status, servants, or prostitutes. In all but *Richard III* and *King John*, women occupy only marginal roles in Shakespeare's English histories, which often focus on what constitutes a good king and portray the political strategizing it takes to overthrow a tyrannical or inept king; in the Henry VI plays, Queen Margaret's dominance of her husband, her affair, and her leading of an army are all seen as unnatural, monstrous warnings against foreign brides. Such public conflict and confrontations over political power in Shakespeare's time were the province of men. David Bevington states that, although women only have marginal parts in the history plays, nevertheless the women's presence in even those few scenes "highlight for us important thematic contrasts between the public and private spheres, power and powerlessness, political struggle and humane sensitivity, the state and the family."[6] Scenes featuring women in the history plays provide a critical commentary and often an alternative perspective to that of the men on issues of family, politics, and conflict. These scenes also comment on the women's feelings of powerlessness in times of political crisis, with its inevitable effects on their family. As one example, halfway through *Richard II*, when the Queen and her ladies overhear the news that Richard has been captured by Bolingbroke and is set to be deposed soon, the Queen asks, "Am I the last that knows it?" (*Richard II* 3.4.94). Indeed, she is, having been forgotten by the men involved in confrontation with one another.

Shakespeare's history plays contain no female protagonists, in part because of the virtues emphasized for women in Renaissance England, which included being silent and obedient.[7] In addition, women's legal status as the property and subject of their husbands nullified their ability to act as independent agents.[8] As Rackin notes, "In the Renaissance masculine superiority tended to be mystified in the spirit, female oppression justified by the subordinate status of the body"[9]; men were associated with the mind and spirit, women with the body, as inferior both mentally and physically. In Renaissance public debates about the nature of women and women's roles, two of the favorite metaphors used to describe the "virtuous wife" included "the snail or the tortoise, both animals that never leave their 'houses' and are totally silent."[10] Given these prevalent ideas about women, it's no surprise that there are no female protagonists in Shakespeare's history plays.

Indeed, women are the protagonists only in Shakespeare's tragedies (Cleopatra, Juliet, Cressida) and when paired with male counterparts (Antony, Romeo, Troilus) who take top billing in the plays' titles, and in the comedies, where strong women aid in restoring order to their worlds—part of the *comic* aspect, since women were more commonly associated with disorder, silence, and the body, as opposed to men's association with order, speech, and the spirit or intellect. Even in the tragedies where women share the title, their roles are limited; Cleopatra is the only adult woman with significant power and she is not English. The English chronicles of history focused on patriarchal culture, namely kings and military leaders, and their sons. As much as possible, women were omitted from this record despite, and perhaps because of intense anxiety about, their absolute necessity for producing legitimate male heirs.

Clear demarcations between the public sphere of men and the private sphere of women are also recognized in *Deadwood*, especially in the first two seasons. Season one features the only woman of wealth and status in the camp, Alma Garret, confined mostly to her second floor hotel room, spending her days in relative isolation and boredom. She watches the street below from behind glass, as though she is a collector's item acquired by her husband Brom, but she rarely sets foot on it and never without a male escort. In season two, Martha Bullock is seen primarily within the house Seth built for her. The prostitutes that make up the main population of women in the camp are seen in the brothels where they work, rarely outside of that. Season two features the following exchange in the Chez Ami brothel, owned and operated by Joanie Stubbs and a female partner. Customer Francis Wolcott condescendingly says to Joanie, "What a tiny corner of operation for such an amusing mind. I'll promise as I sojourn here to bring you stories of the world of men"; Joanie replies cheerily, "I'll just be here in my girl's world diddling myself" ("New Money" 2.3). Wolcott's conception of women as mentally inferior to men, with Joanie perhaps being an entertaining exception, has its foundation in both Renaissance and Roman ideas about male superiority. As a madam seeking to appeal to her potential client's repeat business, Joanie knows she must present herself as playful, positive, and sexually available. She acknowledges the private confines of her existence, that "girl's world," where she has little to occupy her time without the presence of a customer. Women's sphere in the domestic or the commercial is located in the private, enclosed areas of brothels or homes, where they serve men's needs in a variety of ways.

In *Richard II*, the only women included are those of aristocratic title, Richard's aunts, the Duchess of Gloucester and the Duchess of York, and Richard's Queen; all three are associated with emotional appeals to men. None have scenes with one another. The older women make highly emotional appeals to John of Gaunt and King Henry IV or complain to the Duke of York regarding vengeance or justice for murdered husbands and protection of treasonous sons. Richard's Queen bemoans her husband's loss of status as she learns it from overhearing the gardener's gossip, parts tearfully with Richard, and is sent back to France. All of these aristocratic female characters simply respond to the actions of the men in their lives, seeking justice for their husbands or sons in appeals of pathos. Rackin notes that the few women in Shakespeare's histories are presented as "subverters of the historical and historiographic enterprise—in short, as anti-historians. But [the voice that] Shakespeare does give them ... challenges the logocentric, masculine historical record."[11] The men adhere to policy and practice, avoiding pathos altogether. The women amplify, or magnify, the issues of justice and fairness being played out by the men.

In *Henry IV* parts one and two, the two main female characters, the Hostess/Mistress Quickly, and Lady Kate Percy, Hotspur's wife, serve in the dual roles of the magnifying glass for men. Women's attentiveness to men can support their elevated self-esteem or allow the women to recognize changes in men's routines, behaviors, or appearances, identifying aspects of the self that men may be trying to conceal or deny. The Hostess's admiration of Falstaff's role-playing at the tavern contributes to his inflated view of himself, magnifying him, while Lady Percy's keen observations of the minute details of her husband's out-of-character behaviors allow her to draw accurate conclusions about his absences and secrecy. In addition to these two women, *1 Henry IV* also presents two other women: the mysterious, nameless Welsh woman Mortimer has wed and whose language he does not understand, the allure of the foreign woman expressed by even Hotspur while sitting with his own wife, and Doll Tearsheet, a prostitute competed over by men in the tavern subplot of the second *Henry IV* play. In *Henry V*, the Hostess/Mistress Quickly makes another appearance, primarily to report Falstaff's death and serve as comic relief continuing her malaprops. *Henry V* introduces Princess Katherine, Henry's bride-to-be as part of his victory terms over France, also a source of comic relief related to her attempts to learn English. Bevington notes that "Women stand on the periphery of affairs ... and yet the scenes in which they appear offer important perspectives on male competitiveness and ambition."[12] This perspective is shared by women occupying both social levels, the high and the low, of their respective male counterparts. They serve as objects of men's desire, prizes of war, comic relief, foolish victims of men's scheming, dangerous distractions from men's political responsibilities, threats to their masculinity, and, occasionally, comforts to men.

Deadwood's setting in the 1870s mining camp by its very nature limits the number and variety of women initially. Series creator David Milch has "point[ed] out that in 1876 the Deadwood population was 90 percent male; of that 10 percent who were women, nine out of ten were prostitutes."[13] Women and girls who appear in over thirty episodes of *Deadwood* include five: Jane Canary, Trixie, Alma Garret, Sofia Metz, and Joanie Stubbs. Jane Canary and Trixie are the first women in Deadwood we meet, both living hard lives among a community dominated by men. A second tier of women appear in fifteen or more episodes: Jewel, Martha Bullock, and Dolly. Jewel occupies a special place among the Deadwood women; only five episodes out of the series' thirty-six feature characters' names[14] and Jewel is the only female character to be included in that number. An entire episode is dedicated to Jewel's determined pursuit of medical aids to make walking easier for her ("Jewel's Boot is Made for Walking" 1.11), a storyline that takes two episodes to conclude and contributes significantly to the series' growing sense of community building. All these women, with the possible exception of Jane, are dependent upon men for their continued existence, in one way or another. Jane, though, like some of the women in Shakespeare's comedies, adopts cross-dressing to make her way in the masculine world.

Privileged Women's Associations with Loss and Grief

In both the Henriad and *Deadwood*, women of privilege are repeatedly connected to loss and grief, a warning, perhaps for less privileged women against envy or ambition in addition to reminding the audience of the cost of men's ambition to others. The first woman we encounter in *Richard II* is the grieving and angry Duchess of Gloucester, asking John of Gaunt, her brother-in-law, to enact some form of vengeance over her husband's murder. She curses Mowbray, whom she blames, and declares that vengeance depends upon Hereford (Bolingbroke), Gaunt's son, whose challenge of Mowbray she supports. She is presented as an older, wronged widow, fluctuating between deep grief and righteous fury, and frustrated by Gaunt's refusal to demand justice for her husband's and his brother's murder. When John of Gaunt tells the Duchess of Gloucester that he's more moved to vengeance by his fraternal loss than by her general call to action, the Duchess focuses her rhetoric on that aspect of their relationship:

> Ah, Gaunt, his blood was thine! That bed, that womb,
> That metal, that self mold that fashioned thee,
> Made him a man; and though thou livest and breathest,
> Yet art thou slain in him [*Richard II* 1.2.22–25].

She emphasizes a specifically maternal connection the two brothers share in referencing "That bed, that womb, / That metal, that self mold fashioned thee," reminding him of the shared biological origin that shaped them. She pushes that connection, noting that in sharing the same blood it's as though, through the Duke of Gloucester's murder, John of Gaunt has also been murdered. Her critique suggests that this is an offense that he should be taking more personally than it appears he is, to her, at least.

One of the first women we meet in *Deadwood*'s pilot episode is the wealthy and isolated Alma Garret, wife of dandy Brom Garret. Alma, too, exists in an altered state, thanks to frequent self-administered laudanum as a coping mechanism for the circumstances beyond her control, which include being married to Brom to settle her father's debts and the isolation she experiences in a rough mining camp as the sole woman of privilege there. As Anne Helen Petersen has observed, the portrait of Alma the series presents initially emphasizes her marriage as "a high-class form of societally sanctioned prostitution" and underlying her fine clothes, education, and social status, "the vacancy in [Alma's] eyes and the draping of her dressing gown recall that of the whores."[15] Our first views of Alma show her restricted to their second floor hotel room, where she watches the busy main street below from behind the windowpane. She is triply insulated from the life of Deadwood: through Brom's wealth, the limited and removed space of the second floor hotel room, and her use of laudanum. When she learns that her husband has spent all of their cash purchasing a gold claim, her only response is a casual, "Oh well" ("Deadwood" 1.1). Petersen also observes, Alma's "self-seclusion and boredom [emphasizes] the limited options available to even the most refined of women."[16] Through the course of the series, Alma loses two husbands, a lover, a pregnancy, and her gold claim. The only other woman of privilege regularly appearing in the series is Martha Bullock, widow of Seth's older brother whom Seth married to protect; Martha arrives in Deadwood in the second season to find her husband fighting in the thoroughfare and in love with someone else. Martha is shown primarily confined to the Bullock house, caring for Seth, her son William, gardening, cooking, and cleaning, negotiating her way cautiously in what is apparently still a new and awkward relationship with Seth. Later in the series, Martha also loses her young son to a freak accident, making her an object of pity for the entire camp, whether they know her or not. Both of these women of status are marked by significant loss physically, wearing all black for an extended period of time, identifying them even to strangers first and foremost as mourning women.

In her first appearance in *Richard II*, Richard's Queen appears distracted in the modern sense of the word, her thoughts elsewhere, bordering on sorrowful, using the imagery of a corrupted pregnancy to describe her anxiety about her husband's reign. We see her again later in the play with her women in the garden, seeking external distraction from her troubled thoughts. Instead, she overhears the gardeners talking about Richard's capture by Bolingbroke, which is news to her. She seems forgotten or overlooked in the political coup that has taken place without her knowledge. Richard sends word that she is to return to France only a few lines before Bolingbroke orders the same. She is simply an unnecessary side piece to be removed from the board once the game is over and the men are done playing. Her emotional parting with Richard is intended to stir pathos in the audience. She does not want to see him harmed or to be parted from him.

In the first scene where the Queen speaks, Bushy reminds her of her promise to Richard to "lay aside life-harming heaviness / And entertain a cheerful disposition" (*Richard II* 2.2.3–4), to essentially, "keep smiling," presenting herself as a pleasant visual image for the male gaze, regardless of how she really feels. However, the Queen finds she cannot keep that promise of maintaining a pleasant expression to please Richard. She admits that she remains troubled by unnamed fears, which she cannot hide behind a smile:

> Yet again methinks
> Some unborn sorrow ripe in Fortune's womb
> Is coming towards me, and my inward soul
> With nothing trembles [*Richard II* 2.2.9–12].

Her imagery is that of an unnatural pregnancy, an "unborn sorrow ripe in Fortune's womb," suggesting a shift in the King's fortune and therefore a shift in hers as well is due. Shortly following a continuation of this exchange between the Queen and Bushy, joined by Green, the scene changes to York learning that the Duchess of Gloucester has died. The Queen's extended metaphor of the birth of sorrow and woe connects her to the Duchess of Gloucester, who earlier in the play says that she dwells with sorrow and grief, feeling desolate.

In *Deadwood*, Alma Garret tells Hickok that she views herself as "an accomplice," explaining that "A wife inevitably feels she's had some part in what befalls her husband. I'm answerable hereafter on different terms" ("Here was a Man" 1.4). Her answer clearly resonates with Hickok, also newly married, and considering himself on a downward spiral. He agrees to represent her investigating Swearengen's role in Brom Garret's death and in identifying a trustworthy assayer for the gold claim. Similar to the Duchess of Gloucester's request for vengeance over her husband's sudden death and likely murder, *Deadwood*'s Alma Garret requires a male agent to act on her behalf, as she explains to Jane Canary, "I've no one else in the camp" ("Here was a Man" 1.4). Again, in an historical context women cannot enact their own quest for justice and must instead rely on men to take action on their behalf.

In *2 Henry IV* the young widow Lady Percy reminds her father-in-law what his betrayals have cost them both in the past, the death of Hotspur, insufficiently supported in the rebellion. She recalls:

> The time, father, that you broke your word,
> When you were more endeared to it than now,
> When your own Percy, when my heart's dear Harry,
> Threw many a northward look to see his father
> Bring up his powers; but he did long in vain.
> Who then persuaded you to stay at home?
> There were two honours lost, yours and your son's [*2 Henry IV* 2.3.10–16].

She advises her father-in-law to stay away from the conflict, reminding and chastising him for his past failure to behave "honorably," which cost them both Hotspur. She continues to remind him exactly what not only they but the nation, too, lost in the death of Hotspur in a lengthy description of Hotspur as the mirror to which all young English noblemen aspired. Her act two scene three speech marks her as the bearer of the torch of Hotspur's memory and honor, a living memorial to him. This is also the role Richard asks of his Queen—to tell his story—which I discuss later in this chapter.

Privileged Women Portrayed as Helpless and Passive

In many of the instances above, men's political and economic games mean the creation of both young and old widows, with no recourse to justice or revenge, unless a man enact it for them. Even in a comedy we see this helplessness and passivity identified with women, when Beatrice tells Benedick in *Much Ado About Nothing* of her desire to challenge her innocent cousin's slanderers, saying, "Oh, God, that I were a man! I would eat his heart in the marketplace" and "Oh, that I were a man for his sake![...] I cannot be a man with wishing, therefore I will die a woman with grieving" (4.1.305–306; 316; 321–322). When loved ones are threatened by men in these plays, there is no active recourse for the women to take except weeping. They can only sit idly by and wait for news of the next event.

In *Richard II*, Richard charges his queen with returning to her home in France, thinking him dead, and with keeping his story alive by telling it "in winter's tedious nights" so that "to quit their griefs / Tell thou the lamentable tale of me / And send the hearers weeping to their beds" (5.1.40; 43–45). This charge makes her responsible for telling his version of the story, rather than the one they might find in the history chronicles approved by Bolingbroke. He calls it specifically a "winter's tale," often associated with women. Rackin points out that "Isolated from the arena of power, [the Queen] can foresee the outcome of the historical action before it occurs, and she can report it after it is complete, but she can do nothing at all to affect its course."[17] The Queen bears witness, but can take no part in the action herself, similar to Lady Percy in *2 Henry IV*.

In season one of *Deadwood*, Alma Garret, with Sofia, watches from her hotel room window as her father and Seth Bullock talk in the thoroughfare after they've all had dinner together. She attempts to speak to Sofia in a pleasant tone of voice but the edge of anger and bitterness is clear as she says, "If we had a kitchen, Sofia, after supper we would retire to it, to chores and gossip and the most *minute* domestic matters, while the men walked and smoked and argued more important matters. And, incidentally, decided our fates" ("Jewel's Boot was Made for Walking" 1.11). We see her awareness of how her life is determined by the men in it, not by herself, despite how she's attempted to assert herself otherwise. The last part of that speech seems casually tacked on, as though the women's fate isn't significant in any way. She adds, quietly and also pleasantly, the tone belying the content of her speech, "If we didn't hate them too much to be curious about the world, we'd wonder what they had to say" ("Jewel's Boot was Made for Walking" 1.11). The way that her tone is at complete odds with the content of her speech also tells us something about the cultural conditioning of women to sound pleasant at all times and to avoid expressing anger. Alma's speech here, even to Sofia who cannot understand her, suggests her knowing subversion of those cultural standards.

In the second season, Alma Garret's voice-over narration to her late husband Brom on the eve of her wedding to Ellsworth reveals her fear and awareness of her lack of control over her life. She says, "I'm afraid. I am so afraid that my life is living me, and soon it will be over, and not a moment of it has been my own" ("Boy-The-Earth-Talks-To" 2.1). She felt helpless in her arranged marriage to Brom and she continues to feel helpless even as she chooses to marry to protect her child and herself. She's also chosen, though, to see the pregnancy to term, despite the likely medical risk it means taking.

Contrast upper class Alma's passivity and fear to the prostitute Trixie's action and boldness, repeatedly throughout the series. Trixie shoots the john who is beating her in the pilot and although Swearengen beats her and takes her gun away, warning her not to get another one, she immediately requests another one from Jewel. Then she gives it to Swearengen, as if to show him her ability to defy him and protect herself, as if to say that she always chooses when and how to obey his orders. It is Trixie who takes the initiative in persuading Ellsworth to agree to marry Alma to legitimize her pregnancy; likewise, it is Trixie who takes immediate retaliation against Hearst for the murder of Ellsworth, while the rest of the camp seems paralyzed at the sight of the popular miner's body. Given her role in drawing Ellsworth further into Alma's life, it's likely that Trixie felt responsible for what ultimately happens to the older miner.

Repeatedly in both the Henriad and *Deadwood*, women of privilege are associated with loss, grieving, helplessness, and passivity, dependent upon men to take action on their behalf while they remain passive witnesses to the men's action. Class distinctions are also emphasized between the women of *Deadwood* in relation to passive and active roles.

Privileged Women's Failure to Hold Men's Attention

In Shakespeare's history plays, women are also often trying, and usually failing, to get men to stop and listen to them. And the men are always hurrying off to somewhere else, usually to interact with other men in the public sphere. Women at all social levels frequently find their advice or pleas for justice or mercy ignored by men. As the Duchess of Gloucester segues from a request for justice into descriptions of her grief, Gaunt attempts to take his leave of her. She stops him with "Yet one word more" (*Richard II* 1.2.58), in a futile attempt to hold his attention. In these plays, women are often trying to persuade men to stay and listen to them, while the men often seem impatient to leave the company of women and return to the world of men, a place where they match wits or strength of will with equals to gain or sustain power. This scenario of women trying to get men to stay and men trying to leave is applicable to Richard, Gaunt, and York in *Richard II*, to Henry "Hotspur" Percy in *1 Henry IV*, to Falstaff and Northumberland in *2 Henry IV*, and to Pistol in *Henry V*. The history play is a "men's world" in which women's only influence is through "her power to dismay through verbal abuse ... but it achieves nothing."[18] Ultimately in *Richard II*, the Duchess claims that she will retire to dwell with her constant companions of grief and desolation. She seems resigned to existing in the altered state that deep sorrow has cast upon her, giving herself over to it in ways that Gaunt has not.

On *Deadwood*, Alma Garret attempts to advise her husband, Brom, away from pursuing the refund of his gold claim purchase. He follows her murmured advice over his shoulder to take a walk, gathering his thoughts and preparing his argument before confronting Swearengen. He turns in her arms to lay his head on her shoulder, as though he is her child, not her lover. Later, though, when he says he's following up on Swearengen's recommendation to reconnoiter the rim of the claim, she argues quietly but assertively, "I don't agree with this plan" ("Reconnoitering the Rim" 1.3). Standing in their hotel room with her hair down and her clothing disheveled, smiling, and keeping her voice light, Alma asks, "Oughtn't we possibly to take a different view of this, Brom? Consider we've had an adventure for $20,000 and let matters rest there?" She adds, "I don't think we should linger here" ("Reconnoitering the Rim" 1.3), intuiting negative outcomes if they remain. When he insists he's not leaving without his money, she moves over to the bureau to sit and prepare another dose of laudanum, allegedly for a headache. The next time she sees him, he's a bloody corpse thrown over the back of a horse, leaving her a young widow on her own in Deadwood.

The first time we hear from a woman of status in *1 Henry IV* is when Henry "Hotspur" Percy asks how his wife is, and informs her that he must be leaving within two hours time. Lady Percy complains to her husband about his absence from her bed, saying, "Tell me, sweet lord, what is't that takes from thee / Thy stomach, pleasure, and thy golden sleep?" (*1 Henry IV* 2.3.40–41). Lady Percy's detailed observations provide insight into Hotspur's feelings toward the rebellion. She notes his absence from her, loss of appetite, air of melancholy, and sleeplessness. He has abandoned her, banished himself from their bed, preoccupied with rebellion-planning. She notes, too, that he has seemed at war within himself regarding the rebellion. She says, "Thy spirit within thee hath been so at war" as well as noticing that "in thy face strange motions have appeared, / Such as we see when men restrain their breath / On some great sudden hest" (*1 Henry IV* 2.3.56, 60–62). Lady Macbeth observes something similar of her husband, when she says, "Your face, my thane, is as a book where men / may read strange matters" (*Macbeth* 1.5.60–61). She warns him here that his bloody thoughts of treason and ambitious gain show as "strange matters" on his face. Lady Percy observes "strange motions" on her husband's sleeping face, as he, too, prepares for rebellion and war, taking unnatural actions against a sitting king of royal blood. Lady Percy speaks to him again, asking him to hear her. He responds in a distracted, but playful manner, dismissing her question. Her suspicions regarding her brother Mortimer's claim to the throne are accurate, but Hotspur does not confirm this. He tells her nothing of his plans but agrees to let her join him after a delay. Essentially, he does not take her observations or inquiries seriously. By the end of *1 Henry IV*, Prince Hal has killed Hotspur in battle, making Lady Percy another widow. In *2 Henry IV*, Hotspur's mother, Lady Northumberland, ceases her attempts to persuade her husband from joining the rebellion with "I have given over; I will speak no more. / Do what you will; your wisdom be your guide" (2.3.5–6). Obviously, she has tried to persuade her husband in the past, but he refuses to listen to her.

Treatment of or Association with Women Used to Define Men's Character

In the Henriad and *Deadwood*, the treatment of and association with women are used to define men's character. One of the defining characteristics of Shakespeare's tragedies is that women are treated cruelly by men; we see something similar in the English history plays. Ina Rae Hark claims that "*Deadwood* does tend to use women and minorities as exemplars of redemption for its large, flawed white male cast of characters rather than investing in them as people in their own right."[19] Women and minorities are present to marginally frame and magnify the main white male characters' stories.

In *Richard II*, the women presented are wives or widows, connected to the political action only by marriage. None of them have any impact on the unfolding of political gains or losses in the play. They are, for the most part, dismissed, ignored, or humored, as the play progresses, by men in power. The Duke of York privileges his public role as loyal subject and servant over his private role of husband and father when he attempts to silence his wife's pleas to protect their only son from charges of treason. He refers to his wife as "Thou fond mad woman" (*Richard II* 5.2.95) and "unruly woman" (*Richard II* 5.2.110), scolding and chastising her attempts to defend their son, as he tries to get away from her and go to court to inform King Henry IV.

In *1 Henry IV*, it is primarily Falstaff and Hotspur who are associated with women and shown in more than one scene exchanging dialogue with a woman. Prince Hal is associated with women of the tavern through his companionship with Falstaff. Andrews notes that "Marginalized and confined to peripheral spaces, women are figured as dangerous because they threaten to take men away from public duty and to lose them in private pleasures (60)."[20] Hotspur is playfully dismissive of his wife's concerns about his plans for rebellion, he refuses to answer her questions, and he tells her that he loves her not, saying, "This is no world / To play with mammets and to tilt with lips" (*1 Henry IV* 2.3.91–92). "Mammet" means doll, but plays also on the Latin *mamma*, meaning breast. Then he turns serious to say that he won't have her question him further where or why he goes where he does. Then he says she can come after him tomorrow, asking if this will content her. This makes him seem weak, as though he attempts to assert his authority over her one minute, only to give in to her curiosity the next by including her in his trip to Wales. Although "[Hotspur] seems drawn to women (certainly he loves Kate) but yet he patronizes and devalues them."[21] In scenes at the tavern, where we see Falstaff with the Hostess and prostitutes, and in Wales, where we see Hotspur with Lady Percy and the Welsh lady, Mortimer's wife, the men are idle, engaged in hedonistic leisure, not pursuing ambition. They are distracted by the pleasures found in women's company. *The Bedford Shakespeare* notes that "early modern thinking about the body held that sexual activity reduced a man's physical prowess and that spending too much time with women made a man effeminate."[22] It is, perhaps, because of this association with distraction that the plays don't show Henry Bolingbroke with any women, ever, despite the fact that he has multiple sons; similarly, the *Henry IV* plays limit Prince Hal's interactions with women to verbal exchanges with Mistress Quickly/the Hostess or nameless prostitutes until he's a victorious Henry V in France, talking with Katharine about their impending marital alliance as part of the peace negotiations.

Season two of *Deadwood* opens with Al Swearengen's observations to Dan Dority that Bullock has been neglecting his responsibilities in favor of becoming Alma Garret's lover. To Dority, Swearengen says, "They're afloat in some fairy fucking bubble, lighter than air—him, her snatch, and his stupid fucking badge"; Swearengen then calls out Bullock from his balcony, "Lucky trouble didn't jump out earlier, huh, Bullock? Might've found you mid-thrust in other business" ("A Lie Agreed Upon, Part I" 2.1). His public insult of Bullock produces the desired results, drawing the younger man into his office. Jacobs notes that "In class instances of the [Western] genre women represent the stable, civilizing forces and threats or harm to them provide a moral rationale and justification for violent action. Equally they can figure as forces that threaten the domestication and diminishment of heroic masculine activity."[23] Privately, Swearengen clarifies to Bullock what his insult is critiquing: "with you at her ear—among other points of entry—instead of doing your civic duty…" ("A Lie Agreed Upon, Part I" 2.1). The saloon owner had assumed that Bullock would collaborate in steering the camp's economic and political future when he agreed to become sheriff, however, Bullock's affair with Garret has become a distraction. Although Swearengen and Tolliver are almost constantly in the presence of the prostitutes they run, their role as brothel owner establishes a power dynamic with the women, who exist mainly to be ordered about by their pimps, demonstrating the men's power over them to other men. As Dudley notes, control of female bodies emerges quickly as a "central thematic motif" in *Deadwood*.[24] Neither Swearengen nor Tolliver are dangerously distracted by even those prostitutes upon whom they have developed an emotional dependence.

Interestingly, *The Hollow Crown* television production of *1 Henry IV* takes great pains to show in the first tavern scene that prostitutes are associated with Falstaff but not with Prince Hal, who is shown striding down the streets of Eastcheap, entering the tavern, and going upstairs to awaken Falstaff from a bed he's sharing with a prostitute. Aside from his frequent presence at the tavern and his staging of engaging lustily with a prostitute as a guise to distract the guard searching for Falstaff, there is no association of Prince Hal with any women in this production (or in the text of the play) until he becomes King Henry V, successfully invading France and claiming Princess Katharine as a prize-bride.

In Falstaff's treatment of Mistress Quickly, we can track his moral decline between *Henry IV* parts one and two. In the scenes with Mistress Quickly in the second *Henry IV* play, Falstaff promises her marriage, and despite the humor of the scene, "we cannot forget that Falstaff is victimizing a gullible woman,"[25] something the Chief Justice clearly articulates when he says, "You have, as it appears to me, practiced upon the easy-yielding spirit of this woman and made her serve your uses both in purse and in person. [...] Pay her the debt you owe her, and unpay the villainy you have done her" (*2 Henry IV* 2.1. 112–114; 116–118). She is already at a disadvantage in this society by gender and socioeconomic status, yet Falstaff has racked up a debt he has been refusing to pay with anything other than wit, he mocks her misunderstanding of words regularly, and he has accused her of stealing from him. His treatment of Mistress Quickly in this play marks him as more of a narcissistic parasite and less a jovial source of entertainment.

In *Henry V*, the king uses rhetoric aimed at the harm war brings to women in two of his speeches challenging the French, using threats against women to intimidate the French soldiers and politicians. In the first act of the play, upon receiving the Dauphin's gift of tennis balls, taunting Henry for his rumored playful youth, the king includes in his promise of war against the French, "for many a thousand widows / Shall this his mock mock out of their dear husbands, / Mock mothers from their sons" (*Henry V* 1.2.284–286). Much later in the play, Henry threatens the governor of Harfleur to persuade him to surrender the town to the English forces. In particular, he uses threats against the women of Harfleur when he says surrender now, or

> The gates of mercy shall be all shut up,
> And the fleshed soldier, rough and hard of heart,
> In liberty of bloody hand shall range

With conscience wide as hell, mowing like grass
Your fresh fair virgins and your flow'ring infants [*Henry V* 3.3.10–14].

And he goes on to add whose responsibility that consequence would be: "What is't to me, when you yourselves are cause, / If your pure maidens fall into the hand / Of hot and forcing violation?" (*Henry V* 3.3.19–21). He continues addressing "you men of Harfleur" (*Henry V* 3.3.27), saying that if they don't surrender, "Look to see / The blind and bloody soldier with foul hand / Defile the locks of your still-shrieking daughters" (*Henry V* 3.3.33–34), painting a vivid picture of the harm the French will incur if they defy the English. When the governor surrenders, Henry orders Exeter to "use mercy to them all" (*Henry V* 3.3.54). Yet Henry has deliberately used descriptive rhetoric targeting the violation of the young virgins of Harfleur to achieve his goal of taking the town without a battle. Rhetorically at least, Henry has shown his willingness to use women as a means to an end.[26]

In many ways the women of *Deadwood* provide a means of measuring the character of its men. The four women and one girl that appear in over thirty episodes of *Deadwood*, Jane Canary, Trixie, Alma Garret, Sofia Metz, and Joanie Stubbs, are white women who have suffered loss or abuse at the hands of adult white men. Trixie and Joanie are prostitutes. Sofia's family is slaughtered by road agents robbing them. At least three of the women, Jane, Alma, and Joanie, later reveal abuse or exploitation at the hands of adult males while they were still girls. André Bazin writes of the Western film that "the distinction between good and bad applies only to the men. Women, all up and down the social scale, are in every case worthy of love or at least of esteem or pity"; he adds that "Paradoxically Anglo-Saxon puritanism, under the pressure of historical circumstances, reverses the Biblical situation. The downfall of the woman only comes about as a result of the concupiscence of men."[27]

Three of *Deadwood*'s main female characters cope with the circumstances in which they find themselves with the use of mind-altering substances, developing addictions to alcohol (Jane) or laudanum (Alma and Trixie). Two deal with the hopeless situations in which they find themselves by attempting suicide: Trixie in "Suffer the Little Children" (1.8) with an overdose and Joanie in "Suffer the Little Children" (1.8) and again in "Tell Your God to Ready for Blood" (3.1), both times with a gun, a tellingly phallic choice. As adult women who have survived abuse and exploitation at the hands of men, they form a protective circle around Sofia.

Audiences recognize the corrupted-to-the-core evil men Cy Tolliver, George Hearst, Francis Wolcott, and Mr. Lee, in large part due to their reprehensible treatment of women as expendable objects in service to men's needs. Cy threatens to kill some of his prostitutes on a regular basis and he does beat and kill the two grifter teenagers Miles and Flora, who attempt to steal from him. Even more so, he obviously *enjoys* using those kids to threaten Eddie Sawyer and Joanie Stubbs, forcing Joanie to kill Flora and then preventing her from killing herself. In his anger at Joanie's managing to open her own brothel and leave the Bella Union, his smooth civilized veneer cracks, as he mutters, "Don't believe there's no good women 'til you've seen one with maggots in her eyes" ("A Lie Agreed Upon, Part I" 2.1). On the surface, Francis, like Cy, appears to be a gentleman of some status by his rich clothing and elevated speech. However, Francis viciously murders two prostitutes and one of the madams at the Chez Ami brothel, unable to manage his irrational violent and controlling impulses ("Something Very Expensive" 2.6). We also learn this isn't the first time he has committed such an act. Diane Cook notes that "these men [Tolliver and Wolcott] evoke a mood of constant menace and fear" on the series.[28] Mr. Lee, the pimp responsible for bringing Chinese prostitutes to camp, leaves them in a cage, doesn't feed them or provide medical care for them, ignores protests from the elder established leader of the Chinese in camp, Mr. Wu, and publicly burns the bodies of the women who starve to death ("The Whores Can Come" 2.11).

It is also worth noting that Tolliver, Wolcott, and Lee are in some form agents of George Hearst, an isolated, controlling, and powerful man whose sole focus is on expanding his own financial holdings. As Hark notes, "The first two avatars of Hearst who arrive, Wolcott and Lee, are, respectively, a psychopath who slits the throats and mutilates the genitals of women and a pimp who starves his sex slaves and then throws their bodies into bonfires as if they were no more than kindling."[29] The model Hearst sets is that other people are a means to an end for him. He views Aunt Lou as existing only to serve his domestic needs, growing irritated when reminded that she has a grown son, and he threatens Alma Garret Ellsworth with rape when she comes to see him, accompanied by the sheriff, regarding the possibility of selling her gold mine. He orders violent attacks on both her and her husband, Ellsworth, in order to intimidate her into selling her entire gold claim to him.

The series reveals that, when it comes to the women, "There are gradations to slavery, ranging from Alma being trained by her father to occupy the social elite in order to pay off his debts, to the blatant display of imprisonment and starvation of the Chinese women."[30] *Deadwood* paints a consistently oppressive picture of life for women in the mining camp, regardless of race or socioeconomic status; often considered less than human, they are all too often merely a means to an end for men's profit.

In contrast, there are men in the Henriad and *Deadwood* who clearly treat women with respect and compassion, including Richard II, John of Gaunt, King Henry IV, Prince Hal at the tavern, Lord Northumberland, the

Chief Justice, and King Henry V at the French court as well as Bill Hickok, Charlie Utter, Whitney Ellsworth, Seth Bullock, Sol Star, Doc Cochran, Eddie Sawyer, Mr. Wu, and Silas Adams. Richard shows compassion and concern for his queen. John of Gaunt treats the Duchess of Gloucester with respect and compassion, explaining why he can't take any vengeful action on her behalf against the king. King Henry IV is patient, compassionate, and merciful towards his aunt, the Duchess of York. Prince Hal listens to Mistress Quickly, covers Falstaff's bills, and defends her against Falstaff's accusations of robbery. Lord Northumberland allows his grieving daughter-in-law to persuade him to honor his dead son's memory by not joining the rebellion. The Chief Justice chastises Falstaff for lying to and failure to pay debts to Mistress Quickly, recognizing the validity of her claims against Falstaff. Although King Henry V's marriage to Princess Katharine requires only her father's approval as part of the political negotiations following Henry's invasion of France, Henry attempts to court Katharine, asking for her approval, too. Even when she points out to him that it's up to her father, not her, he continues to ask for her acquiescence to the marriage.

On *Deadwood*, Hickok and Utter both care for Jane, with Hickok also serving as a consultant for Alma Garret against Swearengen and Utter stepping up indirectly to aid and defend Joanie Stubbs against Francis Wolcott. Bullock protects Alma Garret against Swearengen and Hearst and respects her decision to discontinue their relationship. Star is protective of Trixie, falling in love with her despite her attempts to dissuade him. Eddie aids Joanie Stubbs in funding her own brothel, seeking independence from Cy. Ellsworth offers to pay Trixie to talk to him when she's obviously been beaten up, he protects Alma's interests at the mine, allows Trixie to persuade him to offer marriage to Alma as a respectable cover for her illegitimate pregnancy with Bullock, and refuses to take advantage of Alma while she's under the influence of laudanum. Jason Jacobs observes that "As partners to" Alma and Trixie, "these complex women, Ellsworth and Star are always clear-sighted and good-hearted and it is perhaps for this reason that the show, in what is left of it, seems less interested in tracking their lives."[31] Mr. Wu is outraged over Mr. Lee's inhumane treatment of the Chinese prostitutes, starving them, profiting from their bodies, and then burning them in the street when they die; the latter proves the final straw for Wu, leading to multiple attacks on Lee. Doc Cochran provides care for the prostitutes in a compassionate manner. He offers free medical care for the Chinese prostitutes. Adams offers respectful comfort and support for Miss Isringhausen when she claims to have been fired and threatened by Alma. Sofia's interactions with adult males are severely limited. We only see Sofia bonding with and having positive, playful interactions with kind-hearted, responsible, and honorable Ellsworth, even before he becomes her adoptive father, Doc Cochran, who provides medical care for Sofia when she is first returned to camp comatose and injured, and the equally kind-hearted, responsible, and honorable Charlie Utter, who aids Jane in spiriting Sofia away from camp to protect her from Swearengen.

Occupying a more gray moral area in their treatment of women are Hotspur, Henry V, Al Swearengen, Dan Dority, and Johnny Burns. Hotspur refuses to tell his wife what he's been doing or where he's been, chides her for asking, but then allows her to join him in Wales, where he's gone to plot rebellion. While in her presence there, he flirts with her, teases her about her language, and expresses desire for a Welsh woman in an aside. Henry V uses verbal violence against women, particularly young, virginal maids, in his threats to the men at Harfleur but he goes out of his way to persuade Princess Katharine to accept him as her husband, when her acquiescence isn't actually necessary. Swearengen beats an already battered Trixie for shooting a john, he threatens further harm to her on more than one occasion, and yet he eventually risks his own life to protect hers, acknowledging verbally some of his prior abuse of her; he refers to her as "a loopy cunt" both times, but in very different tones, suggesting the growth of his relationship with her beyond that of ownership. David Milch has said that "Swearengen's ambivalence toward women is complicated. […] And so we live in that doubleness, where the woman is both a danger to us, a symbol of betrayal, and also a source of comfort."[32]

Swearengen keeps Jewel on staff, despite or because of her disability; he allows her to taunt him openly without repercussions. He acts respectfully toward Alma Garret Ellsworth and even extends his protection to her against Hearst's threats. Sofia "provides an index of Swearengen's evil when he pinches her awake in Cochran's cabin and sends Dority to murder her."[33] However, he never attempts to harm her himself and, eventually, he extends his protection to Sofia against possible harm from Hearst. Hark notes that "Kim Akass has questioned whether soft-pedaling Swearengen's misogyny might reflect anxieties about women in *Deadwood*'s creators, and many of Milch's statements do nothing to contradict such a conclusion."[34] Johnny Burns falls in love with Jen and is unable to follow Swearengen's orders regarding her. Dan Dority shifts from being suspicious and wary of Trixie as a source of danger and/or competition for Al's attention to friendship with her. He's quick to agree to an alternative plan to killing Sofia when Doc Cochran proposes it. But he also demonstrates an unsavory and uncomfortable attraction to teenage Flora. Just as Hearst's henchmen align with his view of others as a means to an end, so, too, do Swearengen's main employees align with his own shifting treatment of women, sometimes violent, abusive, and exploitative, but increasingly compassionate, affectionate, and even protective.

Upper-Class Couples' Difficulty Communicating with One Another

In both *Henry V* and *Deadwood*, we see pairs of upper-class men and women having difficulty communicating with one another. Henry attempts to use his rhetorical skills to court Princess Katharine, who cannot understand most of what he is saying; instead, he may actually be attempting to renew the audience's affection for him in this English-French comic romantic scene at the end of a history play focused on political and military maneuvering.

> HENRY: But, Kate, dost thou understand thus much English; Canst thou love me?
> KATHARINE: I cannot tell.
> HENRY: Can any of your neighbors tell, Kate? I'll ask them [*Henry V* 5.2.193–198].

The shrewd forward-thinking prince from *Henry IV* who planned his apparent reformation in the eyes of the people and persuaded his small number of troops to fight courageously at Agincourt is stymied by a private audience of two, one of whom cannot understand him enough to be persuaded by him. His frustration shows in his flippant reply to her here, suggesting that even the most powerful and privileged of men may have difficulty communicating clearly with a woman he seeks to woo, making him a more relatable figure to the audience and reminding the audience of his likeability after the violent Harfleur threats he issued.

When Martha Bullock arrives in Deadwood, surprising Seth and interrupting both his brawl with Swearengen and his affair with Alma, Bullock escorts her to the house he has built for them. He alludes to letters he has written her, although it's clear that he has only written one; that one we hear in voice-over narration at the end of the episode. In it, he describes in excessive detail the care he has taken with choosing lumber and a design for the house and expresses his desire to provide substitute care and protection for Martha and William in his brother's stead. It is an awkward letter, indicating his discomfort in communicating with a woman he barely knows but conveys his willingness to "do the right thing" in stepping up to his late brother's responsibilities for the family. Yet, the voice-over narration is juxtaposed against his leaving Martha and William at the house so that he may return to Alma's hotel room to reassure her of his recovery from the earlier brawl. We see that he is obviously facing conflicting duties to women in need and he will likely have difficulty making a decision about whose need to privilege.

Later in the series, after the death of William, Martha and Seth sit together in their home, facing their covered windows. She asks if he would still be willing for her to teach the children of the camp, and at his encouragement, adding, "I don't want to lose him but I wouldn't upset them either"

("Boy-The-Earth-Talks-To" 2.12). Seth's brief and increasingly awkward responses finally indicate to Martha that he has no idea what she's trying to convey without further explanation. She clarifies, "I am speaking of wearing mourning until the year has passed," which she worries will dissuade the children from interacting with her out of fear, and then adds, "But I believe if I teach them with love and joy, then I won't make them afraid. And I don't want to lose him" ("Boy-The-Earth-Talks-To" 2.12). He does reach out to her after this exchange, offering both verbal and physical comfort, saying "You'll never lose him," as they hold hands while remaining seated two feet apart from one another, distant but connected ("Boy-The-Earth-Talks-To" 2.12). He does not understand Martha or communicate clearly with her, but he wishes to comfort and support her in both her grief and her desire to teach the children of the camp. This is one example among several others where the couple has difficulty communicating with one another, suggesting an ongoing challenge for them. Seth's desire to do the right thing by his widowed sister-in-law doesn't mean a smooth transition into married life together, whether they are attempting to tease one another lightheartedly during their morning routine or they're sharing a deep grief over the loss of William. These scenes suggest that a successful marriage under the weight of trauma and loss takes continual work, work that mystifies Seth regularly although he prefers to feign understanding of it. Like the courtship scene at the end of *Henry V*, it also serves to make Seth a more relatable and likeable figure for the audience.

The Prostitutes as Props

In the *Henry IV* and *Henry V* plays there are groups of nameless, silent, and often indistinguishable women in the prostitutes that hover on the margins or the background of the scene, usually standing to display themselves and await orders from men. Although the play text and the stage directions don't indicate that prostitutes are present in the first tavern scene of *1 Henry IV*, most productions of this play do feature nameless prostitutes, their bodies displayed as props or set dressing for the men's interaction. In *The Hollow Crown* television production of *1 Henry IV*, a fully clothed Falstaff awakens next to the sheet-draped bare limbs and derriere of a woman, whom he slaps on the rump as he talks to Prince Hal. The 2010 Royal Shakespeare Company's stage version of the play showed Prince Hal emerging from below the stage, fastening his pants, followed closely by a disheveled woman, rearranging her clothing, both grinning. In the tavern scenes in performances, there are usually multiple prostitutes standing around, identifiable by the disarray and dirtiness of their clothing and hair, and how much skin they have on display.

Their presence provides an admiring audience for the teasing, playful interactions between Falstaff, Prince Hal, and Poins, and it contributes to the atmosphere of harmless good-natured fun.

In contrast to this comedic presentation of groups of prostitutes and the romanticization of prostitutes in early Western films and television (Miss Kitty from *Gunsmoke* as one example), *Deadwood*, claims Ina Rae Hark,

> de-romanticizes the "saloon girl" archetype to show its sordid reality: abuse, venereal disease, multiple abortions, drug addiction, suicide. [...] however, the symbolic uses to which the whores' plight are put raise the question of how sincere the writers are in critiquing this sad state of affairs. Rather, they appear to exploit it in the service of telling stories sympathetic to men.[35]

The "heart of gold" good-natured prostitute traditionally found in the Western is much more realistically presented on *Deadwood*, even if en masse without individuation most of the time. The four groups of prostitutes presented on *Deadwood* are set against one another in a hierarchy that primarily emphasizes the behaviors of their pimps.

The prostitutes' appearance in both the history plays and the television series tells viewers a great deal about the conditions in which they live and work. The torn, stained, and worn costuming of the Gem Saloon prostitutes is paired with their bared, bruised, and dirty flesh, suggesting neglect and abuse over an extended period of time. Petersen quotes costume designer Katherine Jane Bryant as describing the Gem's prostitutes' clothing and its lack of fit intended "to convey desperation and vulnerability."[36] This costuming also suggests that these women have been in this role for some time, that they feel hopeless and powerless, and they are accustomed to being poorly and skimpily attired for their clients' accessibility. Their expressions often convey boredom or numbness, suggesting that they are accustomed to the service roles they play to multiple men. The prostitutes at the tavern in both *Henry IV* plays are usually costumed similarly, with loose, dirty, torn undergarments, although they're typically portrayed as playful or jovial—like Joanie Stubbs often presents herself at work—as opposed to tired, fearful, or tense. These women stand at the back or sides of the scene, listening and watching the men featured, while keeping their bodies on display for the men. Peterson says of the Gem prostitutes, other than "Trixie, the whores appear as a ... largely indistinguishable mass, emphasizing their lack of subjectivity."[37] While the Bella Union and Chez Ami prostitutes are dressed more finely with carefully styled hair and appear cleaner than their counterparts at the Gem, they remain largely indistinguishable from one another as well, props to the conversations and threats of their pimp Cy Tolliver with other men. When Lee brings the Chinese prostitutes to camp, their foreign marketability to the white men who constitute the camp's majority is initially presented as something of a comic challenge to Tolliver's idiotic henchmen Con Stapleton and

Leon, as Tolliver seeks to solidify a partnership with Hearst, Lee's boss. The comic outsider-aspect of the Chinese prostitutes fades rapidly, as they are shown remaining packed into the caged cart that conveyed them to Deadwood with no food, water, sleep, or even free medical aid offered by Doc Cochran. As they grow weakened and starve to death, Lee throws them onto a fire like logs, with no attempt made to hide this action. They are used up by men, for male pleasure and profit, simply in a more direct way than that of their white counterparts at the Gem and the Bella Union.

Distinctions Between Women in the Henriad and Women in Deadwood

One of the distinctions between the Henriad and *Deadwood* with regard to female characters is that in the history plays, scenes featuring women often provide comic relief. We see this in *Richard II*, with the Duchess of York pleading to King Henry IV for mercy for her son, arguing that she and her son "outpray" the Duke of York (5.3.109). Even Henry IV comments upon her entry that, "Our scene is altered from a serious thing, / And now changed to "The Beggar and the King" (*Richard II* 5.3.79–80). Mistress Quickly, who appears in the *Henry IV* and *Henry V* plays in some form, also provides comic relief with her unwitting sexual innuendo, such as "I am undone.... A hundred mark is a long one for a poor lone woman to bear; and I have borne, and borne, and borne, and have been fubbed off, and fugged off, and fubbed off ... do your offices" (*2 Henry IV* 2.1.22;30–33;38); in front of the Chief Justice, she tells Falstaff that he will pay his debts to her or "I will ride thee o'nights like the mare" (*2 Henry IV* 2.1.74–75). Mistress Quickly is the butt of the men's jokes about her unintended sexual innuendos. Comic relief in the television series *Deadwood* is more broadly distributed across the ensemble, including Jane Canary, Seth Bullock, Al Swearengen, and Bill Hickok. Comic relief associated with female characters on *Deadwood* is not at their expense but at the expense of others. When General Samuel Fields warns Jane that being seen assisting him in Hostetler's burial won't raise her popularity with her fellow white people in camp, the alcoholic cross-dresser sarcastically replies, "Question I wake to in the morning and pass out with at night: 'What's my popularity with my fellow white people?'" ("A Rich Find" 3.6). Seth explains to Martha his tribulations with arranging the sale of Hostetler's business and his arrest of Hearst; when she asks about a connection between the two events, he offers weakly, "Both their names begin with H?" ("A Rich Find" 3.6). In an exchange with E. B. Farnum, who asks Al, "Anything I should know?," Swearengen, looking his atrocious attire over, replies, "The name of another tailor" ("Mr. Wu" 1.10). After Bullock has shared the doctor's pessimistic prognosis for Sofia Metz, Hickok replies, "From the look of him, you think that doc's been wrong once or twice in his life?" ("Deep Water" 1.2). Women as well as men are portrayed as witty in the series, rather than objects of men's humor.

Most of the distinctions regarding women's roles between the two historically-set dramas reflect the cultural and political environments that produced them. The women play a much more consistently marginalized role in the Shakespearean histories than they do on *Deadwood*, where they demonstrate a strong level of self-awareness regarding their status in that time and place. Krims notes that the Henriad "display a heavy emphasis on masculine aggression and male prerogatives, with a reciprocal stifling of femininity. This is reflected in the minor and often negative roles assigned women."[38] From the margins of the action in the history plays, women are seen pleading with men, distracting men, and all but forgotten in men's conflicts with one another, the latter of which take center stage.

In both the stage drama and the television series, women are positioned, initially, always in relation to men's needs, as mothers, wives, nurses, teachers, friends or colleagues, daughters, objects of desire, or property for profit. The women in *Deadwood*, however, refuse to remain in those confines as the series progresses. At least three of *Deadwood*'s women are dynamic, unlike the Henriad's women, who must remain static given the constant motion and shifting alliances of the men. Hark states:

> Featured female characters do have all the vividness and complexity of their male counterparts. Five play major roles in the series: Jane Canary, Joanie Stubbs, Trixie, Alma Garret Ellsworth, and Martha Bullock. The latter four play variants on the classic Western paradigms of the sexually promiscuous "whore with a heart of gold" and the prim and proper lady from the East; Jane is the outlier, opting instead to assume the gender attributes of a man.[39]

Although most of the main female characters on *Deadwood* are introduced in the recognizable female stereotypes of the Western, their characters are developed and complicated significantly over the course of the series' three seasons, as they gain more independence, agency, and a stronger sense of self. As John Dudley notes, one of *Deadwood*'s prevailing themes explores women's struggles "to achieve subjectivity within a violent patriarchal society."[40] As the series progresses, some of the female characters succeed in their pursuit of self-determinacy.

Sofia Metz, the child rescued after the vicious attack on her family, becomes a symbolic figure of innocence and vulnerability around which the women listed above come together.[41] Jane, Trixie, Alma, and Joanie work to protect Sofia in ways that they were not from adult male predators when they were young. Her existence and their concern for her brings them into contact with one another across social class lines. Hagelin states that "instead of merely dramatizing the ways women are vulnerable to men, the show asks us to replace our assumptions about gender with new networks of sympathy based on class. The collective identity the show valorizes is classed, not gendered."[42] This valuation is evident in the contempt some male characters demonstrate toward the upper classes, with their lack of ambition and their leisure activities.

Sofia is also often a source of motivation for self-improvement for them; Alma quits her laudanum habit with help from Trixie to care more responsibly for Sofia, Jane promises to pay Sofia every time she accidentally uses profanity in her presence, and Trixie's cleaned-up lady-like appearance while she's caring for Sofia leads to her flirtation with Sol Star and her beginning ability to imagine another kind of life for herself. Martha agrees to teach the children of the camp—although the only one we've been shown is Sofia, and Joanie finds some redemption in donating the building she owns for the camp school.

By the third season, some women have begun to branch out into the public forum a bit; Joanie donates the building that housed the Chez Ami to be a school, where Martha teaches. Alma opens a bank and runs it; Trixie aids her, working as a teller. An acting company arrives in the camp, with female actors preparing to perform on stage. We see a movement that extends the space women occupy to include mostly respectable forays into the public forum through support of communal resources, such as the bank, the school, and the theater.

Additionally, some of the women of *Deadwood* demonstrate growth and an increasing sense of independence as the show progresses. Peterson notes that although the show opens with an emphasis on the "subjugation" of women, as the narrative develops the women persist in challenging the patriarchal culture of the camp, "achieving autonomy, self-expression, even, in all its complexity, happiness."[43] This is only true for some of the white women of name, not all of the women. Joanie and Jane find happiness together, Trixie's romantic relationship with Sol Star continues to develop, and it seems that Martha and Seth Bullock have begun to settle into a comfortable marriage together. Alma finds independence through her gold claim and authority through using that money to start Deadwood's first bank. She overcomes a laudanum addiction twice. Although she loses a great deal along the way, including two husbands, one lover, a pregnancy, and her gold claim, Alma finds love and places her trust and herself into the hands of two good men, Bullock and Ellsworth. Despite the extraordinary growth and advancement of characters like Trixie, Alma, Jane, and Joanie, as Jen observes to her fellow prostitutes at the Gem, "Guess if you've got a pussy, even owning a bank don't get you to that table" ("Unauthorized Cinnamon" 3.7), where Deadwood's businessmen and men of influence gather to make decisions about the camp's future. Even the illiterate young prostitute demonstrates an awareness of power and gender disparities, regardless of socioeconomic status, in noting the absence of Alma Ellsworth. Jacobs claims that "For all the writing about the show's eloquent depiction of masculinity, it is in the figuring of women like Trixie and Alma that it achieves depth and eloquence through its depiction of their fascinating and compelling lives."[44] It would take an entire book-length study to analyze the growth and complexity of female characters on *Deadwood*.[45] Jacobs also says that feminism plays an influential role in the shaping of Deadwood's female characters, given their "depth and complexity" is ultimately greater than that of their male counterparts, noting that "it is as if the settlement of their interiority must come prior to the camp's eventual stability."[46] It is possible to mark the camp's development into a town by tracking the presence and growth of women in the series. Dudley goes so far as to claim that the series is actually "a story *about* women"; he applies "Julia Kristeva's notion of abjection" to analyze and interpret the show's "extraordinary pairing of violence and language … as a response to women's emerging subjectivity."[47] In other words, it is the threat of women's growth, self-awareness, and independence that elicits a response of violence and violent language from some of the men. Some of the women are in a state of transition, similar to the state of "becoming" I used to describe Bullock in Chapter 2; similarly, their potential for change and growth is emphasized, to the point where they may be said to be on a par with Bullock in representing the young nation still developing in the late 19th century.

Conclusion

The presence of groups of women also has more than an aesthetically disruptive impact on viewers. As Martha A. Kurtz observes of Shakespeare's English history plays, there is also an important symbolic impact to having so few women on stage with so many men, especially with their costuming drawing attention to them, "giving them a theatrical power that goes considerably beyond the number of lines they speak"; she adds that Shakespeare "emphasize[s] the plight of these helpless women" whose domestic confinement fails to fully protect them from the fallout of men's public actions.[48] Kurtz claims that these few female characters' roles have "the effect of making the women a kind of moral touchstone in the plays."[49] This description is also applicable to the women of *Deadwood*, whose mere appearance provides an aesthetic disruption for viewers, drawing visual attention to them, especially in public places such as the main thoroughfare in the camp where they are surrounded by men. Although there are significantly fewer women of name in the Henriad and *Deadwood*, they perform multiple necessary functions in these works. They provide an emotional appeal through demonstrations of their loss, grief, and helplessness, offering a critique of men's power and responsibility to those affected by their decisions and actions. They frequently comment on women's restricted roles in the past, in 14th century England and 19th century America. Their treatment provides insight or confirmation of men's character, making them moral touchstones in the series. Even their silent presence on stage or in the frame en masse tells audiences something about their cultural context, their dependence upon men, and men's sometimes begrudging dependence upon and occasional fear of women.

If women's status at the beginning of *Deadwood* showed their passivity, vulnerability, and abuse by men, by the series' end at least some of the women have exhibited the capacity for agency, strength, and resistance to the roles they were originally assigned. The audience's perspective of them shifts from sympathy to admiration as part of the series' design and structure, analyzed in the next chapter.

6
Managing Audience Responses through Narrative Space and Events

> "*Deadwood* is finally a story [...] about storytelling—a text that highlights the obsessive violence and power of language but also its limits, its inability to completely represent, define, or contain the abject, the recurring confrontation with the material facts of human existence."[1]

Plays and television series are essentially performative stories, bringing to life a narrative with specific agendas, as I talked about in Chapter 1. They employ a variety of strategies for eliciting a range of responses from audiences. In *Television and American Culture*, Jason Mittell asserts that "Understanding the formal structures texts use to communicate with viewers helps us unpack the ways [...] a drama portrays the world. Formal analysis is a crucial tool of a media-literate viewer."[2] Indeed, most complex narratives invite and encourage sustained audience analysis. In the context of this analysis, I use the term structure to refer to the three organizing elements of space, events, and character[3] as a means of categorizing textual and/or performative similarities between the plays and the television series designed to engage and manipulate audiences. This chapter addresses the use of space and events in narrative structure. Space is embodied in scene sequencing and televisual aspects that direct audience attention and control perspective, while events can be tracked in the form of generic plots centered on conflict, parallel scenes that function similarly, and lack of sufficient closure.

Shakespeare's history plays contain multiple forms of symmetrical balancing in their narrative structuring, a readily identifiable pattern. Referencing Mark Rose's analysis of Shakespeare's scenic divisions as "skillfully balanced diptychs and triptychs," Sherman Hawkins comments on the English Renaissance's enjoyment of such elaborate designs as reflected in the structures of both sets of Shakespeare's history tetralogies.[4] He notes that the plays contain "pair[ed] ... characters,... doubled plots, and contrasted settings...: bipolar opposition seems one law of his 'symmetrical imagination.'"[5] However, it is not sufficient to simply recognize these doublings or patterns in design. We must also ask the question: What is the purpose or function of these pairings? How do they illustrate themes in the work? This demands attention to detail through active, reflective viewing and puzzle-solving.

The structures of the Henriad and *Deadwood* are designed to carefully and deliberately control audience sympathies, establishing them early in the works of *Richard II* and *Deadwood*, to conventionally align with the alleged heroic figure occupying a position of contested justice, the honorable, disadvantaged underdog against established corrupt authority or a gun-wielding mob. From this point, the works are developed to complicate audience sympathies, shifting them steadily from their point of origin to the opposite position. Jennilyn Merten notes that *Deadwood*'s seemingly stock character outlines "fade into the conditions illustrative of good storytelling. Where the sketch remains, it serves to bolster the genre by combining familiarity with unexpected complexity."[6] We may have a marshal in the old west, a mustachioed villain, an honorable young nobleman, a corrupt and arrogant king, but once familiar plots and characters have been introduced, audience expectations are challenged repeatedly.

In addition to problematizing some generic familiarities, the *Henry IV* plays and *Deadwood* share two very similar scenes in particular, related to contemptuous views of outsider males and to the reality of physical human frailty for older male rulers, recognized by the individual himself and respectfully, supportively acknowledged by his younger male heir-figure. These scenes speak to the idea of masculinity as a trait that men grant other men through their interactions, highly dependent on demonstrations of mutual respect. Mittell observes that long-form series allow for character and relationship growth over time, stating that

> Television narratives tend to foreground changing relationships between characters more than focusing on a singular protagonist goal or conflict with an antagonist. This is partly due to the ongoing nature of a series, where it would be difficult to maintain the narrative drive of a single goal or personal conflict. Additionally, viewers can grow to know television characters with much more depth than possible in a single film, and thus the characters' relationships become more defined and central to the ongoing series narrative.[7]

As I've already discussed in Chapter 4 both the Henriad and *Deadwood* are focused around continually shifting relationships between men, especially father-son relationships. Both works also feature large ensemble casts, with characters negotiating constantly changing relationships to one another, especially in relation to political alliances. As the Dudley quote opening this chapter indicates, *Deadwood* emphasizes the effective uses of language, particularly as a weapon, but balances that with frequent acknowledgment of its severe limitations when it comes to fully conveying the complexity of humanity. The result is often incredibly powerful silent scenes and camera techniques that tell us more about character motivation or state of mind than dialog can; we see similar techniques used in recent filmed productions of the Henriad.

Space

When I talk about "space" in relation to narrative structure in this analysis, I'm referring to the settings and order of scenes, characters in place or in transit, and camera angles or focus as devices to manage viewers' attention. When employed effectively, scene sequencing and televisual strategies direct audience scrutiny and control perspective. Character mobility, whether fixed in place or capable of transgressing boundaries, suggests something about individual characters, their relationship to power, and their relationships with one another. Modern television's emphasis on the visual uses the close-up to focus viewers' attention on nuance in actors' facial expressions to convey meaning; some scenes rely solely on visual exchanges or responses to convey that meaning, foregoing all dialogue or non-diegetic music. Camera angles or focus can also direct audience perspective by forced sharing of a specific character's point of view, limiting what we see or hear to what that character is also experiencing. All of these devices work together to elicit specific responses from the audience toward characters, their relationships, and unfolding events in the narrative.

Scene Organization and Character Mobility

Initially, the Henriad and *Deadwood* appear to be a study in contrasts in terms of the issues introduced: How does a country's established ruling order come undone, in the case of the Henriad, and how does a community order emerge out of chaos, in the case of Deadwood? In the first, we have a movement from apparent unity to dissolution, in the second a movement from separation into merging.

Richard II begins with what appears to be a unified country with a strong monarch. In the opening scene, all the main characters are gathered at court, divisions and accusations of treason only beginning to emerge. Scenes shift from Richard's court to the English countryside and seashore, to the garden, to the streets of London, and, finally, to Henry's court. Bolingbroke is almost always in motion, challenging Mowbray, being banished, returning with steady progress toward court to claim the throne. Scenes with the Queen are often pastoral, removed from court to the countryside, and passive, waiting for news. Scenes with Richard are also often passive, with eloquent monologues and dialogue, as he ponders Henry's next move and how he should respond.

In contrast, *Deadwood* opens with main characters in three locations: Montana, the Black Hills trail to Deadwood, and Deadwood, specifically the Gem Saloon. We're given a sense of characters and storylines moving toward convergence in the Deadwood camp. *1 Henry IV* opens at court with the king, beginning with recognizable authorized public power, then shifts in the second scene to the tavern and sloth with Falstaff, the prince, and prostitutes. As Garber notes, "[*1 Henry IV*'s] design is one that emphasizes correspondences between its various worlds."[8] Similarly, the first episode of HBO's *Deadwood* opens with U.S. Marshal Seth Bullock in Montana, taking one final official public action as keeper of the law there and leaving for Deadwood, and closes in Deadwood with Al Swearengen, corrupt saloon owner and pimp, in private but on guard, undressed, in bed, and with a gun under the sheets pointed at the door; this positioning at the opening and closing of the pilot provides a framework for audience attention between the two men, a study in contrasts, and conflict between public versus private concerns and responsibilities. Jacobs asserts that

> One of the key structural attractions of the first two seasons was that the friction and resolution, impasse and transcendence that the characters experience within scenes ripple out into the overall structure of each episode, so that scenes "speak" to scenes, and episodes are in conversation and negotiation with one another.[9]

Garber and Jacobs each note that the ordering of scenes establishes a deliberate pattern of seemingly unrelated locations, characters, and dialogue that are actually in conversation with one another, offering parallels and contrasts to the astute viewer. Mittell says that

> With a heightened degree of self-consciousness in storytelling mechanics, and demanding intensified viewer engagement focused on both diegetic pleasures and formal awareness, [...] contemporary complex narratives foreground the skills of narrative comprehension and media literacy that most viewers have developed but rarely put to use beyond rudimentary means.[10]

Narrative complexity asks more of audiences, engaging us on a different level, whether we're viewing a Shakespeare play or a modern television drama.

In *1 Henry IV* and *Deadwood*, counterpoints in both location and character are immediately established: court and tavern, jail and saloon, Henry IV and Falstaff, Bullock and Swearengen. What connects them? They present opposing worlds, controlled by opposing forces, order and disorder. If Henry rules the court, Falstaff rules the tavern. If Bullock is an enforcer of laws, Swearengen is a violator of them.

ORDER	DISORDER
court	tavern
Henry IV	Falstaff
jail	saloon
Bullock	Swearengen
authorized authority	unauthorized authority
enforcer of laws	violator of laws

What's at stake in both works: Leadership into the future for a community in transition.

In *Richard II*, the king and his cousin, Henry Bolingbroke, are both seen at court, in transit, and back at court together before being separated by Henry IV's imprisonment of Richard. In the plays bearing his name, Henry IV remains at court unless engaged in battle on the field and Falstaff remains in the tavern until he's forced to go to war. Although Prince Hal spends more time at the tavern initially, he travels between tavern, the king's court, and the battlefield in both *Henry IV* plays.

Swearengen, more often than not, remains in place and people go to him, like a king at court. Bullock's domain is the streets of the camp, where he is often seen striding purposefully. Hickok ranges from hotel to street to saloons, although most often he's found in the No. 10 Saloon at the poker table. In addition, the "visual trope signals a split between planning and results throughout the series. Inside, and especially in upper storeys, most of the strategizing by the movers and shakers occurs while the effects of the decisions they make manifest themselves in the crowded thoroughfare."[11] The masterminds behind strategic power plays in Deadwood and the wealthy—not always the same thing—occupy physically elevated positions; they possess an above-street-level view to observe the daily life of the camp, giving them an advantage over those existing only at the street-level.

A pattern begins to emerge in both Shakespeare's history plays and the *Deadwood* series that locates older powerful men as primarily stationary, with the less powerful, more vulnerable seeking out them to settle disputes or exert their influence to effect change. Those older men in positions of power or influence, such as Richard, Henry IV, Falstaff, Swearengen, and Hickok, attract an entourage at their command. Some younger men possess the capacity to travel between oppositional locations of power, which suggests that they are still in the process of becoming, of potential, of determining where their ultimate loyalties lie.

Deliberate sequencing of scenes, locations, character interaction, and tone serves to maximize impact on the audience, eliciting specific responses.

In *1 Henry IV*, the play opens with a somber, formal court scene as the king speaks of having to delay a crusade to the holy land to deal with civil unrest at home. It's followed by a broadly comic scene at the tavern with Falstaff and Prince Hal exchanging witty and affectionate insults before planning a highway robbery for fun. However, it ends with a serious soliloquy from the prince that provides insight into his absence from court and his seemingly disreputable behavior. The next scene returns us to the king's court. Bevington notes that *2 Henry IV* is structured similarly to its predecessor, "alternat[ing] between scenes of political seriousness and scenes of comic irresponsibility, juxtaposing a rebellion in the land with a rebellion in the King's own family," featuring "scenes [that] comment on each other by their nearness and by their mutual concern with lawlessness."[12] We see something similar in *Deadwood*, with serious, tense scenes followed by comic scenes repeatedly as one structural device for controlling audience response.

In season three of *Deadwood*, "A Two-Headed Beast" (3.5) opens with a comic scene. Con Stapleton, former sheriff and constant employee of Cy Tolliver, sits beside a bathtub as one of the prostitutes is bathing. He speaks directly into her voluptuous breasts as if talking through a megaphone aboard a ship, announcing they're approaching an iceberg. In the dvd commentary for this episode, Sean Bridgers describes Peter Jason's campy, over-the-top performance as Con as "a heterosexual Rip Taylor," sometimes referred to as the "King of Camp and Confetti."[13] When Tolliver enters to give Con an assignment, the minion has to acknowledge that he's unfit, given that he's been distracted for the past 24 hours by a "spasm of sex interest" that he claims he hopes will pass quickly ("A Two-Headed Beast" 3.5).

Throughout the episode, scenes with humor are interspersed with tense, frustrated waiting or violent actions. A.W. Merrick attempts to read aloud his latest story for the *Pioneer* to Blazanov as the newspaperman stumbles on the uneven street. Dan Dority angrily refers to Captain Turner as that "sea-creature" in response to Turner's obvious challenge to fight; a furious Bullock doesn't know what to make of the snide asides Swearengen offers about Dority when the sheriff reports a murder to the saloon owner. Two scenes feature the gentle comic teasing of Langrishe to the dying older actor Chesterton. A bumbling scene in the livery with Bullock, Hostetler, Steve, and "the Nigger General," as he refers to himself, searching under the hay for the chalkboard the latter hid earlier is also initially humorous. Another comic scene shows Sol Star sitting up in bed in his new house, raising a hand to knock on the wall to summon Trixie from her room at Shaughnessy's through the secret passage between the two—which Trixie responds to by shouting at how ridiculous she finds this set-up.

But these scenes of light-heartedness are distributed among much more serious, tense scenes. The tone of Merrick and Blazanov's conversation shifts drastically when they discover a fresh corpse. The touchingly comic scenes with the actors frame a long, graphically violent hand-to-hand combat scene in the muddy thoroughfare between Dan Dority and Captain Turner, each representing his boss, both of whom watch the fight from above, on a roof and a balcony. Unexpectedly and violently, at the end of the livery search scene, one character commits suicide, followed by the sheriff's delayed, very public arrest of Hearst at gunpoint. This deliberate juxtapositioning of dramatic scenes with comic ones in both the plays and the television series serve to control audience responses, with the comic scenes lightening the tone or mood, providing a much-needed laugh and making the return to a tense or violent scene that much more strained and jarring, in some cases. The juxtapositioning of these scenes also suggest drawing of sides in the camp in conflict, with Hearst and his followers on one side and Swearengen and his alliances on the other, but the comic scenes suggest pairs or small communal groups, of coming together, at the margins of this building suspense leading to a confrontation of some kind. Sustained tension is useful but challenging; interspersing that tension with comic relief aids in engaging audiences emotionally and encouraging them to keep watching to see what potentially unpredictable tone or mood comes with the next scene.

Shakespeare gives us a microcosm and macrocosm perspective of the need for unity and cohesion in the face of threats to the family and state in *Henry IV*. So does *Deadwood*, as we see Al Swearengen negotiating to sustain his influence over the camp and the camp's independence from outside political maneuvering by government officials in Yankton. Sarah Hagelin states that "*Deadwood*'s odd juxtaposition of affect and violence, of nineteenth-century cadences and twentieth-century invective, of the sacred and the profane, begins to make sense" when viewed through Milch's claim that the modern concept of the self as isolated, alone is just an illusion.[14] She asserts that "*Deadwood* is about the place of the state (or in its absence the community) in our ethical responsibilities to others...."[15] Both sets of work provide audiences with scenes and locations that may seem initially to have little to do with one another, but that ultimately speak to the same themes, often related to community-building or community-dissolving.

Deadwood also presents multiple doubling motifs in terms of location, including the Gem and the Bella Union, shown as competition for one another through their offering of alcohol and prostitutes.[16] While the Bella Union appears superior, because it is cleaner and fancier in its decor, prostitutes' clothing and hygiene, Tolliver's appearance, and the gambling games that are offered, it's an illusion. And in contrast, the Gem's decor, its prostitutes' clothing, and Swearengen's image appear dirty, worn, rough, and primitive; the Gem doesn't pretend it's other than what it looks like, establishing an authenticity to its self-awareness.

The Televisual Medium: Close-Ups and Silent Scenes

The medium of television allows for close-ups and other visual aids to convey a number of details about the scene or character. Often in a televisual narrative, audiences are left to "infer characters' morality and beliefs on the basis of exterior markers, including their appearance, behaviors, and interactions as well as how other characters act toward and talk about them."[17] Wright says that, in Western films or television series, "Much of the coding," or audience understanding of relationships, character motivation, and character reactions, "is done through visuals—clothing, background, movements, expressions...."[18] *Deadwood*'s cinematography and lighting frequently feature close-ups of the actors' expressions and/or body language, with no dialogue or narration, accompanied only by sparse non-diegetic music.

Multiple closing scenes from the series are silent studies of character facial expressions and body language. One of the most powerful final scenes is in "Here was a Man" (1.4). Hagelin notes that in dealing with the famous murder of Hickok, the series "withhold[s] shots of Bill himself, instead showing the community in pairs in a series of two-shots that obsessively frame people looking out windows or through doorways, drawing visual attention to the difference between interior and exterior space."[19] No one is alone, however, in responding to this event. Jane Canary enters the No. 10 first afterwards, stopping right inside the door to grab a bottle and down it, but she's joined silently by Bullock dropping to his knees at the murdered and fallen body of his friend. Obviously, televisual narratives "must cue viewers to infer [a character's] interior state through exterior markers, ranging from the subtleties of [the actor's] facial expression and posture that convey tense, suppressed rage to the dramatic context of whatever [another character has just done]."[20] Timothy Olyphant, who plays Seth Bullock, says that "The challenge of Bullock is his bare simplicity. Can I play a character where I can just hit my mark, be still, look the other person in the eye, and trust that the nuance and complication and all that stuff will still be there?"[21] In this scene of sudden violent loss, Bullock doesn't speak, but his eyes fill with tears and he's trembling slightly. His loss is an unmistakable pain expressed involuntarily and physically, personalizing this famous historical event.

But the most powerful closing silent scene in the series features Trixie, returning to Swearengen's bed after his verbal and physical mistreatment of her leads her to attempt suicide ("Suffer the Little Children" 1.8). He is already reclining in bed when she enters the room. He watches her walk over to his side of the bed, pull a gold nugget from Garret's claim out of her handbag and place it on his nightstand. He grabs her arm, turning her to face him, looks into her eyes, then forces her hand away from where it's hiding the wound she inflicted on herself. He sees it, realizing what she attempted, and looks back at her face. She slaps him, hard, then walks to the other side of the bed, and removes her clothes. Watching her the entire time, he pulls the sheets back for her. She climbs under them and curls up on her side, her back to him. Dialogue would only have weakened what this scene conveys about their relationship, so different from the pilot episode's portrayal of it; the power balance has seismically shifted between them. Just as silent scenes can convey a great deal of information through attention to visual details, so, too, can close-ups or zooms direct audience attention to visual cues.

In *The Hollow Crown*'s (2010) *Richard II*, close-ups enhance Patrick Stewart's intense performance as John of Gaunt, chastising the young king for his mistreatment and degradation of the glorious England he inherited. This final powerful speech of John of Gaunt's suggests the tipping of the scales against Richard, beginning his decline and Bolingbroke's ascension. Gaunt's unwell appearance, sweating from fever, lank hair, trembling, and gasping for breath, remaining seated in front of the king, combined with his unwavering determination to speak truth to power unsettles both Richard and the audience.

Voiceover narration also directs audience attention to relationships between dialogue and visual images that otherwise would appear to have no connection. Given that Elizabethan audiences would have known about Henry V's death at a young age, but most modern audiences would not, the director's choice for *The Hollow Crown*'s version of *Henry V* to open with the Chorus (John Hurt) narrating the first lines of the play as a voice-over against the images of the young monarch's funeral makes sense; the juxtapositioning of these lines with that image illustrates the outpouring of grief over his loss, before taking viewers back to the beginning of his reign to explain how he came to be so beloved. By beginning at the end, it effectively raises the "how did we arrive here" question of history, offering the answer of divine punishment for Henry IV's usurpation of the throne and Richard II's failure to effectively lead.

Point-of-View/Perspective

In some productions of Shakespeare's plays, directors rearrange the scenes in an attempt to achieve a certain effect with the audience response; often scenes are rearranged with the claimed purpose of helping the audience follow more clearly and easily what is happening in terms of political relationships in the history plays. In *Richard II*, the first two scenes are often inverted by directors to reveal to the audience first that King Richard is commonly held to be a corrupt ruler, implicated in the murder of the Duke of Gloucester before Bolingbroke challenges Mowbray as bearing some responsibility for the Duke's murder. Some critics assert that flipping these scenes is a mistake, explaining that:

> Our confusion about what is happening is essential to Shakespeare's method in staging the events of *Richard II*. We are mystified and then enlightened. The disparity between the formality of the opening dispute and the guilt it conceals is one of the keys to appreciating the dramatic spectacle. Shakespeare is here alert to the mystifications of power; the tendency of political authority to sustain itself by means of ritual, symbolism, and—above all—theater.[22]

Shakespeare intends for the audience to be confused about whom to trust in this history play opening with nobility in conflict with one another. Richard appears in control, a respected and fair ruler, arbitrator of justice; Bolingbroke appears disgruntled but honorable, seeking justice on behalf of his uncle. We are mistaken on all accounts by this introduction to the characters and the situation—and that is *exactly* where Shakespeare wants the audience, thinking we know what we are seeing in the opening scene, only to correct us in the next scene, leaving us uncertain about whom to believe in this conflict.[23] This reminds me of Hagelin's observation of 21st century television's strategy of the "affective miscue," which "encourage[s] its audience to ask one question, only to reveal this to have been the wrong question to ask all along."[24] Deliberate confusion of audience perspectives, or setting up audience expectations only to then challenge them, is a strategy shared by complex narratives that seek to engage the audience in more sophisticated ways than mere passive viewing.

Deadwood opens on Montana Territory in May 1876 in a U.S. Marshal's office with Marshal Seth Bullock and prisoner Clell Watson before moving to the Black Hills in July 1876 with a wagon line into Deadwood, focusing on Jane Canary and Wild Bill Hickok, then sweeping into the mining camp itself, the Gem Saloon, with filthy successful prospector Ellsworth and Gem owner Al Swearengen. Jacobs observes that the opening shot of the pilot episode at first glance provides clear markers of the Western genre: an empty dirt street running past a saloon and a scaffold, a cowboy-costumed person on a horse pass unobtrusively by a jail, recognizable by the barred windows.[25] It's a familiar setting for a Western, but absent the activity we've come to expect in such a scene. The gallows and the barred windows suggest the enforcement of laws is central to the story ahead. The narrative opens in the still and quiet aftermath of a physical confrontation between a horse-thief and the lawman. Jacobs notes of the opening scene in the Montana jailhouse where we see Bullock pausing in writing something, we aren't shown what he's writing; "instead the world behind him is brought into clarity (the technique is called 'racking focus' and will become the show's most prominent stylistic signature)."[26] I mentioned *Deadwood*'s use of the rack-focus shot in Chapter 1; with such a shot there is "a narrow depth of field, [and] part of the image will be out of focus. Over the course of a continuous shot, the camera operator can alter the focal plane to shift what part of the image is sharp and clear, effectively guiding viewer's perception by changing focus from one character to another."[27] Another first season example of the rack-focus shot on *Deadwood* is the foreground focus on Alma's shaking hand reaching for the coffeepot in the hotel restaurant that then shifts to background focus on Bill Hickok's face as he watches her and recognizes her symptoms of addiction, the same ones that made Charlie Utter offer to pour the coffee for Bill earlier ("Deep Water" 1.2). This shot provides an unexpected connection between strangers, the wealthy socialite and the legendary gunslinger, recognized by only one of them. Jacobs writes that "[t]he rack-focus gesture constantly reminds us that we fail if we try to locate the meaning of life exclusively in one [...] experience: there is more going on around us that may bear upon things[,] ... not all of it ... clearly defined."[28] This shifting lens focus directs audience attention to the fact that there are always at least two points of view as well as emphasizing one character watching and reacting to the actions of another, or connections between the two characters recognized by only one of them. And the character who observes more, knows more, has the advantage over others who remain oblivious to such connections.

The use of close-ups, zooms, and camera angles contribute to audience identification with and understanding of character motivation, responses, and perspective. Writing about Western film, Pippin claims that the "technique—the invitation [through zooming close-ups on facial expressions] to an identification which is then frustrated, undermined, or in some way turned against the identifier—is both a frequent device in the film and often overlooked."[29] That zoomed-in close-up of facial expressions draws the audience into a study of nuances, making viewers identify with a character, then challenging that first identification and complicating the audience's relationship to any given scene.

The audience also shares a perspective through character location in several scenes. Melody Graulich observes that "Many characters stand at windows in *Deadwood*—first and second story—or posture on balconies, each with his or her unique point of view about 'the show' they're watching [...] These settings indicate a concern for surveillance, control, and power; they also announce the series' obsession with point of view."[30] Many of the characters observe from a distance actions taking place in the street, often without sufficient context, leaving them to draw their own conclusions, which aren't always accurate. Their perspectives are limited by their location and distance; audience perspectives are limited by editing and camera angles in ways that are often overlooked. On *Deadwood*, characters and shots are usually in motion, as Michael K. Johnson notes, "the emphasis on flows and networks [in the camp] is reflected stylistically by a frequently moving camera: pans, zooms, tracking shots, handheld cameras, moving crane shots."[31] The camera's perspective, like the camp, is almost constantly in motion, constantly changing, with new arrivals and departures on a regular basis.

While edits in the form of jump-cuts from some scene and location to another or shifts in camera angles disrupt viewing for audiences, both *2 Henry IV* and *Henry V* feature disruptions to the dramatic illusion on stage through figures that speak directly to the audience, narrating what characters in their roles cannot. *2 Henry IV* breaks from the pattern established in the two preceding history plays by opening with a speaking allegorical figure, Rumor, warning the audience of her danger. She conveys both truth and lies, without distinguishing between the two, noting the danger she represents of instilling false hope or fear. At the end of *2 Henry IV*, a character called Epilogue addresses the audience, seeking to dispel rumors that the character of Falstaff is based on Sir John Oldcastle. Of course, by drawing attention to the character and the real person, the association between the two is made concrete for the audience, negating what the Epilogue claims to be attempting. *Henry V* features a Chorus that interrupts the play five times, each time commenting on the limits of theater to fully and adequately represent historical events such as war, asking for the audience's imaginative assistance to fill in what is lacking in the dramatic narrative. The disruptions in both of these plays that Rumor, Epilogue, and the Chorus create draw attention to the illusion of theatrical spectacle and the distance between what the audience knows from experience, legend, or study, and what is being presented to them on the stage. These figures direct the audience attention in a different way to the stage's presentation, by emphasizing its artifice. As Mittell notes of 21st century American television, "Everything we see is shaped by the techniques of camerawork and editing, which highlight some aspects of the world while leaving others off-screen. Even when representations are accurate, the way television represents the world always shapes our perceptions more than how a perfect reflection would."[32] For every close-up that directs our attention to a particular character's response to events, the rest of the scene and the characters in it are occluded. Moving a play from a live staged performance to a filmed and edited one emphasizes this perspective shift. In some ways, camera angles and focus in televisual adaptations of the plays also disrupt the performance by forcing audience attention to a specific detail, rather than leaving that decision to the audience viewing the whole scene before them.

Although a Western, *Deadwood* lacks the long shots of the horizon audiences have come to associate with this genre. Instead, the mining camp of Deadwood is cradled in the steep Black Hills, boxed in by the rising mountains on all sides. Where we might be accustomed to seeing wagon trains traveling steadily across an open plain, in the Black Hills above Deadwood, we're shown a traffic jam of wagons and riders as far as the eye can see, leading both away from and into the camp. It foreshadows what we'll see in the camp itself. As David Drysdale notes, "the cinematography is often claustrophobic," with the camera following the main thoroughfare in the increasingly overcrowded camp filled with people, animals, wagons, equipment, buildings under construction, trade booths, and even mines."[33] The audience enters the crowded and muddy streets of the camp along with Seth Bullock, seeing it through his eyes as a newcomer overwhelmed by the busyness of it all.

The first episode privileges Seth Bullock's perspective in entering Deadwood, leading Witschi to claim that "the most prominent narrational voice" is Bullock's.[34] Witschi adds that Bullock's writing in a journal and insisting on taking down Watson's last words, both in the opening of the pilot episode, "firmly establish Seth Bullock as a literate man, a principled and compassionate man, and above all a man interested in preserving and passing along the stories of individuals."[35] We see further evidence of his interest in preserving and telling stories through his letter to the family of the murdered Cornishman in the third season.

In the television adaptation of *The Hollow Crown*'s *Richard II*, directed by Rupert Goold, we're given a shot of Richard lying on the ground, face up, at Bolingbroke's feet at court, where Bolingbroke is demanding that Richard "perform" an official transfer of the crown to him. The camera is directly above Richard (Ben Whishaw) in a close-up of his face, but with the crown also in the shot, not on his head, but off to the side, as though resting on the ground. However, it's not touching the ground, but appears to float above it. This dream-like quality to the scene's visual elements suggests many possible interpretations, among them raising the concept of the divine right of kings, whereby their power comes from God's appointment of them as monarchs, a central theme of this history play. The crown doesn't touch the earth, but remains suspended mysteriously above it. This image deliberately plays with audience perspective and distracts our attention from either man claiming the crown, to the crown itself and the nature of authority. Richard, too, is floating just barely above the floor in the close-up portion of this scene, with the crown suspended above and to the right of him, suggesting that the crown is indeed his by divine right.

Deadwood, too, plays with audience perception through its use of "off-kilter camera positions, visually distorted or out-of-focus images, and unusually high and low angle shots"[36] and "fast-blurred pans"[37] to represent characters' altered states of concussions, illness, or discomfort. Sometimes the extreme close-up also influences how we view a character; initial close-ups of Al Swearengen, in "Deep Water" (1.2), for example, are too close, making him appear looming and threatening, enhancing our view of him as dangerous, creating a discomfiting desire to put some distance between him and us. In the final scene of "A Lie Agreed Upon, Part I" (2.1), the camera shows Alma Garret's hotel room, where we see Sofia Metz covered and sleeping on a chaise lounge, but the view is somehow distorted. It becomes moreso as Alma's torso in a red dress with a black corset crosses the scene and the camera moves to follow her, revealing the shot was focused on Sofia's reflection in the dressing table's mirror, rather than Sofia directly. The camera follows Alma to answer the door, with the shot focused looking over her shoulder to Bullock's cut and bloody face. He pulls her into his arms. She reaches blindly behind her with one arm to pull the hotel room door to, so as not to wake Sofia. This is one example of many shots utilizing distortion, angles, window or doorframes, and mirrors to challenge and alter the audience's perspective. We think we're seeing a direct shot, unfiltered "reality," until we're shown that we've mistaken a reflection for the real thing. These types of shots also tend to emphasize a significant shift in at least one character's life, requiring an adjustment of her or his perspective, too. In this case, it's Alma's life that is changing, again; she has the responsibility of Sofia as her ward and her lover Seth Bullock is at the door, after having engaged in a brawl with Al Swearengen that left both men bloody and bruised. The fight ended as the stagecoach arrived bearing Seth's wife and son, necessitating a decision about the future of Alma and Seth's relationship and the competing demands of love, honor, and responsibility for Alma, since Seth leaves the decision about their future in her hands.

In the Henriad and *Deadwood*, the use of space is embodied in scene organization and televisual aspects that direct viewer attention and control perspective. Scene sequencing indicates that scenes are deliberately juxtaposed with one another to contrast or, more often, emphasize correspondences between seemingly disparate worlds and characters. Settings and characters are often aligned in counterpoint to one another, with older powerful men as more stationary, and younger men more mobile, seeking out those in power. Alternating scenes of comedy and seriousness may both focus on community-dissolving or community-building in different ways. Both works contain multiple doubling motifs, to be discussed further in the next chapter on character. The televisual medium's use of close-ups and silent scenes or scenes with non-diegetic music, used very sparsely on the series, serve to emphasize the importance of the visual element to convey meaning. Point of view is affected by scene sequencing, camera focus, angles, and movement intended to deliberately confuse the audience, defamiliarizing the familiar, complicating perspectives by doubling them. These techniques disrupt viewer perspective just as dramatic personifications of Rumor, the Chorus, and the Epilogue do. Some aspects of scene organization and structure are influenced by genre plot conventions and other devices that fall under the category of events, or actions in these works.

EVENTS

The order of events or actions also contribute to narrative structure and managing audience responses. The predictability of generic plot structures for the English history play and the American Western film applied to television series can be used to meet or establish some audience expectations and/or be disrupted to create tension, suspense, or comedy; the best narratives offer some combination of the familiar and the unfamiliar. In both kinds of drama, the history play and the Western, conflict between the individual and the greater communal good serves as a driving force in the plot. Surprisingly these generically distinct narratives about men's relationships with one another in pursuit of power share a couple of parallel scenes emphasizing masculinity as determined by peers and cross-generational interactions highlighting the mortality of powerful older men. Finally, both narratives feature a lack of sufficient closure, leaving viewers wondering what comes next in the stories they offer.

The English History Play Plot Structure

English history plays tend to feature the kings whose names are the play's titles, often providing the story of that man's rise to power, and, in some cases, his fall, as well. Shakespeare's First Folio contains ten plays in the history category, two individual plays, *King John* and *Henry VIII*, and two sets of plays, the so-called minor tetralogy, consisting of *1 Henry VI*, *2 Henry VI*, *3 Henry VI*, and *Richard III*, and the so-called major tetralogy, consisting of *Richard II*, *1 Henry IV*, *2 Henry IV*, and *Henry V*. All of these plays deal with England's past, between the late 12th and the early 16th centuries, emphasizing the country's transformation from medieval to early modern.[38] Most history plays begin with at least the appearance of political stability that is challenged by rebel factions, usually in support of one of the king's relatives replacing the current monarch and, often, end with the death of the monarch in the title. For this reason, some of the histories may also be viewed as tragedies. The history play *Richard II* has also had the title or subtitle of *The Life and Death of King Richard the Second*.

In general, Shakespeare's history plays feature civil war or the threat of it, rather than external challenges to the monarch and country. Repeatedly, they illustrate the dangers of a divided nation. Michael Hattaway claims that Shakespeare's history plays "lay out, in all their complexity and tenuousness, the devious paths by which the crown descended to Elizabeth."[39] *Richard II* opens in apparent political stability in King Richard II, whose reign is quickly, confusingly, and subversively challenged by a cousin. Shakespeare emphasizes the weaknesses and strengths of both men laying a claim to the throne, sharply contrasting kingly behaviors and qualities of Richard and Bolingbroke. *Henry IV* follows Bolingbroke's troubled tenure as king and father, ending with his death and his son being crowned Henry V. But *1 Henry IV* seems to focus more on the comedy of Falstaff, a form of the Vice character from earlier mystery and morality plays, and Prince Hal's resistance to acting as a responsible prince, playing at the role of the prodigal son. Finally, *Henry V* shows the new young king deliberately focusing the country's attention on France, an external adversary, to unite the various political and cultural divisions in England, as his father advised. The play ends with Henry's victory over France, and the promise of his marriage to Princess Katharine, the latter a convention of Shakespeare's comedies rather than his histories.

The history plays frequently alternate scenes at court, following the lives of the royal family and courtiers, with scenes on the street, with commoners' perspective of their ruling families and political conflict. Often these plays also employ what initially appear to be sharp contrasts between characters or perspectives that ultimately may reveal surprising parallels in plot or theme. Thematic concerns in the history plays tend to include the divine right of kings and nationalism. As I mentioned in Chapter 1, some notable American figures have viewed the American cowboy as the equivalent to the English knight.

The American Western Plot Structure

Initially *Deadwood* seems to follow some of the basic conventions of the Western as identified by Wright, involving three main "characters" in the form of the hero, the society, and the villain.[40] Wright describes the plot structure of the classic Western as beginning "with the hero coming into a social group, a fledgling society..." to whom he is a stranger.[41] In the pilot episode, Bullock and Hickok arrive separately in Deadwood; while Hickok is already a familiar figure to some of the camp's population from newspaper photographs and stories circulating about him, Bullock is an unknown quantity. Wright notes that "the hero is revealed to have an exceptional ability, often gunfighting, expert shot, etc. As a consequence of this ability, the society recognizes the hero as a special and different kind of person."[42] Within a very short span of time, the community witnesses Bullock's skills as a gunfighter or expert shot when they see him paired with Hickok in an encounter with Ned Mason in the thoroughfare. Another part of the classic Western plot is that "the society does not completely accept the hero," as we see with Doc

Cochran's cautionary comment to Jane about trusting Bullock.[43] Of course, "there is a conflict of interests between [a] villain and the society" and "the villain is stronger than the society" in the form of Swearengen initially but Hearst eventually.[44] Ultimately, "a strong friendship or respect between the hero and the villain" emerges, as we see between Bullock and Swearengen, who come to rely upon one another.[45]

Al Swearengen initially meets the classical Western villainous requirement in that he is "committed to personal gain by any means and at any cost, usually at the cost of progress, decency, and law."[46] He does not, however, remain in that relationship with the camp community, especially once Tolliver and then Hearst are introduced to fulfill that function, without any backstories supplied to explain their motivations or behaviors of treating other people as means to self-serving ends. We're not meant to sympathize with them, thus contextualizing backstories are withheld from the audience. Instead, changes in Swearengen's character move the series away from the classical Western plot and into the most sophisticated fourth plot construct that Wright recognizes for the Western, that of the professional plot. In the professional plot, "the thieves" or what would have been the villains in the classical plot structure, can be "good guys," especially if the coding of good and bad contrasts includes distinctions between kind and unkind people.[47] Wright says that the villains or thieves "may not always be legal and honest, but then neither are the heroes. In fact, the villains are no longer necessarily bad ... and they may not even be unkind."[48] Although Swearengen seems brutally violent and cruel in the first season of the series, his character begins a gradual shifting, exemplified by his kindness to some of the vulnerable in the camp, including Trixie, Jewel, Doc Cochran, and the Reverend Smith. *Deadwood* actually demonstrates a progression from the appearance of the more simplistic classical Western plot in its pilot episode towards the more complex professional plot by the end of its run if we look at the change in Swearengen's character and the alliances formed. Development of Swearengen's character is discussed later in Chapter 7, under the subheading of "Controlling and Shifting Audience Sympathies."

As I mentioned in Chapter 1, both narratives deliberately open with familiar scenes to play with and unsettle audience expectations for how the characters will act, what their relationship is to one another, and how events will continue to unfold. Audiences are expected to recognize certain elements of the introduction to the tetralogy and the series, only to have those expectations tested immediately, alerting them that they are seeing something different, something new. *Deadwood*'s opening shot on the streets of a small town in Montana presents a familiar Western setting: a jail with a lone, injured lawman and prisoner under potential assault at night from an angry, drunken, and armed mob demanding the prisoner, attempting to circumvent the process of law in delivering his punishment. Viewers might anticipate that the lawman will attempt to maintain control over the situation, dispersing the mob while defending the prisoner from their violent intentions.[49] Most viewers don't expect the marshal to lead him to the porch of the jail, declare his guilt, and pronounce the sentence as though this one authority figure embodies the judge and executioner as well. Also surprising is the marshal's physical assistance, jerking Watson's body downward to aid in breaking his neck quickly and efficiently. Not only that, but the marshal demands participation in taking responsibility for passing the dead man's last words and wishes on to his relatives from the mob. And he gets it, however reluctantly. His emphasis on the humanity of the prisoner and the appropriate follow-up of providing last words to relatives mark him as a moral figure. Audience expectations of the marshal in the old West as a moral authority figure are met then challenged then affirmed, engaging audiences to watch more closely, wondering how else the narrative might prove unpredictable. We see something similar in *Richard II*, where the king is meant to serve as the arbitrator of justice but is revealed to be deliberately subverting justice, and in *Henry V*, where the king appears to be pressuring the clergy to carefully provide the justification he seeks for going to war with France. The message audiences are left to ponder, both from the English history plays and the television series' presentation of effective leadership, is whether some degree of corruption is necessary to achieve the greater common good.

The Role of Conflict

Drama in any form requires conflict and resolution of that conflict as the narrative progresses. The Henriad is built on the beginning of the Wars of the Roses, the struggle for political control of England between the Lancaster and York branches of the Plantagenet royal family. These history plays raise questions about leadership based on effective experience in both the military and political theaters versus the concept of divine right, that kings are identified through God's grace in placing them on the throne through bloodline and inheritance of that position. But these plays also question political posturing as just that, a carefully orchestrated illusion cultivated to provide the appearance only of virtue, following Machiavelli's guide for princes. Henry Bolingbroke and his son Prince Hal are portrayed as master manipulators when it comes to gaining power and support, or extending their political reach. What is unclear, however, is whether audiences are supposed to admire them for this ability, or respond critically to it.

Deadwood is also structured around conflict, between order and the law and disorder and lawlessness. Although series creator David Milch claimed that when he switched from the concept of the establishment of order in community in Rome to the American West, he "changed the organizing principle from the cross to gold," Hagelin argues that this claim is part of the "affective miscue the show uses to mount its argument in favor of radical communalism"; she goes on to claim that gold isn't the series' binding agent, especially after the murder of Wild Bill in episode four.[50] Like the history plays, the television series features conflict followed by resolution of the conflict in a repeated pattern. The first season is structured around the seeming opposition of Bullock and Swearengen, hero and villain, law and crime, order and disorder, before the two men recognize some of their common objectives and forge an alliance together. The second season's dramatic conflict begins to shift, to highlight locals' interests challenged by outsiders, specifically political and economic machinations seeking to take control of the camp, represented by Yankton and Hearst's employees.[51] We're shown outsiders coming to Deadwood and challenging the not-yet-established status quo of power relationships in both seasons one and two, with Bullock as the first outsider and Yankton and Hearst's men combined as the second set of outsiders threatening Swearengen's position of power in the camp. Finally, the third season's conflict is clearly between the locals in the camp, led by Swearengen and Bullock, against Hearst himself, his ambitions, and his desire for total control. Season three of *Deadwood* concludes with only the promise of a reprieve from the oppressive force of Hearst himself in the camp, of course. The series was cancelled without sufficient advance warning for the conclusion of its various narratives. Fans were left frustrated with speculations of what might have come next, especially after rumors of a couple of made-for-television movies to provide closure to those lingering unresolved story arcs fizzled.

Parallel Scenes

Two sets of strikingly similar scenes from *1 Henry IV* and *Deadwood* serve the same kinds of functions in the overall narratives. The first similar scenes use the opposition of insiders versus outsiders to provide comic relief, and, through emphasizing appearance, behavior, and language differences, to allow insider male characters to assert their identification with conventional masculinity, as though that might be doubted by their on-stage/screen male peers. The second similar scenes strengthen ties between men, especially cross-generationally, and call attention to the inevitability of aging and the mortality of all, even the most powerful men.

The first set of similar scenes involves men who are outsiders, out of place in some way, and who are condemned by insiders, or men who more clearly belong to the settings. We're given a contrast between insiders and outsiders, but also an insider's condemnation of the outsider to other men, contempt that often aligns the outsider with the feminine and pronounces him as weak for that alignment. Of course, this tells us more about the anxieties of the man who is condemning the outsider than about the outsider himself.

In *1 Henry IV*, when King Henry has accused Henry "Hotspur" Percy of deliberately withholding prisoners of war from him, in violation of the King's orders and the customs of war among the nobility, Hotspur defends his actions. He says he meant no offence to the king, but he was so irritated by the messenger sent to deliver the request that he refused. He describes himself at the time as exhausted and filthy from battle and, in contrast, the messenger as "…neat and trimly dressed, / Fresh as a bridegroom…. / He was perfume'd like a milliner" (*1 Henry IV* 1.3.30–31, 33). He reports the messenger's rude behavior, smiling "as soldiers bore dead bodies by" and criticizing them as "untaught knaves, unmannerly / To bring a slovenly unhandsome corpse / Betwixt the wind and his nobility" (*1 Henry IV* 1.3.38; 39–42). The messenger's appearance, hygiene, expression, and critique of the tired soldiers' care for their fallen peers as an insult to him indicate just how out of place and inappropriate the messenger is, given the context. If this isn't sufficient to show Hotspur's disdain for the messenger's speech and behavior, he goes on to describe the messenger as using "many holiday and lady terms" in questioning Hotspur, emphasizing the man's inability to understand battle, soldiers, or war (*1 Henry IV* 1.3.43); he is as removed from familiarity with the sacrifices men make in such circumstances as women are. At the end of an exhausting battle, Hotspur says he was approached by a clean, perfumed, fashionably beardless, snuff-snorting non-combatant, who demanded his prisoners, while denigrating the sight and smell of corpses on the battlefield as being too close to his exalted person. Hotspur claims he had every right to be infuriated and insulted by this pretentious and inappropriate messenger, who then went on to claim that but for "these vile guns" he himself would have been a soldier (*1 Henry IV* 1.3.63–64). It's obvious this individual is out of place and out of touch with the realities of war. The battlefield is as alien to the courtier as his appearance and behavior is to the soldiers; he fails to adapt to the prevailing circumstances. If Prince Hal is one kind of foil for Hotspur, this messenger is another, obviously ill-suited to the tasks of the battlefield, but also condescending and rude to the soldiers' efforts and sacrifices. In addition, Hotspur's diction indicates his disdainful identification of this messenger with femininity; he references the man as "perfumed" (*1 Henry IV* 1.3.33) and "smelling so sweet" (*1 Henry IV* 1.3. 53) twice, saying the messenger questioned him in "lady terms" (*1 Henry IV* 1.3.43) and "talked like a waiting gentlewoman" (*1 Henry IV* 1.3.54) when it came to the realities of war. Hotspur himself identifies with masculinity, as a "man's man," a soldier proud of the calculated risks he and his men have taken and the sacrifices they've made, which the messenger seems to be oblivious to. His disgust with the messenger's non-masculine behavior and speech, in particular with his disrespect for the weary and injured soldiers he is in the midst of, takes the form of misogynistic criticism and a refusal to hand over his prisoners to this annoying "popinjay" (*1 Henry IV* 1.3.49), a term for a gaudily beautiful parrot also often applied to a person perceived to be "shallow, vain, or conceited."[52] Hotspur admits his emotional state at the time as grieving, angry impatience and that he himself was wounded.

In the pilot episode of *Deadwood*, Milch provides us with an equally out of place individual, when Dan Dority reports to Swearengen that "the New York dude" is waiting to see him. Al asks if he ordered whiskey, which Dan confirms; Al then asks, condescendingly and with an accompanying miming of the second description here, "Did he down it, or is he sipping at it?" to which Dan laughs, acknowledging the latter ("Deadwood" 1.1). As Al approaches the man in question downstairs, the saloon owner says to Dan, "Brom Garret of Manhattan, scourge of the Deadwood Pharo tables" ("Deadwood" 1.1). In a short span of time, Garret has been associated with the east twice, first New York by Dan and then, more specifically, Manhattan by Al, identifying him not just as an outsider, but also as an urbanite. When Garret excitedly asks if Al has heard that Wild Bill Hickok has arrived in the camp, Al replies, tauntingly, "Oh, yes I did. Does that give you the vapors?" ("Deadwood" 1.1). Even dim-witted Garret picks up on that insulting tone, asking if the saloon owner is angry about something. When finalizing the deal for his gold claim, Driscoll spits in his hand; Garret hesitates to do the same, prompting Driscoll to ask Swearengen, "What's his fucking problem?" ("Deadwood" 1.1). Driscoll also refers to Garret as "the goose-looking man in the shiny suit" twice ("Deadwood" 1.1). Garret is almost always attired in a clean, impractically light-colored, three-piece, new-looking, and stylish suit[53] with a hat, his hair carefully combed into place, his moustache neatly trimmed. He's the perfect inherited-wealth dandy, in both appearance and behavior, naive and gullible when it comes to gold mining and Al Swearengen's elaborate scam involving Dan Dority, E.B. Farnum, and Tim Driscoll in order to profit off Garret. Garret is the stereotypic gentrified, purposeless man-out-of-place in the wild West, the "dude" that he's referred to as repeatedly by Swearengen's staff, a mark for their boss's manipulation and robbery.

Conventionally, in Western films, any association between male characters and the East suggests weakness that likely cannot survive the rough life on the frontier. Johnny Burns also later describes him to Swearengen as "that cherry New York dude" ("Reconnoitering the Rim" 1.3). In writing about the conventions of Western film, Wright says, "The East is always associated with weakness, cowardice, selfishness, or arrogance. The Western hero is felt to be good and strong because he is involved with the pure and noble wilderness, not with the contaminating civilization of the East."[54] Brom Garret is associated with the East through references to Manhattan and New York, and, perhaps in part because of this association, treated with contempt by Swearengen, Dority, Burns, and Driscoll. Bullock, the alleged hero of this series, is from Etobicoke, Ontario, Canada—north and west of New York, but not that removed from it—and more commonly associated with Montana, even further west than Deadwood, a mitigated association with the East. Even he expresses contempt for the East when he refers to Garret's family as "those society people in New York City, who live with their heads up their asses anyway" ("Sold Under Sin" 1.12). Clearly, he has no patience for the wealthy upper classes who have little to no understanding of laboring for one's keep.

Brom, more of an outsider than most in Deadwood, attempts to pick up and use the language of insiders, when he repeats what Al has said of Tim Driscoll, "He *is* shitfaced" ("Deadwood" 1.1) and later, what Ellsworth has said of mining the property, to Dan, "She hasn't even showed me any flake. Oh hell" ("Reconnoitering the Rim" 1.3). He mimics Ellsworth's feminization of the land the claim is on but adds a sense of entitlement and whining complaint with the word "even." These are the only two times Brom uses profanity or slang terms. His diction is usually more elevated and formal, for example, his use of the terms "needn't," "quite," "conspirators," "duped," "confer," "charlatan," "colluded," and "cahoots," which are parroted by Al Swearengen to his face with "I don't *collude*. I don't *cahoot*" ("Deep Water" 1.2), and by Bill Hickok and Charlie Utter after he's left with "I don't think he took your point—*quite*" and "I think he *quite* missed it" ("Reconnoitering the Rim" 1.3). Like Swearengen, Utter and Hickok are older, experienced insiders on the frontier, aware of the distance that separates them from Garret and playing with his elevated and formal diction to comment on it.

The foil for Brom Garret is not Al Swearengen or Seth Bullock but Whitney Ellsworth, an older, filthily-clothed prospector, a real hands-on miner who strikes gold early in the pilot episode. Ellsworth is experienced, knowledgeable, independent, and capable. He's the assayer recommended by Swearengen to Bullock as trustworthy and adept. He demonstrates an ability to read others well, recognizing when Alma is showing signs of pregnancy, and exhibiting compassion when he offers to marry her to protect her reputation. Unlike Brom, he recognizes when Alma is high and refuses contact with her in that altered state of mind, regardless of her sensual invitation to him. He is comfortable with profanity and slang (consider his introduction of "pissed off" to Alma[55]) but also uses elevated diction on occasion (his use of "nefarious" and "liable to rebuke" to Trixie[56]); he demonstrates some understanding of adjusting his speech depending on his audience and his intentions.

Ellsworth is uncompromising about some things, especially when it comes to the safety of others for whom he is responsible, evident in his anger towards Francis Wolcott and George Hearst's treatment of miners at the Comstock. He demonstrates no qualms about standing up for what he believes in and calling those out who exhibit no regard for human life. Ellsworth is well-respected in the camp as an experienced and efficient miner, a responsible community member, one who is kind to children and respectful towards women—regardless of their social status or occupation, willing to take in a stray dog, trustworthy, honest, and even willing to sacrifice his own independence and comfort to assist and protect the more vulnerable. He takes his responsibility to the child Sofia seriously. If Brom's murder is a blip in the narrative that primarily affects Alma, Ellsworth's deals a blow felt at the very heart of the camp.

In these comparable scenes, we see experienced male insiders mocking and rejecting inexperienced male outsiders, applying feminine gender conventions to those men as a means of further setting themselves apart from those whom they criticize. The feminine conventions they both reference have to do with speech, appearance, and behavior indicating weakness of character in a man. These outsiders' presumptiveness and sense of entitlement elicit anger from the insider critiquing them, perhaps due to envy at the advantages those outsiders have had through wealth, social status, and privilege to observe some of life's harsh realities at a safe distance. Similar to the messenger who annoyed Hotspur, Garret's appearance and behavior mark him as a passive, removed, narcissistic member of the upper class, in Deadwood for fun and adventure, perhaps also causes for contemptuous homophobic/misogynistic responses from men who are active and engaged entrepreneurs seeking to make their way. Consider that in season three, Swearengen shows contempt for neither Jack Langrishe nor Gustave the tailor, both of whom possess effeminate characteristics, but both of whom also clearly have dedicated occupations, something that Swearengen respects, which seems to support Hagelin's claim that "the collective identity the show valorizes is classed, not gendered."[57] These scenes remind us that masculinity is conferred upon, or denied, men by other men's opinions of them, and sometimes that respect is influenced by vocation in connection with social class.[58]

In a second set of similar scenes, we see a young, healthy man visiting the bedside of an older, ailing, and powerful man. These scenes emphasize the mortality of even powerful men, their dependence on others, the testing of the younger men by the older men, and demonstrations of respect and loyalty from the younger men towards the older men, despite the elders' obvious vulnerability. If the two are or have been in conflict with one another, the scene provides resolution to that conflict, allowing the two to reassure one another of their alliance against other outside threats to the community's stability.

In *2 Henry IV*, we have a young, healthy heir apparent visiting the older, ailing bedridden ruler. King Henry is paranoid and defensive about his physical weakness, asserting his mental capabilities to continue ruling. In *Deadwood*'s season two, we see the young, healthy, resilient Bullock visiting the older, ailing, bedridden Swearengen, who is paranoid and defensive about his physical weakness, asserting his mental capabilities to continue information gathering and interpretation. In some ways this scene serves to emphasize the concept of the king's two bodies, the political body of power that is eternal, always claimed by someone, and the physical mortal presence of the current ruler. We see rulers weakened in both cases, but still asserting their right and ability to rule, despite visible evidence to the contrary. The King has swooned and required rest. Swearengen fought with Bullock, falling over the second floor balcony to the street below, but he's also suffering from kidney stones, the combination of which has managed to incapacitate him for two episodes, leaving him bedridden and unable to speak.

In *2 Henry IV*, act four scene four, Henry IV "swoons," and Warwick says, "Be patient, princes. You do know these fits / Are with His Highness very ordinary. / Stand from him, give him air; he'll straight be well" (4.4.114–116). Before the scene has ended, the king has awakened and requested they carry him elsewhere, to bed, to rest. Clarence notices "his eye is hollow, and he changes much" (*2 Henry IV* 4.5.6). Prince Hal arrives and offers to sit with the sleeping king. The prince speaks as he watches over his sleeping father, noting that "thy due from me / Is tears and heavy sorrows of the blood," again using the language of emotional debt or what he owes his father (*2 Henry IV* 4.5.37–38). He promises that "nature, love, and filial tenderness" move him to "pay plenteously" those debts to his "dear father" (*2 Henry IV* 4.5.39–40). He adds that in this reciprocal relationship, his father's debt to him is the crown itself, connecting them by his father's possession of it and his bloodline (*2 Henry IV* 4.5.41–43). He picks up the crown and leaves the room with it as he swears to protect what his father leaves him in order to pass it to his own children in the future. The king wakes and assumes the worst, asking why he was left alone, where the prince has gone, and who took his crown. Paranoid, defensive, and hurt, he asks, "Is he so hasty that he doth suppose / My sleep my death?" (*2 Henry IV* 4.5.60–61). He says that the prince's theft combines with his own illness to bring about his death. He adds a meditation on the contentious relationship between sons and fathers:

> See, sons, what things you are!
> How quickly Nature falls into revolt
> When gold becomes her object!
> For this the foolish overcareful fathers

> Have broke their sleep with thoughts,
> Their brains with care, their bones with industry;
> For this they have engross'ed and piled up
> The cankered heaps of strange-achieve'd gold;
> For this they have been thoughtful to invest
> Their sons with arts and martial exercises—
> When, like the bee, toiling from every flower,
> Our thighs packed with wax, our mouths with honey,
> We bring it to the hive, and like the bees,
> Are murdered for our pains. This bitter taste
> Yields his engrossments to the ending father [*2 Henry IV* 4.5.64–78].

The king compares the hard work of fathers to store up the means to sustain their sons, only to be killed by those very sons, to the labor of bees to sustain the hive. The gold or honey both seek becomes the envious and ambitious goal of the sons to impatiently take from them. There is no appreciation expressed for the labor undertaken by the fathers on behalf of their heirs. This idealized comment suggests that fathers are always thinking ahead, selflessly, about the future for their heirs, but that the heirs are only thinking of the present and themselves. Yet Prince Hal's earlier speech and actions reveal that he is thinking of protecting his father and passing the crown on to his own son someday. His father is mistaken about his motivations.

When they meet again and the king accuses the prince of taking the crown prematurely, caring nothing for his father, the prince asserts his grief and loyalty towards Henry IV. He swears that if he desires the crown more than his father's honor, "Let me no more from this obedience rise, / Which my most inward true and duteous spirit / Teacheth this prostrate and exterior bending" (*2 Henry IV* 4.5.145–147). He describes his fear at finding his father seeming to be dead and explains that he took up the crown to scold it for the weight it laid on his father. He swears that if he coveted it, "Let God forever keep it from my head" (*2 Henry IV* 4.5.173). The king replies, assured, "thou mightest win the more thy father's love, / Pleading so wisely in excuse of it!" (*2 Henry IV* 4.5.178–179). He warns his son that "Yet, though thou stand'st more sure than I could do, / Thou art not firm enough," concerned about the need to sustain the support he has and to garner better, stronger support for his claim to the throne (*2 Henry IV* 4.5.201–202). He advises Prince Hal to make "thy course to busy giddy minds / With foreign quarrels, that action, hence borne out, / May waste the memory of the former days" (*2 Henry IV* 4.5.212–214). In *Henry V*, his son takes that advice to heart, pursuing a war with France to unite his followers in an effort to reclaim an area that once belonged to England. A common external enemy serves to unite England's various political factions.

On *Deadwood*, in season two, Al Swearengen is incapacitated by kidney stones combined with the fight he had with Seth Bullock. For two episodes,[59] he is removed completely from the action in Deadwood, leaving his minions to scramble for guidance, worrying about his health. He is unable to communicate verbally or physically at all during this time, which serves to emphasize the importance of Al's communication skills and his political acumen. Sheriff Bullock pays him a visit to check on him, since his screams of pain were heard clearly throughout the camp as Doc Cochran attempted to treat his condition with assistance from Dan, Johnny, and Trixie. Still partially paralyzed and exhausted from his physical ordeal, Swearengen puts on a defensive front to Bullock and seems pleasantly surprised by the younger, healthier man's show of respect, deference, and willingness to do as Swearengen advises without resistance.

Upon first waking after his physical ordeal to find Doc Cochran, Johnny Burns, and Dan Dority in his room, Dan smiling at him, Al suspiciously demands, "You fuck me while I was out?" ("Complications" 2.5). When Bullock comes to call, Swearengen jokes, "You got gall, coming before me, prettier than ever" and Bullock responds with concern, "Are you all right?" ("Complications" 2.5). Swearengen dismisses the younger man's concern with, "On the fucking mend, that's all to say on that" ("Complications" 2.5). Then he launches into quizzing Bullock about the new commissioner's arrival in camp, the alliances he's already begun to form, and who is likely to be publicly blamed if the commissioner is harmed; he demonstrates clearly that his mental sharpness has not been dulled by his physical ailment. He advises Bullock to keep an eye out for the commissioner, whose public notice on the gold claims is likely to agitate many in the camp against him. A common enemy serves to unite these two adversaries further. He scolds the sheriff with "Don't be fucking clever with me" and then smugly says, "Bedridden I know more than you" about political developments in camp that have escaped Bullock's notice ("Complications" 2.5). Later in the same episode, Bullock returns to report to Swearengen, "The commissioner's all right" and to speculate on the Yankton political maneuvering that involves Deadwood while they share a bottle of whiskey together ("Complications" 2.5), a masculine communion substitution. When Bullock leaves, Swearengen assures him that he'll assist with the responsibility of keeping watch over the camp and its conflicts once he's feeling better; Bullock returns the assurance by expressing his faith in Swearengen's recovery ("Complications" 2.5).

In both of these scenes between ailing, bedridden, and powerful older men and healthy younger men, contentious verbal exchanges between the two focus on their past relationship, verging on renewing that past conflict, before mutually respectful assurances of loyal alliances emerge, followed by the elder man advising the younger as to the future of the community through stable political authority. Combining forces against a common external threat also serves to unite pre-existing divisions.

6. Managing Audience Responses through Narrative Space and Events 155

These two scenes between the sick or dying and the healthy may also speak to other, earlier scenes in both narratives. The Henry IV and Prince Hal scene serves as a corrective to the John of Gaunt and Richard II scene. In *2 Henry IV*, the prince demonstrates appropriate respect and care towards his elder, calming Henry's anxiety about his son's motives for removing the crown from his bedside. Prince Hal's behavior contrasts starkly with Richard's lack of care and respect towards his elder, John of Gaunt, in *Richard II*, and his violent response to Gaunt's accusations of the king's mismanagement and degradation of England. On *Deadwood*, Bullock's demonstration of respect and care for Swearengen's recovery, despite their recent adversarial relationship, contrasts sharply with the lack of respect and care Cy Tolliver displays toward his former thieving partner Andy Cramed, once Cramed has clearly contracted smallpox. Instead of providing treatment and care for the younger man, Tolliver orders him transported into the forest and abandoned. Tolliver never exhibits any sense of communal responsibility in the ways that both Bullock and Swearengen do.[60]

Altogether, these four scenes convey ideas about masculinity, power, respect, and alliances, while also providing some comic relief from the more intense, dramatic scenes bookending them. The first pair of similar scenes emphasize appearance, behavior, and language differences between socially-accepted males and those excluded, allowing some male characters to assert their identification with conventional masculinity, as though that might be doubted by their male peers. The second set of similar scenes not only features the frailty of the human body through older, powerful, and ill or dying men, whose power cannot help them in these conditions, but also reinforces the bonds these men share with their younger counterparts.

Lack of Sufficient Closure

Given that both the Henriad and *Deadwood* tell historically-set stories, neither offers a satisfactory conclusion, as both must leave out the rest of the story leading up to the present day. Hawkins notes that the history plays have a surprising lack of sufficient closure.[61] The story begun in *Richard II* is a prequel to Shakespeare's first set of history plays focusing on Henry VI and Richard III, which end with the destruction of Richard and the promise of restoration of a rightful king in Richmond, who becomes Henry VII. Richmond's marriage to Elizabeth ends the Wars of the Roses, providing unification of claims to the throne, leading to Henry VIII and then Elizabeth I, as though a definitive successive order is unmistakably restored. The second set of history plays, then, seems to end in a strong, united rule under Henry V, only to lead into the original set with a weak king overwhelmed by civil war and only the promise of restored unification. The second tetralogy attempts to stage a recovery of community, restoring what dissolved into civil war in the first tetralogy.[62] However, in *Henry V*, the former Prince Hal is able to possess the throne via not just his father's legacy but also through his own capabilities as an effective ruler, a surprisingly modern concept, determining rightful rulers not by inheritance but by capability.

HBO's *Deadwood*, of course, was cancelled in its third season, although Milch had envisioned a fourth. The network promised two television movies to allow storylines to be concluded, but those have yet to materialize despite tantalizing rumors about the possibility of them practically every year since the series went off the air in 2006. The series ended season three with the departure of Hearst but with an ominous sense that his physical exit was not the end of his reign in the camp. In addition, the communal resistance to Hearst's dictatorialism is dealt a demoralizing, paralyzing blow when Hearst has Ellsworth murdered. As Alan Sepinwall and Matt Zoller Seitz put it, "the camp loses its will to fight"[63] at the sight of Ellsworth's corpse. What's left to tell about Deadwood in this period? Plenty: Trixie and Sol's relationship, Martha and Seth's relationship, the opening of the theater and its first production, Jane's death, Cy's general nefariousness, Deadwood's continued progress toward annexation and statehood, Bullock and Swearengen's continuing relationship, Star's political ascension, the fire that destroyed much of Deadwood, and Bullock's friendship with Teddy Roosevelt, historical events that could have provided a framework for continued storylines and character development. Sepinwall and Zoller Seitz also observe that

> Years later, Milch would say that the stories of Hearst and Langrishe were linked: "It's seemed to me that when the bosses seem to be in charge, there's always room for art as a compensatory dynamic. I think that's what we do best in our society, the best of us as storytellers, present an alternative to the story the bosses are telling."[64]

Perhaps the best stories do exactly that, not just providing escapism or idealistically sanitized versions of the origins of community, but creative alternatives that address the past and the present simultaneously, offering hope and inspiration for viewers. Both sets of work end in suspension, waiting for the next chapter to be told.

Events of the narratives include generic plots centered on conflict, parallel scenes that function similarly, and lack of sufficient closure. *Deadwood* adapts the Western plot featuring varied relationships among the hero, the villain, and the society, specifically the professional plot, allowing for alliances between the hero and villain. Both the history plays and the television series emphasize the conflict between law and order, disorder and order. Parallel scenes offer comic relief and allow some male characters to assert their identification both as insiders and with conventional masculinity. Conflicts between younger and older generations reignite when older men are presented as physically vulnerable, only to have the conflicts resolved and loyalty reassured by the younger men. In addition, focusing on external threats allows alliances to be formed or reformed with a common enemy to defeat. Finally, these narratives share a lack of closure, suspension of the ongoing story.

Conclusion

By analyzing specific aspects of structure, we gain insight into the overarching design of the whole tetralogy or series. What are the organizing principles? An apparent study in contrasts gives way quickly to recognition of the increasingly complex use of mirroring/doubling to complicate audience perception while emphasizing the challenges and necessity of community, of collaboration, of the collective experience of humanity. These works demonstrate their sophisticated ability to engage audiences by defamiliarizing the familiar in terms of visual images and generic plot development, ordering of scenes to elicit specific responses from audiences, and emphasizing point-of-view, through dramatic disruptions such as allegorical figures on stage and through camera focus or angle of shots for televisual narratives, providing multiple perspectives on recurring conflicts and resolutions. The seemingly endless and complex doubling of scenes and characters as foils to one another complicates audience understanding of human nature, adding a rich density to repeated readings or viewings of these texts. In addition, these complex narratives also share an emphasis on character development through costuming and character foils and blurred lines as they seek to not just control but also deliberately shift audience sympathies regarding characters as the series of plays or episodes progress.

7
Managing Audience Responses Through Character

"Verbally and structurally, the play explores the rhetorical figure of chiasmus, or the pairing of opposites in an inverted and diagonal pattern whereby one goes down as the other goes up and vice versa."[1]

CHARACTER

In this chapter, I'm using the term character in relation to structure, referring to the ways in which costuming details convey insight into a character's defining traits, motivations, or behaviors, as well as how sharply contrasting characters' conflicts with one another aid in defining each. In some cases, what begins as a distinct contrast between two such characters gives way to a gradual recognition of similarities between the two, blurring the boundaries originally established to set them apart. In addition, this section examines devices that are used to establish and then shift audience sympathies from one character or set of characters to another as the narrative progresses.

Costuming and Character

Bullock and Swearengen's costuming contributes significantly to how audiences view their personalities; Janie Bryant, costume designer for *Deadwood*, says that "Bullock's four-button frock coat is like an armor.... His coat is black, but there is a lot of texture in the fabric."[2] His multi-layered outfits suggest attempts at both protection and containment. The layers combined with the textured nature of his clothing suggest a depth and complexity to this character, too—that he is more than he might initially appear to be. There is a certain vanity in his appearance as well. Al Swearengen, in contrast, seems not to care about his clothing. He, too, wears a waistcoat and blazer but to an entirely different effect. Sometimes there's an open-necked long-john underneath the waistcoat, with the top buttons of the undergarment undone, which seems "a little more sleazy. It's a fuck-you."[3] It also makes Swearengen seem barely contained, his suit providing only the thinnest veneer of civility. He doesn't seem to require the illusion of physical containment that Bullock does because he is more experienced at self-control than the younger man. The outfit suits Swearengen's character, too, in that his personality is so large it can't be confined. The back of his waistcoat is a surprising deep red satin material, a hidden richness, reflecting the robust nature of his personality. His presence dominates the scenes he's in. Look at the cover art of any of the books about the *Deadwood* series; his image is on every single one of them. It's impossible to think about *Deadwood* without picturing him immediately.

In terms of costuming to convey character, in most productions of *Richard II*, Richard is dressed in light-colored, highly embroidered or decorated flowing gowns or tunics, clothing that signifies his status as monarch, per sumptuary laws of the Elizabethan period. He is attired for leisure at court. His language aligns with his clothing; it's elaborate, with complicated syntax, demonstrating his educational training with rhetoric, and the necessity of such speech at court. Richard is far more loquacious and eloquent, speaking 758 lines to Bolingbroke's 413, almost twice as many.[4] When he finally dons armor, it, too, signifies his status as king, but he wears it awkwardly, suggesting his lack of fitness as a military commander. In contrast, we're usually shown a Henry Bolingbroke at ease in military attire, right from the beginning of the play, as he issues a terse challenge to Mowbray. Bolingbroke is most often dressed in plain armor and plain dark, earth tones, practical and prepared for face-to-face battle. His language often matches the straightforwardness of his attire; it is frequently direct, to the point, with short sentences in subject-verb-object syntax.

Character Foils and Blurred Lines

Richard II features the opposing cousins Richard and Henry Bolingbroke who clearly contrast one another in appearance, costuming, speech, and demeanor. Richard is loquacious, with a strong sense of how to perform power and authority through speech and appearance, but passive, reacting to events rather than initiating action. Henry is a soldier, a man of action and few words, and prone to subversive tactics to achieve his ends. With *1 Henry IV* Shakespeare sets up four characters to compare and contrast immediately: Henry IV, Falstaff, Hotspur, and Prince Hal.[5] It's as if Shakespeare has taken Richard and Henry and split them into four characters, which he shuffles around in various combinations of comparison and contrast, raising questions about optimum combinations, vices, and virtues, leadership qualities, and the older men's competition for attention, time, and influence on the younger men. Falstaff and Prince Hal bear some traces of Richard while Hotspur and the king, a more mature, empowered version of his younger self, bear traces of the younger Bolingbroke. Falstaff and Prince Hal possess Richard's sense of theater, performance, and the power of rhetoric to persuade. They are also passive, or appear passive, in the case of Prince Hal. Hotspur and the king are men of action who excel at military endeavors; neither are consistently powerful or persuasive rhetoricians. One possesses an excess of honor in the form of pride while the other is anxious about being perceived as lacking honor. Both are often shown to be distracted from matters at hand, Hotspur by imagined slights and his temper, the king by his seemingly wayward heir. They share real or imagined betrayal from close male relatives. Reading the Henriad this way corresponds with Hawkins' reading of the first history tetralogy, where he finds that "a single character or action in 'Henriad' is often mirrored as it were prismatically—by several in the fragmented world of *Henry VI*."[6] This complex layering of character foils and doubling adds a dense richness among the relationships in the Henriad.

In *Deadwood*, audience attention is initially divided among Seth Bullock, Wild Bill Hickok, and Al Swearengen, each presented with virtues and vices, none fully exemplifying the idealized hero or villain. Hickok isn't exactly heroic, although he does exhibit kindness, compassion, and support for the more vulnerable. However, he has a ruinous gambling addiction and a fading sense of self-preservation, of which he is well aware.[7] In this sense, Bullock is eventually able to exhibit a greater sense of self-control through restraint than Hickok is shown as having. Swearengen is self-centered and brutally violent, but also reflective, adaptive, and increasingly self-aware. Bullock seems to represent a median between the two older men. While Bullock might initially appear closer in character and behavior to Hickok, it's actually Swearengen that he is more similar to and can learn more from.

A second set of foils emerges with the addition of Cy Tolliver to the series, as a contrast to Al Swearengen in their ownership of competing saloons. Though Tolliver initially appears a more refined, genteel pimp in his clothing and personal hygiene than Swearengen, that appearance is deceptively dangerous. Although both Swearengen and Tolliver frequently insult and threaten their employees and other characters with which they have regular, familiar, and otherwise amiable interactions, there is often "hospitality"[8] or genuine fondness in Swearengen's words, unlike Tolliver's. Swearengen's insults or threats in these cases often sound like a performance of expected aggression while conveying affection for those whom he addresses. Tolliver's refined surface quickly reveals a dark and deep misogyny that he barely masks most of the time, as I noted earlier in this chapter.[9] This is only one example of multiple doublings among characters in the series, which include Al and Alma, Hickok and Ellsworth, Trixie and Joanie, Trixie and Alma, Swearengen and Wu, Dority and Burns, Dority and Adams, Swearengen and Trixie with Tolliver and Joanie, Martha and Jane, Jewel and Doc, Jewel and Trixie, Swearengen and Hearst, Joanie and Eddie with Flora and Miles, Trixie and Jen, and Bullock and Star with Hostetler and Samuel Fields.[10] The complex mirroring of characters throughout the series, like that found in *Richard II* and *Henry IV*, adds a dense richness to the relationships. Why compare these characters? To compare commonalities sharply emphasizes distinctions. Both are important and seen more clearly when placed in juxtaposition with one another.

Controlling and Shifting Audience Sympathies

Shakespeare maintains a firm control over evolving the audience response and sympathies toward specific characters, especially in *Richard II*, which has a chiasmus (x) structure that is deliberate and sets it apart from the other history plays. The chiasmus is "a Renaissance figure of speech signifying a criss-cross."[11] Bevington observes that

> Verbally and structurally, the play explores the rhetorical figure of chiasmus, or the pairing of opposites in an inverted and diagonal pattern whereby one goes down as the other goes up and vice versa. Again and again, the ritual effects of staging and style draw our attention to the balanced conflicts between the two men and within Richard. Symmetry helps to focus these conflicts in visual and aural ways.[12]

The pairing of apparent opposites that then change places in fortune, power, influence, and audience sympathy is one of the identifying and unique features of this play's structure. In productions of the play, Richard's appearance is often feminized, with his long loose hair, rich, delicately embroidered gowns, and bare feet. He's difficult to take seriously as dangerous or threatening in most productions. In contrast, Bolingbroke is usually initially presented as a capable knight or soldier, with short hair, in chainmail, armor or camouflage uniforms, heavy boots, and armed with weapons, obviously prepared for a physical confrontation. If we do see Richard in armor or the like later in the play, it's obvious how awkward he is with it and how it's designed more to present a stunning appearance than for actual combat. The two leads contrast one another in every possible way, including their appearance and speech, emphasizing the play's careful attention to balance and symmetry in characterization.[13]

Shakespeare sets up audiences at the beginning of *Richard II* to sympathize with the banished Henry Bolingbroke, whose only crime appears to be demanding justice, seeking to protect the king, and criticizing Richard as a capable king. Bolingbroke is presented initially as a brave challenger in the name of justice, seeking accountability for his uncle's murder and doing so in appropriate ways, in the open, in front of the king. In contrast, Richard appears to use others for his own entertainment, allowing the challenge between Bolingbroke and Mowbray, setting up the fight, then calling it off just as it is set to begin, as though he's mainly demonstrating his own power and authority to the others present. Bolingbroke's father, John of Gaunt, serves as an advising uncle to King Richard; he attempts to serve the king but also support his son in this action. Gaunt's sorrow at his son's banishment elicits an immediate merciful subtraction of two years from Bolingbroke's sentence. When John of Gaunt dies during that banishment, Richard breaks the practice of primogeniture by claiming Gaunt's estate instead of allowing it to pass to his eldest son. Richard is initially presented as self-centered, lacking compassion, and corrupt; Bolingbroke is positioned as the underdog, daring to challenge corrupt power, even if indirectly. As an eldest son in banishment during the last years of his father's life who has had his inheritance taken away in his absence, Bolingbroke is presented as the more sympathetic character. Upon returning to England, Bolingbroke keeps insisting that he's broken his banishment only to claim what is rightfully his, inherited from his father; it's difficult to argue against that, as York discovers.

When Richard learns of John of Gaunt's physical decline, his response is greedy and self-serving rather than sorrowful or concerned. He says, "Now put it, God, in the physician's mind / To help him to his grave immediately!," adding that "The lining of his coffers" will provide uniforms for soldiers in the Irish-English war; he concludes with "let's all go visit him. / Pray God we may make haste and come too late!" (*Richard II* 1.4.59–60; 61; 63–64). In his confrontation with Gaunt, wherein Gaunt speaks truth to power in criticizing Richard's mishandling of England's finances, Richard is provoked to respond harshly, even physically attacking the elderly, dying Gaunt in some productions. A few minutes later, when he's informed that Gaunt has died, he dismissively says, "So much for that" (*Richard II* 2.1.155). He immediately orders Gaunt's property seized and when York protests this violation of primogeniture, Richard replies with "Think what you will," ordering the moveables taken anyway (*Richard II* 2.1.209). The king's reputation with others is also negative. Ross notes to Northumberland and Willoughby that the king has grievously taxed the commons and fined the ancients, having lost the hearts of all his people (*Richard II* 2.1.246–248). Willoughby calls the king himself "bankrupt" (*Richard II* 2.1.57). Northumberland notes that "reproach and dissolution hangeth over him" (*Richard II* 2.1.258) and calls him "most degenerate king!" (*Richard II* 2.1.262). Clearly, Richard II is not behaving as a responsible king should, as his aristocratic subjects recognize.

Midway through the play, however, Shakespeare forces us to switch sympathies, when Richard realizes he has lost the support of forces he relied upon to defend his claim to the throne. He urges his remaining followers "All souls that will be safe, fly from my side" (*Richard II* 3.2.80), the first time we see him think of protecting others rather than demanding his orders be followed regardless of the harm they entail. He also begins the first of his powerful meditations upon mortality here, acknowledging his foolish pride and conceit, prompted by learning of the executions of his friends Bushy, Green, and the Earl of Wiltshire. He says, contemplatively:

> Let's choose executors and talk of wills.
> And yet not so, for what can we bequeath
> Save our deposed bodies to the ground?
> Our lands, our lives, and all are Bolingbroke's,
> And nothing can we call our own but death
> And that small model of the barren earth
> Which serves as paste and cover to our bones.
> For God's sake, let us sit upon the ground
> And tell sad stories of the death of kings—
> How some have been deposed, some slain in war,
> Some haunted by the ghosts they have deposed,
> Some poisoned by their wives, some sleeping killed,
> All murdered [*Richard II* 3.2.148–160].

Richard uses the word "deposed" three times, foreshadowing the outcome of this conflict between himself and his cousin Bolingbroke. He emphasizes talking, especially the importance of telling stories of past kings' deaths, grouping himself with them as one preparing to die an unnatural death. His reflection turns to Death as the only true sovereign, ruling over all while merely allowing kings to think they hold any meaningful power:

> For within the hollow crown
> That rounds the mortal temples of a king
> Keeps Death his court, and there the antic sits,
> Scoffing his state and grinning at his pomp,
> Allowing him a breath, a little scene,
> To monarchize, be feared, and kill with looks
> Infusing him with self and vain conceit,
> As if this flesh which walls about our life
> Were brass impregnable, and humored thus,
> Comes at the last and with a little pin
> Bores through his castle wall, and—farewell, king! [*Richard II* 3.2.160–170].

Richard describes the crown as "hollow" or empty, something he has only just recognized; it is a prop for playing a part granted by the grotesque-jester figure of Death, as a sort of trick or joke. He acknowledges Death's reign over all, even kings, and how Death permits, for a time, the vanity of kings playing at control and authority, as if they are immortal. He employs diction associated with death fifteen times in this thirty-two line soliloquy, essentially in every other line. He recognizes his own mortal nature, that he has need for food as well as friendship, and that he experiences loss and grief as others do. This speech marks the beginning of Richard's fall from power but also his elevation in audience sympathy and admiration.

While it appears that he recognizes that he is defeated and will be deposed and killed by his cousin, and that he has simply surrendered to the inevitable in this speech, that is not the case. When he and Bolingbroke finally come face-to-face again, he boldly and defiantly names his cousin's actions for what they are when he demands

> ... show us the hand of God
> That hath dismissed us from our stewardship;
> For well we know, no hand of blood and bone
> Can grip the sacred handle of our scepter,
> Unless he do profane, steal, or usurp [*Richard II* 3.3.72–81].

The concept of the divine right of kings asserts that monarchs are appointed by God; Richard calls out Henry as a violator of this divine order and a thief. He goes on to curse those who support Bolingbroke's treasonous rebellion with civil war, bloodshed, and loss of generations of their children. He says to a belatedly kneeling Bolingbroke, "Up, cousin, up. Your heart is up, I know" (*Richard II* 3.3.193), openly criticizing Bolingbroke's ambition to usurp the throne.

Once Henry has taken Richard prisoner and claimed the throne for himself, he demands that Richard participate in a non-existent ritual handing over the crown and its authority. Richard recognizes the ridiculousness of Henry's desire for a performance of transferred power and authority. To the horror of all present at court, Richard performs the coronation ceremony in reverse, giving away the crown, beginning with "Now mark me how I will undo myself" (*Richard II* 4.1.204). Richard takes control of the scene and delays letting go, just as he does with the crown demanded by Bolingbroke. This remarkable scene emphasizes Richard's innate sense of theatricality and training to rhetorically perform power at court with Henry's inability to speak or perform power in comparison. It is a riveting tour de force, completely unexpected at this point in Richard's fall. Told he must abdicate the throne, Richard holds out the crown, calling, "Here, cousin, seize the crown. Here, cousin" (*Richard II* 4.1.182), as if calling a pet of some kind or taunting a playmate. Yet, when Bolingbroke does reach out to take it, Richard does not let go; instead, he says

> On this side my hand, and on that side thine.
> Now is this golden crown like a deep well
> That owes two buckets, filling one another,
> The emptier ever dancing in the air,
> The other down, unseen and full of water.
> That bucket down and full of tears am I,
> Drinking my griefs, whilst you mount up on high [*Richard II* 4.1.184–190].

The image is a powerful one, with the two cousins both holding onto the crown, the symbol of authority and sovereignty, compared to a well with two buckets balanced against one another; as one rises, so the other must descend. Richard recognizes his position in this analogy as the descending heavy-with-weeping container. Yet, something is off in this analogy. Empty buckets aren't generally raised in wells; full ones are. This odd aspect of the comparison reminds listeners that this is an usurpation, an unnatural unseating of a rightful monarch. The empty bucket representing Bolingbroke may also suggest Richard's critique that his cousin does not have what it takes to reign successfully. As the scene continues, Richard refuses to read the charges against himself despite Northumberland's repeated demands that he do so; he weeps, he compares himself to Christ persecuted, he asks for a looking glass, which he then breaks, and he sharply puts Bolingbroke down every single time his cousin attempts to engage him in some kind of formal, elaborate, regal rhetoric.

Finally, when Bolingbroke gives up and orders some of the court to "convey" Richard to the tower, the deposed king notes with bitterness, "Oh, good! 'Convey'? Conveyers are you all, / That rise thus nimbly by a true king's fall" (*Richard II* 4.1.318–319). Bevington claims that it's as though Richard's identity as a powerful royal figure must be lost or removed before he can recognize and appreciate his own mortality, something he shares with all other humans.[14] Alone, held prisoner, Richard meditates on human mortality again, saying

> I wasted time, and now doth time waste me;
> For now hath Time made me his numb'ring clock.
> My thoughts are minutes, and with sighs they jar
> Their watches on unto mine eyes, the outward watch
> Whereto my finger, like a dial's point,
> Is pointing still in cleansing them from tears.
> Now sir, the sounds that tell what hour it is
> Are clamorous groans that strike upon my heart,
> Which is the bell. So sighs and tears and groans
> Show minutes, hours, and times. But my time
> Runs posting on in Bolingbroke's proud joy,
> While I stand fooling here, his jack of the clock [*Richard II* 5.5.49–60].

Richard acknowledges regret for how he spent his time, foolishly, as he now feels at the mercy of time and mortality. The measures of his suffering are all that mark the passage of time, turning him into a human timepiece, with wordplay on time marked on his face/face of a clock. Productions often show that Richard's appearance has also degenerated, his long hair matted and unkempt, his clothing worn and dirty, testifying to his fall from power and his status as prisoner, emphasizing his vulnerability. Richard converses with the groom who visits him, learning that Bolingbroke rode Richard's horse Barbary to his coronation. He is disappointed to hear the horse bore Bolingbroke proudly, but then realizes it's no fault of the steed's, noting "I was not made a horse, / And yet I bear a burden like an ass, / Spurred, galled, and tired by jauncing Bolingbroke" (*Richard II* 5.5.92–94). This humility further serves to redeem Richard in the eyes of the audience. It's followed closely by the entrance and attack of his three assassins. Richard kills two of them before falling to the third, surprising audiences with his will to live and his ability to defend himself at all, especially when outnumbered.

At the play's beginning, it is impossible to imagine how one might sympathize with Richard. Clearly, he has been cruel, disrespectful, and dismissive with regard to the dying John of Gaunt and the primogeniture practices of the English aristocracy. By the play's end, however, it is equally impossible to imagine how one might *not* sympathize with Richard in his eloquent recognition of mortality and futility despite being born into a position of power; we are all human and mortal, ultimately. When he taunts his usurping cousin for desiring a mock-performance of the legitimate transfer of power, we can't help but feel that Bolingbroke has asked for the taunting and he deserves it. In some ways, York serves readers as a character "who helps to direct our viewpoint, because his transfer of loyalties from Richard to Bolingbroke structurally delineates the decline of Richard's fortunes and the concurrent rise of Bolingbroke's."[15] York's loyalties switch quietly and unobtrusively during the play, with the audience's sympathies shifting at the same time, but in the opposite direction.

Rumor or reputation comes to play an important thematic role in both *2 Henry IV* and *Deadwood*. In *2 Henry IV*, while Shakespeare continues to employ character foils, Bevington claims "the foil relationships in this play focus less on honor ... than on two related matters: rumor or reputation, and justice."[16] Similarly, the reputation of the Deadwood camp becomes of paramount importance by season three's series as the camp moves closer to annexation amidst the pressures brought to bear by commerce baron George Hearst, a darker villainous contrast to Swearengen. Both Swearengen and Hearst attempt to harness the power of rumor to achieve their goals. Hearst's early representatives in the camp, Wolcott and Tolliver, facilitate rumors to encourage mine owners to sell their claims quickly and cheaply. Swearengen uses the threat of rumor to foster the perception that the camp is unstable and dangerous, an unsuitable place for business, not ready for annexation to the U.S.

On *Deadwood*, in the early episodes Seth Bullock is presented as an upright, respectable enforcer of the law, and protector of the innocent, while Al Swearengen is introduced as a violent, amoral, paranoid, dangerously unpredictable, and ruthless criminal. With the opening shot of the pilot focused on Bullock in a marshal's office, a public setting, and the closing shot featuring Swearengen reclining in his bed, a private setting, it seems that we've clearly been given a hero and a villain, likely to remain in conflict for the duration of the series. However, the moral ambiguity of the two lead male characters equals that found in *Richard II*; as Bevington explains, "Shakespeare ... clouds [Richard and Bolingbroke's] respective responsibilities for murder."[17] Bullock identifies holes in Ned Mason's story about the Metz family massacre and forces Mason to tell his story to a full bar; he volunteers to ride out and search for any surviving children. It's he who finds Sofia and carries her halfway back to the camp. He checks on her with Doc Cochran the next day. Swearengen beats an already beaten Trixie for shooting a john, and the camera angle places the audience in Trixie's position, on the floor, with Al's boot on her neck, holding her by one arm pulled upwards. But then it shifts us into the position of Al, looking down at Trixie with our foot on her throat as she croaks out her promise to be good. The camera switches back and forth, in a one-shot alternating between their perspectives, repeatedly. Later, Swearengen casually reminds Dan, almost as an afterthought, "Oh, and Dan? Don't forget to kill Tim" ("Deadwood" 1.1). Swearengen also visits Cochran's himself to pinch Sofia into opening her eyes, threatening Jane, who is trying to protect the child, and ordering Dan to murder Sofia, to Dan's horror. When Dan and Doc offer a roadblock to Al's orders regarding Sofia, Al accepts it, and kills Persimmon Phil himself, removing any danger of being associated with Phil and the Mason brothers' independent action of murdering and robbing the Metz family. It's worth noting that this is one of the few instances where we see Al doing the dirty work himself. Sarah Hagelin notes that *Deadwood*'s "first season slowly and subtly reveals this setup to have been what [she] call[s] an affective miscue—a strategy that the serialized television of the twenty-first century uses frequently to encourage its audience to ask one question, only to reveal this to have been the wrong question to ask all along."[18] Viewers have been given what they expect to see in this genre: an idealistic young hero and a violent, scheming villain with experience on his side.

However, as the series progresses, Al Swearengen is shown to be smart and articulate, adaptable to the changing conditions of the camp. His power shifts from primarily residing in force and violence or the threat of violence, to witty wordplay and savvy political interpretation. As early as "Plague" (1.6), Swearengen begins to show himself to be civic-minded as he calls a meeting of the leading businessmen in camp to address the outbreak of smallpox, placing the interests of the camp alongside his own need to profit. Compare his initiative to collaborate and address the problem rather than cover it up, as Tolliver has done. Subsequent episodes continue to soften his harsher character traits and emphasize his virtues. In "Bullock Returns to the Camp" (1.7), Swearengen gives a job to a teenage drifter, whom he is kind towards. In exchanges with the boy, Swearengen reveals his desire to mentor younger men. Swearengen tells the boy, Miles, that if he runs a brothel, "something you got to know about specialists—they pay a premium, and they never cause fucking trouble" ("Bullock Returns to the Camp" 1.7). In the same episode, though, he physically harms Trixie by grabbing and squeezing her crotch for lying to him about Alma's dependency on laudanum and he threatens her, saying, "Don't kid yourself, Trixie. Don't get a mistaken idea" ("Bullock Returns to the Camp" 1.7). It's a slow process of softening Swearengen's image without sacrificing the destructive danger he continues to represent.

Likewise, Bullock clearly isn't a wholly moral character, problematized almost immediately in the pilot when he acts as judge and executioner, hanging Clell Watson, yanking his body down to break his neck efficiently. Shortly after arriving in Deadwood, he (or Hickok) shoots Ned Mason off his horse. Bullock supports Hickok's request for back-up, regarding his perceived threat from Tom Mason, and supports Hickok's claim that Mason meant him harm, even though Mason hadn't actually drawn his gun at the No. 10. Already married, he has an affair with Alma Garret. He beats Otis Russell and E.B. Farnum in blind rages. He threatens to kill Jack McCall. At times he behaves as a man controlled by his urges rather than one capable of exerting reason over them.

In "Suffer the Little Children" (1.8), Swearengen proposes an alliance with Bullock, which the younger man seems to accept by not refusing it outright. In "Jewel's Boot is Made for Walking" (1.11), when Swearengen learns of Trixie's affair with Sol, his facial expression suggests that he is hurt. Confronting them about it and demanding payment from Sol, he reveals his emotional investment in Trixie when he says,

> What can any one of us really fucking hope for, huh, except a moment here and there with a person who doesn't want to rob, steal, or murder us? At night it may happen ... trusting each other enough to tell half the truth. Everybody needs that. Becomes precious to them. They don't want to see it fucked with ["Jewel's Boot is Made for Walking" 1.11].

This scene between the saloon owner, Star, and Trixie may be the first inkling of vulnerability the show provides with Swearengen. The dialogue suggests that Trixie has been someone Al could confide in, "telling half the truth," and that her seeking out Star has broken his trust in her in a personal way that her earlier shooting of a john did not. Dudley also points out that Al's self-criticism in this example, in permitting his intimate relationship with Trixie

7. Managing Audience Responses through Character   169

to become "precious" to him, sets him apart from Cy, who never holds himself accountable for anything.[19] In other words, Al blames himself for allowing this vulnerability with Trixie and assuming her ongoing sexual and emotional loyalty to him. He exhibits a growing sense of self-awareness in this speech, despite its carefully deliberate distancing from any first-person statements.

In the same episode, the scene above is quickly followed by another providing further discernment into Al's character and vulnerability, in the form of the infamous monologue he delivers during oral sex performed on him by Dolly. The audience is given insight into Swearengen's thoughts and background as he cryptically opens with, "Now, I see what the fuck's in front of me, and I don't pretend it's something else" ("Jewel's Boot is Made for Walking" 1.11). He goes on to explain that he's switching from Trixie as his preferred prostitute and confidante to Dolly, the woman fellating him, suggesting that his first sentence relates to having been hurt by Trixie's seeking out Sol Star and developing feelings for him. He continues to talk about "being a man," doing what needs to be done regardless of feelings, redirecting his focus from Trixie to the the Reverend Smith, whose illness is progressing, as he says

> The minister's got to die. I mean, that's the, that's the fucking point. [...] Why go on like that? Who's going to benefit from that? You got to kill it and put an end to it. You— you don't linger on about it. You don't go fucking around weeping about it. [...] You've got to behave like a grown fucking man about it. You've got to shut the fuck up ... ["Jewel's Boot is Made for Walking" 1.11].

It's clear that Al sees the Reverend's condition as one requiring action, in the form of a mercy killing and that he's having to talk himself into performing the action. But notice that he says "it," rather than "him." There is deliberate ambiguity as to how to interpret "it"; it could be an attempt to dehumanize Smith, with Swearengen preparing to carry out the mercy killing he deems necessary. Or it could refer to the hurt, sorrow, frustration, and helplessness the rest of his speech seems to convey towards the situation with Smith and with Trixie. He adds, "I don't look back. I do what I have to do and I go on" ("Jewel's Boot was Made for Walking" 1.11). He's essentially giving himself a pep talk to suppress his grief, reminding himself how to "behave like a grown fucking man about it." Cook says Swearengen's killing of Smith reveals "a profound sympathy for human suffering that lies beneath his customary brutality,"[20] especially given that Swearengen reveals his brother suffered from a similar condition.

His talk then shifts again, to Dolly, and the Chicago orphanage where he found her. He tells her that the woman who ran the girls' orphanage and a brothel previously ran a boys' orphanage, too. Then he reveals that he knows that because his own mother left him at the boys' orphanage. In a five-sentence excerpt from this longer monologue, Swearengen uses some version of the word "fuck" fifteen times, excessive even by his usual standards, indicating his agitated emotional state. He reveals that in leaving a handful of bills and coins with him and mentioning the exact number twice ("seven dollars and sixty odd cents"), which he had to turn over to Mrs. Anderson, his mother essentially paid the orphanage and brothel manager to take him, the reverse of the position he occupies as a pimp ("Jewel's Boot is Made for Walking" 1.11). His contradictory recounting of his mother's destination (prostitution or remarriage in Georgia versus sailing around the world—itself a sexual euphemism—to either become an authority figure or a prostitute) suggests versions of a story that he has told himself over time as to why she would leave him.

The story he tells Dolly connects his past to her own through the Chicago orphanage, but it also suggests a connection between his childhood struggle with fear and powerlessness and how he's feeling in the present, faced with both Trixie's emotional and physical abandonment and the task of dealing with the Reverend Smith's worsening condition. It relates to his earlier comment about the necessity of moving forward without looking back or feeling bad for what he has to do.

In a second such monologue in season three, Swearengen is seated behind his desk, facing sideways and appears to be talking to himself, with his blazer, waistcoat, and long johns unbuttoned and completely open. Eventually, Dolly is revealed as kneeling out of sight in front of him as the scene continues. Again, he is speaking about a situation that elicits fear from him, facing Hearst again after his and Captain Turner's ambush assault on Swearengen, when he ponders, "Invites me and Tolliver for a chat. What the fuck is in his head? Does he think he broke me? Does this cocksucker think he broke me? And now we're at his beck and call?" ("Full Faith and Credit" 3.4). He pauses to critique Dolly's method as ineffective, given his lack of physical response, but then returns to the subject uppermost in his thoughts, the invitation from Hearst and its possible meaning. He continues his speculation with "Does he construe my forbearance as weakness is what the fuck nags at me. Or my considerations of alternatives for being fucking intimidated, because the time's coming when he sees what I'm up to beyond any fucking mistake, [...] Does he think I'm afraid?" ("Full Faith and Credit" 3.4). He isn't sure how to interpret Hearst's opinion of him if he were to decline the invitation, as appearing weak or intimidated, and, again, he's thinking of the longer term results that he is working toward, against Hearst. His inability to develop an erection despite Dolly's ministrations also speaks to his preoccupied state of mind.

Later in the same episode, he turns away from Dolly's second failed attempt at fellating him, and he picks up where the first monologue left off. He says, "I knew what was coming, too, fucking captain holding me down. I knew what the fuck was next. [...] They hold you down you, you can't get at them to help yourself. [...] They hold you down from behind, then you wonder why you're helpless. How the fuck could you not be?" ("Full Faith and Credit" 3.4). He refuses to admit that he was taken by surprise by Captain Turner and Hearst although he questions the feeling of wondering why he was suddenly helpless, moving beyond the emotional aspect of the memory to reason, in asking how could you not be helpless in those circumstances. His current fear leads him into the past again and he reveals a bit more about his sense of abandonment, referencing a proctor physically restraining him as he imagined his mother changing her mind and calling to him from a ship ("Full Faith and Credit" 3.4). By the end of this monologue—which only contains four forms of "fuck," Al clearly has tears in his eyes, recalling the feelings of longing, helplessness, and powerlessness from this episode in his childhood, imagining his mother changing her mind, calling to him, the proctor keeping him from going to her. Or rather, he was imagining she actually wanted to keep him with her, but the proctor kept him from confirming that. He has revisited the association of helplessness with Hearst and the adults keeping him from his imagined mother, calling to him to come to her, both of them longing for one another. Dolly attempts to offer some comfort by sharing, twice during his speech, that she, too, hates to be held down. Swearengen even responds apologetically and gently to Dolly's comment, saying that he probably does that to her, too, holding her hair. She denies it, which makes him smile a little, concluding the scene with "Well, bless you for a fucking fibber anyway" ("Full Faith and Credit" 3.4). His emotional vulnerability and surprising kindness to Dolly humanize him further in the audience's eyes.

In season two, Swearengen's fight with Bullock and his incapacitation by kidney stones for two full episodes also emphasize his physical vulnerability. By the time he's functionally convalescing in "Something Very Expensive" (2.6), the audience is anxious to see him back in action and reacting to some of the issues that have arisen during his illness. It also helps to soften his image when the audience is given two other villains who appear far worse in comparison: sadistic misogynist Cy Tolliver and the profit-driven egomaniac George Hearst. Swearengen even comes to protect some of the vulnerable in the camp, such as Jewel, Doc Cochran, and the Reverend Smith, and, in season three, Trixie, Ellsworth, Alma, and Sofia. In addition, once we see the stoic manner in which Al deals with Hearst and Captain Turner's ambush assault on him, we're reminded both of his vulnerability and his immense strength.

As Al Swearengen's physical health deteriorates, his likeability increases and his power changes mediums, from the knife, violence, and executions to wordplay, interpretation of others' words and actions, and political strategizing, non-violent power plays behind the scenes.[21] Similarly, Hawkins describes *Richard II* as featuring a main character who loses his power and position due to a character flaw or corruption, but then manages to "regain both audience and sympathy and his own soul."[22] Swearengen shows a certain level of adaptability on his part in response to the changing nature of the Deadwood camp. In the early episodes of season one, he shows people what he's capable of doing; he has the reputation of a killer. From the moment the telegraph lines go up, Al's power in the camp begins to change, but it doesn't lessen. Hawkins says of the history plays that rebellions are controlled more "by eloquence and cunning, by the word rather than the sword."[23] Al's physical health starts to decline—he needs a magnifying glass to read, then reading glasses, then gets sidelined by the kidney stones, exacerbated by his fight with Bullock, then he is figuratively castrated by Hearst cutting off his middle finger. If we view Swearengen as emasculated by having his phallic power figuratively taken from him, we might find its parallel in Richard II's loss of the crown as symbolic of his power; both men become more sympathetic after these losses. Swearengen, introduced as a brutal, self-serving, powerful, and feared villain, evolves into a charismatic and witty central figure, necessary to the camp's progress, father-figure to the alleged hero figure Bullock, among others. Critics agree that although Al Swearengen "appears at first to be the crassest of villains [...] Milch encourages us to read him as heroic."[24]

The authors of both works carefully and deliberately control audience sympathies, establishing them early in the works of *Richard II* and *Deadwood*, to be conventionally with the alleged heroic figure occupying a position of contested justice, the disadvantaged noble underdog against established corrupt authority or a gun-wielding mob. From this point, the works are developed to complicate audience sympathies, shifting them steadily from their point of origin to the opposite position in relation to another significant male character.

In addition, if audiences viewed Bullock as representative of the young nation in the process of becoming in the first season of the series, by the end of the third season it seems clear that some of the women in the camp have also proven to be in the same position. Their adaptability, growth, and potential for further growth equals, if not surpasses, that of Bullock, perhaps making them an even more dynamic symbol of the young nation developing as it expands westward. While most of the main female characters on *Deadwood* are introduced in the recognizable female stereotypes of the Western, they gain more independence, agency, and a stronger sense of self as the series progresses. As John Dudley notes, one of *Deadwood*'s prevailing themes explores "the struggles of women to achieve subjectivity within a violent patriarchal society."[25] By the third season, some women have begun to contribute civically through creating and staffing the school, the bank, and the theater, sites of community interaction. They occupy the same state of "becoming" I used to describe Bullock in Chapter 2; similarly, their potential for change and growth is emphasized, to the point where they may be said to be on a par with Bullock in representing the young nation still developing in the late 19th century.

Conclusion

As an element of differentiating characters for the audience, costuming and other appearance details can provide clues about a character's motivations or behaviors. In some cases, the initial distinctive boundaries established between characters may fade and blur over time, emphasizing their commonalities rather than their differences. The most striking structural similarities of the Henriad and *Deadwood* are parallel scenes that serve similar functions in reinforcing masculine identification for main male characters and the narrative devices designed to carefully and deliberately establish and then shift audience sympathies from their point of origin to the opposite position as the narrative progresses.

The first time we read a Shakespearean play we see only the generic picture of what happens on the surface, the plot itself. The second reading allows us to study details—a specific scene's import or a dialogue or soliloquy's effectiveness. Finally, we step back to use what we know from the first two readings to analyze the bigger picture—the play as a whole, how it reflects or converses with other plays around it regarding themes, structure, devices, characters, etc. In identifying and looking closer at these structural similarities between the Henriad and *Deadwood*, we gain a better understanding of the narrative strengths of these works, especially in drawing audiences into engagement with the stories they offer.

Conclusion

Thinking about and viewing *Deadwood* through the lens of Shakespeare's Henriad provides a number of benefits. Comparing commonalities and divergences between historically-based genres, the 16th century English history play and the 21st century cable television Western, helps viewers understand how such genres deliberately portray the past in a specific way to confirm, challenge, or even manipulate audience views of history. These comparisons should also make us think about the role of national myth in our collective consciousness and, hopefully, make us question its idealized and alleged wholly-noble origins and accuracy in terms of inclusion and exclusion.

Shakespeare's English history plays feature a decidedly Tudor-positive perspective to appeal to Queen Elizabeth I and to engage audiences in order to turn a profit. Alternative stage versions of England's history leading up to Elizabeth's reign are either impossible to include or subversively referenced. Milch's *Deadwood* clearly privileges, as most Westerns have, a white European perspective on the American expansion westward in the 19th century, one that emphasizes capitalism and free trade initially, even as it seeks the high ratings that would allow it to continue to generate profit. Despite the ways that both of these performative narratives are tied to the culture that produced them and designed as commercial ventures, the more voices we have contributing to the stories we tell of our collective national history, the closer we get to a complete understanding of the past. It still can't be a whole, clear picture of the past, though; it will always be fragmented, with missing pieces. To pretend otherwise is to privilege one perspective over others, silencing other stories. Millichap writes that "Milch rewrites the accepted history of his America in *Deadwood*, moving from the decaying cities of the East to the final frontier of the great West ... but discovering the same patterns of human violence that deny the American Dream."[1] Such rewritings allow us to imagine further variations of historical narratives and the contributions of both familiar and unknown individuals to national origins.

In addition, we can appreciate and understand better the central characters of Seth Bullock and Al Swearengen, and the evolving father-son relationship between them, if we consider the parallels they share with Hotspur and Prince Hal and with Bolingbroke/Henry IV and Falstaff. Such a perspective may also explain some aspects of audience response to these two characters. I've had countless conversations about the possible source of Bullock's simmering anger, seemingly an ever-present facet of his personality; many viewers have posed the same question that Swearengen does in the pilot episode to Star: "What's your partner so mad about all the time?" It's a mystery, the same way that Hotspur's unrelenting fury is, perhaps, a quirk of personality or perhaps rooted in experiences during formative years. If we look at Swearengen as Falstaff, the audience's increasing fondness toward him becomes easier to understand. Many viewers claim Swearengen as their favorite character, despite his initial violent and misogynistic introduction. As he proves himself politically astute and clever, his surprisingly vulnerable and witty presence increasingly comes to dominate the *Deadwood* series.

The longing for cross-generational connection, the challenges of clear and sufficient communication, and conflicting, competing personal interests hover constantly over father-son relationships in *Richard II*, the *Henry IV* plays, and *Deadwood*. Recognizing their similarities in one dramatic portrayal can enable us to better comprehend how those same dynamics are playing out in another; Swearengen is a father-figure to many of the Deadwood camp's young males. It's a role that seems to come naturally to him and that he enjoys. He mentors others constantly in relation to running a business, marketing strategies, and political wrangling. If we flip the channel to a reality series like *Pawn Stars* or *Gold Rush*, we can see the same type of issues played out each week in a present-day setting, without scripted actors performing the parts. The historical, scripted portrayals of conflicted father-son dynamics speak to a universal psychological experience, one that will always have an audience.

Shakespeare's second English history tetralogy contains few women's roles and the parts they play are severely restricted to emphasize the private, emotional costs of men's political powerplays, men's failure to listen to women, and women's grief, helplessness, and passivity. In comparison, most of the similarities between these late 16th century English dramatic representations of women in such plays and that of early 21st century American televisual representations of women in *Deadwood* are appalling.[2] However, the distinctions between the two are encouraging, when we consider the growth, independence, and capabilities of female characters on *Deadwood* and what that suggests about the culture producing the series. That, too, is worthy of a book-length study.

Finally, our culture's recent interest in the anti-hero on film and television—*Breaking Bad*'s Walter White, *The Soprano*'s Tony Soprano, *Mad Men*'s

Don Draper, and *Deadwood*'s Al Swearengen, to name only a few, has been fostered in part by the provision of a compelling backstory to explain such characters' motivations; this love of the anti-hero seems to many people to be a new phenomenon. It isn't, not when we consider the Vice character from medieval morality plays, the same figure that *Richard III* was based on, and to which Prince Hal/Henry V bears some similarities in his early soliloquy about manipulating his public image. Complex narrative structures provide opportunities to sway audience sympathies across a broad spectrum, especially in an age where viewers are well aware that the image or audio in front of them may not be a direct, unfiltered, or unaltered one, that it may even be designed to deliberately mislead them in some way. If viewing, analyzing, and discussing the complexities of a smart television drama can transfer into questioning what we're seeing and hearing in other venues, how messages are constantly being presented to us, what we know or accept as truth versus what we assume, and where there is clear discontinuity in the image or audio or disruption of the narration—these kinds of awareness should help us practice and extend our critical thinking skills in everyday life.

As I said in the introduction, the goal of this book is to encourage *Deadwood* viewers to learn more about how Shakespeare's history plays parallel aspects of the series so that they may rewatch the series with the insight the plays provide into mythmaking, political power negotiations, gender roles, and performative texts' portrayal of a nation in transition. For Shakespeare fans, the goal of this book is to encourage them to consider *Deadwood* as a complex text worthy of further study in its address of many of the same themes found in the Henriad regarding establishing order out of disorder, the inevitable corruption of authority in this process, the complicated, conflicted importance of father-son relationships, the importance of honor, and the marginalization of women.

Appendix: *Deadwood* Episodes

HBO. Paramount Studios. 2004–2006.

Season 1

"Deadwood." 1.1 Dir. Walter Hill. Written by David Milch.
"Deep Water." 1.2 Dir. Davis Guggenheim. Written by Malcolm MacRury.
"Reconnoitering the Rim." 1.3 Dir. Davis Guggenheim. Written by Jody Worth.
"Here was a Man." 1.4 Dir. Alan Taylor. Written by Elizabeth Sarnoff.
"The Trial of Jack McCall." 1.5 Dir. Ed Bianchi. Written by John Belluso.
"Plague." 1.6 Dir. David Guggenheim. Written by Malcolm MacRury.
"Bullock Returns to the Camp." 1.7 Dir. Michael Engler. Written by Jody Worth.
"Suffer the Little Children." 1.8 Dir. Daniel Minahan. Written by Elizabeth Sarnoff.
"No Other Sons or Daughters." 1.9 Dir. Ed Bianchi. Written by George Putnam.
"Mr. Wu." 1.10 Dir. Daniel Minahan. Written by Bryan McDonald.
"Jewel's Boot is Made for Walking." 1.11 Dir. Steve Shill. Written by Ricky Jay.
"Sold Under Sin." 1.12 Dir. Davis Guggenheim. Written by Ted Mann.

Season 2

"A Lie Agreed Upon, Part I." 2.1 Dir. Ed Bianchi. Written by David Milch.
"A Lie Agreed Upon, Part II." 2.2 Dir. Ed Bianchi Written by Jody Worth.
"New Money." 2.3 Dir. Steve Shill. Written by Elizabeth Sarnoff.
"Requiem for a Gleet." 2.4 Dir. Alan Taylor. Written by Ted Mann.
"Complications." 2.5 Dir. Gregg Fienberg. Written by Victoria Morrow.
"Something Very Expensive." 2.6 Dir. Steve Shill. Written by Steve Shill.
"E.B. was Left Out." 2.7 Dir. Michael Almereyda. Written by Jody Worth.
"Childish Things." 2.8 Dir. Timothy Van Patten. Written by Regina Corrado.

"Amalgamation and Capital." 2.9 Dir. Ed Bianchi. Written by Elizabeth Sarnoff.
"Advances, None Miraculous." 2.10 Dir. Daniel Minahan. Written by Sara Hess.
"The Whores Can Come." 2.11 Dir. Gregg Fienberg. Written by Bryan McDonald.
"Boy-the-Earth-Talks-To." 2.12 Dir. Ed Bianchi. Written by Tedd Mann.

Season 3

"Tell Your God to Ready for Blood." 3.1 Dir. Mark Tinker. Written by David Milch and Tedd Mann.
"I am Not the Fine Man You Mistake Me For." 3.2 Dir. Dan Attias. Written by David Milch and Regina Corrado.
"True Colors." 3.3 Dir. Gregg Feinberg. Written by Regina Corrado and Ted Mann.
"Full Faith and Credit." 3.4 Dir. Ed Bianchi. Written by Ted Mann.
"A Two-Headed Beast." 3.5 Dir. Daniel Minnihan. Written by David Milch.
"A Rich Find." 3.6 Dir. Tim Hunter. Written by Alix Lambert.
"Unauthorized Cinnamon." 3.7 Dir. Mark Tinker. Written by Regina Corrado.
"Leviathan Smiles." 3.8 Dir. Ed Bianchi. Written by Kem Nunn.
"Amateur Night." 3.9 Dir. Adam Davidson. Written by Nick Towne and Zack Whedon.
"A Constant Throb." 3.10 Dir. Mark Tinker. Written by David Milch and W. Earl Brown.
"The Catbird Seat." 3.11 Dir. Mark Tinker. Written by Bernadette McNamara.
"Tell Him Something Pretty." 3.12 Dir. Mark Tinker. Written by Ted Mann.

Chapter Notes

Preface

1. Tim O'Shei, "Breaking Free of his Demons, David Milch stays in the Hollywood Game," *Buffalo News*, April 25, 2016.
2. David Milch, *Deadwood: Stories of the Black Hills* (2006); David Lavery, ed., *Reading Deadwood: A Western to Swear By* (2006); Jason P. Vest, *The Wire, Deadwood, Homicide, and NYPD Blue: Violence Is Power* (2011); Ina Rae Hark, *Deadwood* (part of the TV milestones series, 2012); Jason Jacobs, *Deadwood* (BFI TV Classics series, 2012); Jennifer Greiman and Paul Stasi, eds., *The Last Western: Deadwood and the End of American Empire* (2012); Paul Cantor, *The Invisible Hand in Popular Culture* (2012); Melody Graulich and Nicolas S. Witschi, eds., *Dirty Words in Deadwood: Literature and the Postwestern* (2013); Sarah Hagelin, *Reel Vulnerability: Power, Pain, and Gender in Contemporary American Film and Television* (2013); Mary M. Dalton, Max Dosser, Katie Nelson, and Rebecca Steiner, eds., *Critical Media Studies: Student Essays on Deadwood* (2016).

Introduction

1. Garber, 28.
2. And not just Shakespeare's, of course, but classic literary works in general.
3. *Deadwood* at IMDB.com. The series also received 22 Emmy nominations, winning 7, and a Golden Globe.
4. See Brad Benz, "*Deadwood* and the English Language," *Great Plains Quarterly*, 2007: 239–251; Daniel Salerno, "'I Will Have You Bend': Language and the Discourses of Power in *Deadwood*," *Literary Imagination*, 2007: 12.2: 190–209, Ina Rae Hark, *Deadwood*, Ch. 3; and Alan Sepinwall, *The Revolution was Televised*. Milch has noted that many people who lived in Deadwood at the close of the 19th century "might have been illiterate, but they knew the King James Bible and Shakespeare, and that's what shaped the way they thought and the way they presented themselves" (qtd in Landsberg, 543).
5. Landsberg, 544.
6. Mittell, *Complex TV*, 209.
7. Graulich, xxx.
8. Mittell, *Television and American Culture*, 310–311.
9. Ibid., 365.
10. Ibid., 365–366.
11. Stanford Friedman, 757.
12. Ibid., 758.
13. See Feinstein and Singer interviews with Milch.
14. Mittell, *Complex TV*, 216.

Chapter 1

1. Pippin is describing the Western film genre but this is easily applicable to *Deadwood*, too. He is drawing on the ideas of André Bazin in *What Is Cinema?* (146–147).
2. Hattaway, "The Shakespearean History Play," 9.
3. Westerfelhaus and Lacroix, 20.
4. Edgerton and Marsden, 40.
5. Lewis, 16.
6. Bevington, "Introduction to *The First*

Part of King Henry the Sixth," 510. Bevington references earlier English history plays such as the anonymous *Famous Victories of Henry V, Gorboduc* or *The Misfortunes of Arthur, Cambises,* and *Tamburlaine.*

7. *The Bedford Shakespeare,* 416.

8. Bevington, "Introduction to *The First Part of King Henry the Sixth,*" 508–509.

9. Mittell, *Television and American Culture,* 288–289.

10. Mittell, *Complex TV,* 53–54.

11. Mittell, in part quoting Steven Johnson's work, *Complex TV,* 35.

12. See James L. Keidel, Philip M. Davis, Victorina Gonzalez-Diaz, Clara D. Martin and Guillaume Thierry, "How Shakespeare Tempests the Brain: Neuroimaging Insights," *Cortex* 49.4 (April 2013): 913–919.

13. Pippin, 19.

14. See *Directed by John Ford,* a 1971 documentary by Peter Bogdanovich.

15. Landsberg, referencing Richard Cullen Rath's *How Early America Sounded* (2003), 532.

16. Witherspoon, 105.

17. See Wendy Witherspoon, "The Final Stamp: *Deadwood* and the Gothic American Frontier" and Nicolas S. Witschi, "'Down These Mean Streets': Film Noir, *Deadwood,* Cinematic Space, and the Irruption of Genre Codes," both in *Dirty Words in Deadwood.*

18. Shapiro, 196.

19. Ibid., 196.

20. Ibid., 197. Shapiro also notes that Remington provided illustrations for Wister's stories in *Colliers* magazine, "which represented the West as an evolving (and whitening) social order."

21. Berger, 20.

22. Bevington, "Sources: *Richard II,*" A-39.

23. Kurtz, 269.

24. See Milch's *Deadwood: Stories of the Black Hills* for more on Milch's historical source material.

25. Berrettini, 255.

26. Klein, 99.

27. Rackin, *Stages of History,* 90.

28. Ibid., 90.

29. The mass is out of place, historically, as Cataline came before Christ, as noted by Peter Burke in *The Renaissance Sense of the Past* (1969) 1–2.

30. Rackin, *Stages of History,* 91.

31. Rackin and Howard, 15.

32. Rackin, *Stages of History,* 93.

33. Ibid., 86.

34. Ibid., 103.

35. Ibid., 103–104.

36. "Zipper," *The Oxford English Dictionary* indicates, came into use in the 1920s. I wondered, too, about Ellsworth's use of "headlight" as slang for a black eye when he is talking to Trixie, but I've been unable to confirm when that usage emerged. The intercontinental railroad was established in the 1870s and train engines had headlights.

37. Mizejewski, 198.

38. Ibid., 191.

39. Ibid., 204.

40. Ibid., 191.

41. Berger, 239.

42. Kurtz, 268.

43. See John Ames, *The Real Deadwood: True Life Histories of Wild Bill Hickok, Calamity Jane, Outlaw Towns, and Other Characters of the Lawless West.*

44. Jacobs, *Deadwood,* 23.

45. Ames, 17.

46. Klein, 96.

47. Ibid., 96.

48. Millichap, 105.

49. Garber, 321.

50. Salerno, 193.

51. Graulich introduction to *Dirty Words in Deadwood,* xlii.

52. Hattaway, 12.

53. Bevington, 740.

54. Leslie Dunton-Downer and Alan Riding, eds., *Essential Shakespeare* (2004), 118.

55. Ibid., 128.

56. Ibid., 118 and 128.

57. Slotkin, 401–402. Wild Bill asks where Bullock served as U.S. Marshal and when Bullock answers, Bill replies, "Come to your senses now?" ("Deadwood" 1.1).

58. Witherspoon, 111.

59. Witschi, 125.

60. Pippin, 25.

61. Ibid., 20.

62. Ibid., 22.

63. Drysdale, 134–135.

64. Jacobs, *Deadwood,* 30. Milch also refers to language as "a lie agreed upon" in an interview with Singer.

65. Cook, "Moral Relativism in David Milch's *Deadwood,*" and Westerfelhaus and

Lacroix,"Waiting for the Barbarians: HBO's Disquiet as a Post-9/11 Ritual of Disquiet."

66. See Phyllis Rackin, *Stages of History*, 69.

67. Rackin and Howard, 12.

68. Ibid., 12.

69. Dudley, 94. In a footnote, he adds, that the relationship between the Gem's "familial dynamics" and the developing identity of the local community and its national adoption serves to emphasize repeatedly the relationship of the individual "narratives of loss" that linger for so many characters with the series' broader historical place in the settling of the frontier (101-102).

70. Jacobs, *Deadwood*, 145.

71. Worden, 222.

72. Jacobs, *Deadwood*, 28, 26, 28.

73. Cook, 2. Cook explains that Newcomb and Hirsch are building their analysis of television as a cultural form on the work of anthropologist Victor Turner and the work of television's "bardic function," per John Fiske and John Hartley.

74. Hagelin, 144. She also says that "the collective sins of slavery and the genocide of the Native American population are never far from the edges of the frame" (144).

75. Cohen, 303.

76. Ibid., 313.

77. Ibid., 301.

78. Hark, 64.

79. Ibid., 70. See also chapter four and Swearengen's pleased observation of Bullock's growth in being able to put communal interests before personal ones.

80. McGee, 91.

81. Drysdale, 139.

82. Worden, 224; 226-227

83. Worden, 227.

84. McGee, 137.

85. Worden, 232.

86. Ibid., 24.

87. Garber, 33.

88. Graulich, xxii.

89. Ibid., xli.

90. Merten, 144.

91. Reiman, 41.

92. Drysdale, 140.

93. Jacobs, *Deadwood*, 141.

94. Cook, 5.

95. Diffrient, 192.

96. See Meghan C. Andrews, "Gender, Genre, and Elizabeth's Princely Surrogates, in *Henry IV* and *Henry V*" *Studies in English Literature, 1500-1900* 54.2 (Spring 2014), 375-399; Marvin B. Krims, "Hotspur's Antifeminine Prejudice in Shakespeare's *1 Henry IV*," in *Literature and Psychology* 40.1-2 (1994), 118-132; and Martha A. Kurtz, "Rethinking Gender and Genre in the History Play," in *Studies in English Literature, 1500-1900* 36.2 (Spring 1996), 267-287.

97. Graulich, xxxiv.

98. See Cook's perspective on Smith's role in *Deadwood*, 12-13, and Bevington's "Introduction to *The Tragedy of Richard the Second*," 742.

99. Westerfelhaus and Lacroix, 34.

100. Ibid., 34.

101. Witschi, 134.

102. Pippin, 99.

103. Cook, 2.

104. Merten, 143.

105. Ibid., 142-143.

106. Westerfelhaus and Lacroix, 35.

107. Jacobs, *Deadwood*, 31.

108. Cook, 7-8.

Chapter 2

1. *The Oxford English Dictionary*.

2. Bevington, 748.

3. Jacobs, *Deadwood*, 4.

4. Vest, 147.

5. He uses a similar rhetorical tactic in *Henry V*, when he praises the small number of English troops present to fight at Agincourt, turning a weakness into a strength.

6. *The Oxford English Dictionary*.

7. Cook, 13.

8. This may also stem from his relationship with his father, who, as he reveals to Hickok, nicknamed him "Sloth," or laziness, an unwillingness to act, one of the seven deadly sins.

9. Bevington, 784.

10. Ibid., 785.

11. Edmondson, 255.

12. Ibid., 255.

13. Ibid., 256.

14. Bevington, 784.

15. Garber, 324.

16. Ibid., 324.

17. Ibid., 333.

18. Graulich, xxviii.

19. Jacobs, *Deadwood*, 2.

20. Garber, 318.
21. Witherspoon, 107.
22. Edmondson, 250.
23. Ibid., 254.
24. Ibid., 257.
25. Jacobs, *Deadwood*, 12.
26. Garber, 328.
27. Ibid., 322.
28. Ibid., 328.
29. Milch, 126.

Chapter 3

1. *Richard II*, 3.1
2. Garber, 244.
3. Ribner, 179.
4. Garber, 249.
5. Ibid., 251.
6. Ibid., 268.
7. Ibid., 351.
8. Witherspoon, 118.
9. Hattaway, 13.
10. Milch, 21.
11. Ibid., 21.
12. Easthope, 43.
13. Jacobs, "Al Swearengen, Philosopher King," 20.
14. McIntosh, 33.
15. O'Sullivan, 123.
16. Ribner, "The Political Problem in Shakespeare's Lancastrian Tetralogy," 177.
17. Ribner, in "Bolingbroke: A True Machiavellian," quotes Machiavelli as writing, "It is not necessary, then, for a prince really to have all the virtues mentioned above, but it is very necessary to *seem* to have them," 181 (italics mine).
18. Diffrient, 185–199; Perlman, 102–112.
19. Garber, 320.
20. Easthope, 43.
21. Ribner, "Bolingbroke: A True Machiavellian," 182.
22. Salerno, 197.
23. Feinstein, "Crossing Genres, 'Deadwood' Dominates."
24. Garber, 325.
25. Ibid., 317.
26. Ibid., 317–318.
27. Ibid., 325.
28. Ibid., 326.
29. Jacobs, "Al Swearengen, Philosopher King," 13.
30. Ibid., 13.
31. Milch, 17.
32. Millichap, 110.
33. Feeney.
34. Garber, 257.
35. Salerno, 199.
36. Graulich, xxvi.
37. Garber, 320.
38. Ibid., 350.
39. Mittell, *Complex TV*, 136.
40. Rackin, *Shakespeare and Women*, 67.
41. *Essential Shakespeare Handbook*, 108.
42. Ibid., 118 and 128.
43. *Deadwood*, "New Money," 2.15; *Deadwood*, "Requiem for a Gleet," 2.16.

Chapter 4

1. Bazin, 146.
2. Rackin, "Anti-Historians: Women's Roles in Shakespeare's Histories," 337.
3. Bly, 92.
4. Ibid.
5. Easthope, 22.
6. Bly, 102.
7. Milch, 121.
8. Ibid., 121.
9. Barra.
10. McGee, 107.
11. Bevington, 786.
12. Ibid., 786.
13. Rauchut, 97.
14. See Bevington, 786, and Garber, 317–318.
15. Bevington, 785.
16. Ibid., 785.
17. Garber, 324.
18. Ibid., 328.
19. Ibid., 321.
20. Bevington, 741.
21. Ibid., 741.
22. Shephard, 10.
23. Havrilesky.
24. Smith, 60.
25. Ibid., 66.
26. Berrettini, 257.
27. Mitchell and Wright, 123.
28. Ibid., 123.
29. Ibid., 121.

Chapter 5

1. Rackin, *Shakespeare and Women*, 51.
2. Ibid., 49–50.

3. *Essential Shakespeare Handbook*, 118.
4. Rackin and Howard, 20.
5. Andrews, para 21.
6. Bevington, 744.
7. See Rackin, "Anti-Historians: Women's Roles in Shakespeare's Histories," 329, and Weisner, *Women and Gender in Early Modern Europe*, 24.
8. Weisner, 31.
9. Rackin, "Historical Differences/Sexual Differences," 50.
10. Weisner, 20.
11. Rackin, "Anti-Historians," 329.
12. Bevington, 786.
13. Hark, 79.
14. *Deadwood*, "The Trial of Jack McCall," 1.5, "Bullock Returns to the Camp," 1.7, "Mr. Wu," 1.10, and "E.B. was Left Out," 2.7. Not included is "Boy-the-Earth-Talks-To" (2.12), Hearst's nickname.
15. Petersen, 273.
16. Ibid., 273.
17. Rackin, *Stages of History: Shakespeare's English Chronicles*, 163.
18. Jardine qtd in Kurtz, 279.
19. Hark, 107.
20. Andrews, para 21.
21. Krims, 119.
22. *The Bedford Shakespeare*, "View," 599.
23. Jacobs, *Deadwood*, 89.
24. Dudley, 96.
25. Bevington, 828.
26. In this respect, *Henry V* may be comparable to *Deadwood*. Some critics have observed that, in Kenneth Branagh's film *Henry V*, this scene takes place at night, amid obvious destruction and exhausted English troops; it's clear that Henry is using violent, vivid language in an attempt to save his men from a battle they're not likely to win. Milch has said that *Deadwood*'s profanity is a defensive means for the men of not drawing their guns.
27. Bazin, 144.
28. Cook, 4.
29. Hark, 80.
30. Jacobs, *Deadwood*, 131.
31. Ibid., 101.
32. Milch, 90.
33. Jacobs, *Deadwood*, 88–89.
34. Hark, 82.
35. Ibid., 79.
36. Petersen, 271.
37. Ibid., 272.
38. Krims, 119.
39. Hark, 82.
40. Dudley, 73–74.
41. Pippin, in *Hollywood Westerns and American Myth* (2010), describes how the baby in John Ford's *Stagecoach* unites women across social barriers, 7.
42. Hagelin, 150.
43. Petersen, 268.
44. Jacobs, *Deadwood*, 103.
45. See McCabe, "Myth Maketh the Woman: Calamity Jane, Frontier Mythology and Creating American (Media) Historical Imaginings"; Smith, "Whores, Ladies, and Calamity Jane: Gender Roles and the Women of HBO's *Deadwood*"; Jacobs, "Alma and Trixie" and "Cy and Joanie"; Hark, *Deadwood*; Dudley, "'Land of Oblivion': Abjection, Broken Bodies, and the Western Narrative in *Deadwood*"; Mizejewski, "Calamity Jane and Female Masculinity in *Deadwood*"; Johnson, "Queer Spaces and Emotional Couplings in *Deadwood*"; Tonkovich, "Who Put the Gun into the Whore's Hand?: Disability in *Deadwood*"; Petersen, "'Whores and Other Feminists': Recovering *Deadwood*'s Unlikely Feminisms"; Guida, "Neither Here Nor There: Calamity Jane and the Western's Liminality in Deadwood."
46. Jacobs, *Deadwood*, 90.
47. Dudley, 75.
48. Kurtz, 270.
49. Ibid., 270.

Chapter 6

1. Dudley, 99.
2. Mittell, *Television and American Culture*, 161.
3. In *Complex TV*, Mittell's definition of narrative contains "four basic storytelling facets that might require orientation: time, events, characters, and space" (263). He refers to these as categories that help viewers make sense of television narratives (263). Given that *Deadwood*'s episodes seem to cover a single 24-hour period each while the Henriad covers roughly 24 years, the "time" aspect is less relevant for the purposes of this book.
4. Hawkins, "Structural Pattern in Shakespeare's Histories," 44.
5. Ibid., 44.

6. Merten, 145.
7. Mittell, *Television and American Culture*, 215.
8. Garber, 315.
9. Jacobs, *Deadwood*, 40.
10. Mittell, *Complex TV*, 53–54.
11. Hark, 27.
12. Bevington, 826.
13. Rip Taylor IMDB.com entry.
14. Hagelin, 148.
15. Ibid., 148.
16. Dudley, 83.
17. Mittell, *Complex TV*, 134.
18. Wright, 49.
19. Hagelin, 151.
20. Mittell, *Complex TV*, 131.
21. Milch, 122.
22. *The Bedford Shakespeare*, 408.
23. Models of this kind of structuring, where one scene seems, to the protagonist and readers/viewers, to present an honest perspective, only to be corrected in the subsequent scene by Truth, is also found in Edmund Spenser's *The Fairie Queene* (1596) and John Milton's *Paradise Lost* (1667).
24. Hagelin, 143.
25. Jacobs, *Deadwood*, 1.
26. Ibid., 3.
27. Mittell, *Television and American Culture*, 188.
28. Jacobs, *Deadwood*, 144–145.
29. Pippin, 135.
30. Graulich, xli.
31. Johnson, 212.
32. Mittell, *Television and American Culture*, 270.
33. Drysdale, 140.
34. Witschi, 133.
35. Ibid., 133.
36. Johnson, 228.
37. Ibid., 232.
38. Widdicombe.
39. Hattaway, 9.
40. Wright, 40.
41. Ibid., 40–41.
42. Ibid., 42.
43. Ibid., 43–44.
44. Ibid., 44–45.
45. Ibid., 44–45.
46. Ibid., 53.
47. Ibid., 119.
48. Ibid., 120.
49. Jacobs, *Deadwood*, 6.
50. Hagelin, 146. She posits that the central theme running through the series is recognition of how the vulnerable body, in suffering, in pain shared, connects individuals in community in the camp.
51. Jacobs, *Deadwood*, 158.
52. *The Oxford English Dictionary*.
53. His costuming is similar to that of Richard II's. It reflects a wealthy, inactive, leisure status.
54. Wright, 57.
55. *Deadwood*, "New Money," 2.15.
56. *Deadwood*, "Something Expensive," 2.18.
57. Hagelin, 150.
58. Kahn, 18.
59. *Deadwood*, "New Money," 2.15, and *Deadwood*, "Requiem for a Gleet," 2.16.
60. Hagelin, 152. She asserts that "the arrival of smallpox in the camp…cements Cy as an outsider, specifically by the way he treats the body in pain … to Cy, pain is isolating, and the way he deals with vulnerable bodies is to banish them. The contrast this forms with Al creates an ethically dubious but artistically effective sense of view affiliation with Al and the tactile, corporeal attitude toward bodies and pain that he represents" (152–153).
61. Hawkins, 16.
62. Ibid., 21.
63. Sepinwall and Seitz, 74.
64. Ibid., 73.

Chapter 7

1. Bevington, 744.
2. Milch, 131.
3. Janie Bryant, costume designer for *Deadwood*, quoted in Milch, 131.
4. *Essential Shakespeare*, 108.
5. See Garber, 317–318.
6. Hawkins, 34.
7. These latter two traits align him with Richard II.
8. Graulich, xxvi.
9. Hagelin, 152–153.
10. For some excellent analysis of these doubles, see Michael K. Johnson, "Queer Spaces and Emotional Couplings in *Deadwood*"; Tim Steckline, "The Thinking of Al Swearengen's Body: Kidney Stones, Pigpens, and Burkean Catharsis in *Deadwood*"; and John Dudley, "'Land of Oblivion': Abjection,

Broken Bodies, and the Western Narrative in *Deadwood*." See also, Graulich's footnote "introduction" li.
11. *The Bedford Shakespeare*, 409.
12. Bevington, 744.
13. Ibid., 744.
14. Ibid., 743.
15. Ibid., 742.
16. Ibid., 827.
17. Ibid., 744.
18. Hagelin, 143.
19. Dudley, 88.
20. Cook, 12.
21. Tim Steckline interprets this differently, saying "After Al's recovery his control of the town increasingly falters, however much his verbal wit and his carnal purgations may recover their vivacity and regularity" (61).
22. Hawkins, 33.
23. Ibid., 6.
24. Steckline, 68.
25. Dudley, 73–74.

Conclusion

1. Millichap, 108.
2. Not all, of course, because we do see strength, stoicism, resilience, compassion, caretaking, and articulately persuasive rhetoric from female characters in both, too.

Bibliography

Ames, John. *The Real Deadwood*. NY: Chamberlain Bros., 2004.
Andrews, Meghan C. "Gender, Genre, and Elizabeth's Princely Surrogates in *Henry IV* and *Henry V*." *Studies in English Literature, 1500–1900* 54. 2 (Spring 2014): 375–399.
Baker, Brian. *Contemporary Masculinities in Fiction, Film and Television*. NY: Bloomsbury Academic, 2015.
Barra, Allen. "The Man Who Made *Deadwood*: The Creator of the Immensely Popular New Western Discusses What Makes It Truly New: An Interview with David Milch." *American Heritage* 57.3 (July 2006): n.p.
Bazin, André. "The Evolution of the Western." *What Is Cinema?* Vol II. Trans. Hugh Gray. University of California Press, 2004. 149–157.
_____. "The Western: Or the American Film Par Excellence." *What Is Cinema?* Vol II. Trans. Hugh Gray. University of California Press, 2004. 140–147.
The Bedford Shakespeare. Eds. Russ McDonald and Lena Cowen Orlin. Boston and NY: Bedford St. Martin's, 2015.
Benz, Brad. "*Deadwood* and the English Language." *Great Plains Quarterly* 27. 4 (2007): 239–253.
Berger, Jr., Harry. *Harrying: Skills of Offense in Shakespeare's Henriad*. NY: Fordham UP, 2015.
Berrettini, Mark L. "No Law: Deadwood and the State." *Great Plains Quarterly* 27.4 (2007): 253–265.
Bevington, David. "Introduction." *The First Part of King Henry the Fourth*, in *The Complete Works of Shakespeare*. 6th Ed. Ed. David Bevington. NY: Pearson-Longman, 2009. 784–787.
_____. "Introduction." *The Life of King Henry the Fifth*, in *The Complete Works of Shakespeare*. 6th Ed. Ed. David Bevington. NY: Pearson-Longman, 2009. 873–877.
_____. "Introduction." *The Second Part of King Henry the Fourth*, in *The Complete Works of Shakespeare*. 6th Ed. Ed. David Bevington. NY: Pearson-Longman, 2009. 826–829.
_____. "Introduction." *The Tragedy of King Richard the Second*, in *The Complete Works of Shakespeare*. 6th Ed. Ed. David Bevington. NY: Pearson-Longman, 2009. 740–744.
Bly, Robert. *Iron John: A Book About Men*. Reprint 1992. Reading, MA: Addison-Wesley, 1990.
Brockway, Cristi H. *Deadwood* transcripts. Available at: save.deadwood.net/transcripts/index.htm.
Cantor, Paul. *The Invisible Hand in Popular Culture: Liberty vs. Authority in American Film and TV*. Lexington: The UP of Kentucky, 2012.
Cohen, Derek. "History and the Nation in 'Richard II' and 'Henry IV.'" *Studies in English Literature, 1500–1900* 42.2 (Spring 2002): 293–315.
Cook, Diane. "Moral Relativism in David Milch's *Deadwood*." *Dark Reflections, Monstrous Reflections: Essays on the Monster in Culture*. Ed. Sorcha Ni Fhlainn. Mansfield College, Oxford: Inter-Disciplinary Press, 2006. 1–19.

"*Deadwood* Transcript Collection." *The Deadwood Chronicles.* Available at: deadwoodchronicles.com/deadwood-transcript-collection/

Diffrient, David Scott. "Deadwood Dick: The Western (Phallus) Reinvented." *Reading Deadwood: A Western to Swear By.* Ed. David Lavery. London and NY: I.B. Tauris & Co. Ltd., 2006. 185–199.

Directed by John Ford. Dir. Peter Bogdonovich. 1971.

Drysdale, David. "'Laws and Every Other Damn Thing': Authority, Bad Faith, and the Unlikely Success of *Deadwood*." *Reading Deadwood: A Western to Swear By.* Ed. David Lavery. London and NY: I.B. Tauris & Co. Ltd., 2006. 133–144.

Dudley, John. "'Land of Oblivion': Abjection, Broken Bodies, and the Western Narrative in *Deadwood*." *Dirty Words in Deadwood: Literature and the Postwestern.* Eds. Melody Graulich and Nicolas S. Witschi. Lincoln and London: U of Nebraska P, 2013. 72–103.

Easthope, Anthony. *What a Man's Gotta Do: The Masculine Myth in Popular Culture.* NY: Routledge & London, 1990.

Edgerton, Gary R. and Michael T. Marsden. "Introduction: Legacy of Western Scholarship." *The Journal of Popular Film & Television* 39.2 (2011): 38–40.

Edmondson III, Henry T. "Why Hotspur Can't Take a Joke: Temperament and Leadership in Shakespeare's *Henry IV, Part 1*." *Public Integrity* 17 (2015): 247–263.

Essential Shakespeare Handbook. Eds. Leslie Dunton-Downer and Alan Riding. NY: DK Publishing, Inc., 2004.

Feeney, Matt. "Talk Pretty: The Linguistic Brilliance of HBO's *Deadwood*." *Salon.* May 21, 2004. Available at: www.slate.com.

Feinstein, Jessica. "Crossing Genres, 'Deadwood' Dominates." *Yale Daily News.* March 26, 2004. Available at: http://yaledailynews.com.

Garber, Marjorie. *Shakespeare After All.* NY: Anchor Books, 2004.

Graulich, Melody. "Introduction." *Dirty Words in Deadwood: Literature and the Postwestern.* Lincoln and London: U of Nebraska P, 2013. xii–xliv.

_____ and Nicolas S. Witschi, eds. *Dirty Words in Deadwood: Literature and the Postwestern.* Lincoln and London: U of Nebraska P, 2013.

Guida, Reece. "Neither Here Nor There: Calamity Jane and the Western's Liminality in *Deadwood*." *Critical Media Studies: Student Essays on Deadwood.* Eds. Mary M. Dalton, Max Dosser, Katie Nelson and Rebecca Steiner. Winston-Salem, NC: Library Partners Press, 2016. 35–41.

Hagelin, Sarah. *Reel Vulnerability: Power, Pain, and Gender in Contemporary American Film and Television.* New Brunswick, NJ: Rutgers UP, 2013.

Hark, Ina Rae. *Deadwood.* Detroit: Wayne State UP, 2012.

Hattaway, Michael. "The Shakespearean History Play." *The Cambridge Companion to Shakespeare's History Plays.* Ed. Michael Hattaway. CUP, 2002. 3–24.

Havrilesky, Heather. "The Man Behind *Deadwood*." *Salon.* March 5, 2005. Available at: www.salon.com.

Hawkins, Sherman. "Structural Pattern in Shakespeare's Histories." *Studies In Philology* 88.1 (Winter 1991):16–45.

Henry IV, Part 1. Written by William Shakespeare, directed by Dominic Dromgoole. Shakespeare's Globe, London, 2010. Taped stage production directed by Robin Lough. A Shakespeare's Globe Production, 2012.

"Henry IV, Part 2." *The Hollow Crown.* Written by Richard Eyre and William Shakespeare, directed by Richard Eyre. Neal Street Productions, 2012.

"Henry IV, Parts 1 and 2." *The Hollow Crown.* Written by Richard Eyre and William Shakespeare, directed by Richard Eyre. Neal Street Productions, 2012.

"Henry V." *The Hollow Crown.* Written by Ben Power and William Shakespeare, directed by Thea Sharrock. Neal Street Productions, 2012.

Henry V. Written by Kenneth Branagh and William Shakespeare, directed by Kenneth Branagh. Universal Pictures UK, 2002.

Hill, Erin. "'What's Afflictin' You?': Corporeality, Body Crises, and the Body Politic in *Deadwood*." *Reading Deadwood: A Western to Swear By.* Ed. David Lavery. London and NY: I.B. Tauris & Co. Ltd., 2006. 171–183.
The Hollow Crown. BBC, Neal Street Productions, 2012.
Howard, Douglas L. "Why Wild Bill Hickok Had to Die." *Reading Deadwood: A Western to Swear By.* Ed. David Lavery. London and NY: I.B. Tauris & Co. Ltd., 2006. 43–56.
Hyde, Anne. "*Deadwood* as History: What the Show Got Right About the Old West—And What It Missed." *Foreign Affairs.* Aug. 15, 2012. Available at: www.foreignaffairs.com.
Jacobs, Jason. "Al Swearengen, Philosopher King." *Reading Deadwood: A Western to Swear By.* Ed. David Lavery. London and NY: I.B. Tauris & Co. Ltd., 2006. 11–2.
_____. *Deadwood.* London: Palgrave Macmillan, 2012.
Johnson, Michael K. "Queer Spaces and Emotional Couplings in *Deadwood.*" *Dirty Words in Deadwood: Literature and the Postwestern.* Eds. Melody Graulich and Nicolas S. Witschi. Lincoln and London: U of Nebraska P, 2013. 208–235.
Kahn, Coppelia. *Man's Estate: Masculine Identity in Shakespeare.* Berkeley, LA: U of California P, 1981.
Keidel, James L., et al. "How Shakespeare Tempests the Brain: Neuroimaging Insights." *Cortex* 49.4 (April 2013): 913–919.
Klein, Amanda Ann. "'The Horse Doesn't Get a Credit': The Foregrounding of Generic Syntax in *Deadwood*'s Opening Credits." *Reading Deadwood: A Western to Swear By.* Ed. David Lavery. London and NY: I.B. Tauris & Co. Ltd., 2006. 93–100.
Krims, Marvin B. "Hotspur's Antifeminine Prejudice in Shakespeare's *1 Henry IV.*" *Literature and Psychology* 40.1-2 (1994): 118–132.
Kurtz, Martha A. "Rethinking Gender and Genre in the History Play." *Studies in English Literature, 1500–1900* 36.2 (Spring 1996): 267–287.
Landsberg, Alison. "Walking the *Deadwood* of History: Listening, Language, and the 'Aural Visceral.'" *Rethinking History* 14.4 (2010): 531–549.
Lewis, Nathaniel. "David Milch at Yale: An Interview." *Dirty Words in Deadwood: Literature and the Postwestern.* Eds. Melody Graulich and Nicolas S. Witschi. Lincoln and London: U of Nebraska P, 2013. 1–17.
Lotz, Amanda D. *Cable Guys: Television and Masculinities in the 21st Century.* NY and London: NYUP, 2014.
MacIntyre, Jeffrey. "The Professor and the Madman: Meet David Milch, the Genius Behind HBO's *Deadwood.*" *Slate.* Aug. 31, 2006. Available at: www.slate.com.
Martin, Brett. *Difficult Men: Behind the Scenes of a Creative Revolution: From the Sopranos and the Wire to Mad Men and Breaking Bad.* NY: Penguin Books, 2013.
McCabe, Janet and Kim Akass. "Sex, Swearing, and Respectability: Courting Controversy, HBO's Original Programming and Producing Quality TV." *Quality TV: Contemporary American Television and Beyond.* London: I.B. Taurus, 2007. 62–76.
McCuskey, Brian. "Last Words in *Deadwood.*" *Dirty Words in Deadwood: Literature and the Postwestern.* Eds. Melody Graulich and Nicolas S. Witschi. Lincoln and London: U of Nebraska P, 2013. 18–43.
McGee, Patrick. *From Shane to Kill Bill: Rethinking the Western.* Malden, MA: Blackwell Publishing, 2007.
McIntosh, Shawn. "Six Shooters and the Fourth Estate: A.W. Merrick and *Deadwood*'s Information Society." *Reading Deadwood: A Western to Swear By.* Ed. David Lavery. London and NY: I.B. Tauris & Co. Ltd., 2006. 33–41.
McKinley, Jesse. "'Deadwood' Gets a New Lease on Life." *New York Times.* 11 June 2006. Available at: www.nytimes.com.
Merten, Jennilyn. "'Right or Wrong, You Side with Your Feelings.'" *Dirty Words in Deadwood: Literature and the Postwestern.* Eds. Melody Graulich and Nicolas S. Witschi. Lincoln and London: U of Nebraska P, 2013. 141–164.
Milch, David. *Deadwood: Stories of the Black Hills.* NY: Bloomsbury, 2006.
Millichap, Joseph. "Robert Penn Warren, David Milch, and the Literary Contexts of *Deadwood.*"

Reading Deadwood: A Western to Swear By. Ed. David Lavery. London and NY: I.B. Tauris & Co. Ltd., 2006. 101–113.

Mitchell, Giles R. and Eugene P. Wright. "Hotspur's Poor Memory." *The South Central Bulletin* 43.4 (Winter 1983): 121–123.

Mitchell, Matthew W. "Some More Light on the Text: Watching HBO's *Deadwood* with and Without the Apostle Paul." *The Journal of Religion and Popular Culture* 25.1 (Spring 2013): n.p.

Mittell, Jason. *Complex TV: The Poetics of Contemporary Television Storytelling*. New York UP, 2015.

_____. *Television And American Culture*. Oxford UP, 2010.

Mizejewski, Linda. "Calamity Jane and Female Masculinity in *Deadwood*." *Dirty Words in Deadwood: Literature and the Postwestern*. Eds. Melody Graulich and Nicolas S. Witschi. Lincoln and London: U of Nebraska P, 2013. 184–207.

Murdoch, David H. *The American West: The Invention of a Myth*. U of Nevada P, 2001.

"The New Language of the Old West." *Deadwood*. The Complete First Season DVD. NY: HBO Video, 2004.

Newcomb, Horace. "Deadwood." *The Essential HBO Reader*. Eds. Gary R. Edgerton and Jeffrey P. Jones 2008. U of Kentucky P, Lexington. 92–102.

O'Sullivan, Sean. "Old, New, Borrowed, Blue: *Deadwood* and Serial Fiction." *Reading Deadwood: A Western to Swear By*. Ed. David Lavery. London and NY: I.B. Tauris & Co. Ltd., 2006. 115–129.

The Oxford English Dictionary. Available at: www.OED.com.

Perlman, Allison. "*Deadwood*. Generic Transformation, and Televisual History." *Journal of Popular Film and Television* 39.2 (2011): 102–112.

Petersen, Anne Helen. "'Whores and Other Feminists': Recovering *Deadwood*'s Unlikely Feminisms." *Great Plains Quarterly* 27. 4 (2007): 267–282.

Pippin, Robert B. *Hollywood Westerns and American Myth: The Importance of Howard Hawks and John Ford for Political Philosophy*. New Haven and London: Yale UP, 2010.

Rackin, Phyllis. "Anti-Historians: Women's Roles in Shakespeare's Histories." *Theatre Journal* 37.3 (1985): 329–344.

_____. *Shakespeare and Women*. Oxford: Oxford UP, 2005.

_____. *Stages of History: Shakespeare's English Chronicles*. Ithaca, NY: Cornell UP, 1990.

_____ and Jean E. Howard. *Engendering a Nation: A Feminist Account of Shakespeare's English Histories*. London and NY: Routledge, 1997.

Rauchut, E.A. "Hotspur's Prisoners and the Laws of War in *1 Henry IV*." *Shakespeare Quarterly* 45.1 (Spring 1994): 96–97.

Reading Deadwood: A Western to Swear By. Ed. David Lavery. London and NY: I.B. Tauris & Co. Ltd., 2006.

Reiman, Donald H. "Appearance, Reality, and Moral Order in *Richard II*." *Modern Language Quarterly* 25.1 (March 1964): 34–45.

Ribner, Irving. "Bolingbroke: A True Machiavellian." *Modern Language Quarterly* 9.2 (June 1948): 177–183.

_____. "The Political Problem in Shakespeare's Lancastrian Tetralogy." *Studies in Philology* 49.2 (April 1952): 171–184.

"Richard II." *The Hollow Crown*. Written by Rupert Goold, Ben Power and William Shakespeare, directed by Rupert Goold. Neal Street Productions, 2012.

Salerno, Daniel. "'I Will Have You Bend': Language and the Discourses of Power in *Deadwood*." *Literary Imagination* 12.2 (2010): 190–209.

Sepinwall, Alan. *The Revolution Was Televised: The Cops, Crooks, Slingers, and Slayers Who Changed TV Drama Forever*. NY: Touchstone, 2012.

_____ and Matt Zoller Seitz. "Deadwood." *TV (The Book): Two Experts Pick the Greatest American Shows of All Time*. NY and Boston: Grand Central Publishing, 2016. 69–75.

Shakespeare, William. *The First Part Of King Henry the Fourth*, in *The Complete Works of Shakespeare*. 6th Ed. Ed. David Bevington. NY: Pearson Education, Inc., 2009. 784–825.

_____. *Julius Caesar*, in *The Complete Works of Shakespeare*. 6th ed. Ed. David Bevington. NY: Pearson Education, Inc., 2009. 1051–1090.
_____. *The Life of King Henry the Fifth*, in *The Complete Works of Shakespeare*. 6th Ed. Ed. David Bevington. NY: Pearson Education, Inc., 2009. 873–918.
_____. *Macbeth*, in *The Complete Works of Shakespeare*. 6th ed. Ed. David Bevington. NY: Pearson, Education, Inc., 2000. 1255–1292.
_____. *Much Ado About Nothing*, in *The Complete Works of Shakespeare*. 6th ed. Ed. David Bevington. NY: Pearson, Education, Inc., 2000. 219–255.
_____. *The Second Part of King Henry the Fourth*, in *The Complete Works of Shakespeare*. 6th Ed. Ed. David Bevington. NY: Pearson Education, Inc., 2009. 826–872.
_____. *The Tragedy of King Richard the Second*, in *The Complete Works of Shakespeare*. 6th ed. Ed. David Bevington. NY: Pearson Education, Inc., 2009. 740–783.
Shapiro, Michael J. "HBO's Two Frontiers: *Deadwood* and the *Wire*." *Geopolitics* 20 (2015): 193–213.
Shephard, Alexandra. *Meanings Of Manhood in Early Modern England*. Oxford: Oxford UP, 2003.
Simmons, J.L. "Masculine Negotiations in Shakespeare's History Plays: Hal, Hotspur, and 'The Foolish Mortimer.'" *Shakespeare Quarterly* 44.4 (Winter 1993): 440–463.
Singer, Mark. "The Misfit: How David Milch Got from *NYPD Blue* to *Deadwood* by Way of an Epistle of St. Paul." *New Yorker*. Feb. 14, 2005. 192–205. Available at: newyorker.com.
Slotkin, Richard. *Gunfighter Nation: The Myth of the Frontier in Twentieth-Century America*. NY: Harper Perennial, 1992.
Smith, Bruce R. *Shakespeare and Masculinity*. Oxford: Oxford UP, 2000.
Smith, Kathleen E.R. "Whores, Ladies, and Calamity Jane: Gender Roles and the Women of HBO's *Deadwood*." *Reading Deadwood*. Ed. David Lavery. 79–92.
Stanford Friedman, Susan. "Why Not Compare?" *PMLA* 126.3 (May 2011): 753–762.
Steckline, Tim. "The Thinking of Al Swearengen's Body: Kidney Stones, Pigpens, and Burkean Catharsis in *Deadwood*." *Dirty Words in Deadwood: Literature and the Postwestern*. Eds. Melody Graulich and Nicolas S. Witschi. Lincoln and London: U of Nebraska P, 2013. 44–71.
Tonkovich, Nicole. "Who Put the Gun into the Whore's Hand?" *Dirty Words in Deadwood: Literature and the Postwestern*. Eds. Melody Graulich and Nicolas S. Witschi. Lincoln and London: U of Nebraska P, 2013. 236–268.
Vest, Jason P. *The Wire, Deadwood, Homicide, and NYPD Blue: Violence Is Power*. Santa Barbara, CA: Praeger, 2011.
Westerfelhaus, Robert and Celeste Lacroix. "Waiting for the Barbarians: HBO's *Deadwood* as a Post-9/11 Ritual of Disquiet." *Southern Communication Journal* 74.1 (Jan.-Mar. 2009): 18–39.
Widdicombe, Toby. *Simply Shakespeare*. Pearson, 2001.
Witherspoon, Wendy. "The Final Stamp: *Deadwood* and the Gothic American Frontier." *Dirty Words in Deadwood: Literature and the Postwestern*. Eds. Melody Graulich and Nicolas S. Witschi. Lincoln and London: U of Nebraska P, 2013. 104–123.
Witschi, Nicolas S. "'Down These Mean Streets': Film Noir. *Deadwood*. Cinematic Space, and the Irruption of Genre Codes." *Dirty Words in Deadwood: Literature and the Postwestern*. Eds. Melody Graulich and Nicolas S. Witschi. Lincoln and London: U of Nebraska P, 2013. 124–140.
Worden, Daniel. "Neo-Liberalism and the Western: HBO's *Deadwood* as National Allegory." *Canadian Review of American Studies* 39.2 (2009): 221–246.
Wright, Paul and Hailin Zhou. "Divining the 'Celestials': The Chinese Subculture of *Deadwood*." *Reading Deadwood: A Western to Swear By*. Ed. David Lavery. London and NY: I.B. Tauris & Co. Ltd., 2006.157–168.
Wright, Will. *Six Guns and Society: A Structural Study of the Western*. Berkeley and Los Angeles: U of California P, 1975.
Zinder, Paul. "The World Is Less than Perfect: Nontraditional Family Structures in *Deadwood*." *The Last Western: Deadwood and the End of American Empire*. Eds. Jennifer Greiman and Paul Stasi.

Index

abjection 127, 184*ch7n*10, 188
Adams, Silas 31, 59, 71, 74, 78, 119, 161
"Advances, None Miraculous" (episode) 178
Akass, Kim 1, 120, 189
alliances 12, 19–20, 28–29, 32, 34, 68, 70, 79, 83, 89–90, 92, 95, 97–98, 100, 115, 125, 130, 135, 145, 147, 152, 154–157, 168
"Amalgamation and Capital" (episode) 65, 178
"Amateur Night" (episode) 69, 100, 178
ambition 11, 27, 31, 39, 61–63, 71–72, 78, 80, 88, 91, 107–108, 115, 126, 147, 164
Ames, John 187
anachronisms 15–17
Andrews, Meghan 104, 114, 187
anger 2, 42–44, 46, 52, 55–56, 60, 73, 83–84, 86, 93–96, 99–100, 111, 118, 151, 175; *see also* mad
anti-hero 5, 175
anxiety 9, 14, 25–26, 70–71, 100, 105, 109, 154
audience 2–3, 5–6, 10–13, 15–18, 20, 25, 28, 32–33, 35, 37, 51, 54, 62–63, 67, 72, 75–77, 79–80, 87–88, 92, 102, 104, 108–109, 117, 121–123, 128–143, 145–146, 150, 158, 160–162, 164, 166–167, 169, 171–176
Aumerle 60, 82, 84–85
authority 4, 7, 9, 12, 20–21, 24, 26, 28, 31, 33, 39, 63–65, 67, 69, 71, 73, 77, 84–86, 115, 126, 130, 133, 138, 141, 145, 154, 159, 162, 164–165, 170, 172, 176, 187–188

Bazin, André: "The Western" 12, 24, 81, 117, 187
The Bedford Shakespeare 115, 187
The Bella Union Saloon 17, 29, 104, 118, 123–124, 135
Benz, Brad 179, 187
Berger, Harry, Jr. 14, 187
Berrettini, Mark L. 15, 96, 180, 182, 187
Bevington, David 10, 49, 85, 88, 104, 107, 134, 161, 165–167, 179–185, 187, 190–191
Blazanov 134

Bly, Robert 82, 182, 187
Bogdanovich, Peter 188
Bolingbroke, Henry 5, 11, 18, 21–22 29, 32–33, 42, 58–67, 69–71, 77, 80, 81, 88, 100, 105, 108–109, 111, 115, 132–133, 137–138, 141, 144, 146, 159–167, 175, 190
"Boy-the-Earth-Talks-To" (episode) 78, 98, 111, 122, 178
Branagh, Kenneth 183*n*26, 188
Breaking Bad 175, 189
Bridgers, Sean 134
Bryant, Janie 158
Bullock, Martha 18–19, 52, 55, 106–107, 109, 121–122, 124–126, 156, 161
Bullock, Seth (character) 2, 5, 14, 17–19, 23, 28–36, 39–41, 43–46, 48–58, 64, 68–71, 75–84, 86–101, 104, 106, 109, 111, 115, 119, 121–122, 124, 126–127, 132–134, 136, 138, 141–145, 147, 150, 152–156, 158–161, 167–168, 171–173, 175, 177, 180*n*57
Bullock, Seth (real person) 14–15
Bullock, William 109, 121–122
"Bullock Returns to the Camp" (episode) 41, 50, 89, 168, 177
Burns, Johnny 40, 62–63, 65, 74, 77, 100, 120, 149–150, 154, 161

camera 2, 30, 53, 131, 139–142, 157, 167
Canary, "Calamity" Jane (character) 17–18, 69, 84, 104, 107, 110, 117, 119–120, 124–126, 136, 138, 145, 156, 161, 167, 188, 190–191
Canary, "Calamity" Jane (real person) 15
Cantor, Paul 187
"The Catbird Seat" (episode) 50, 52, 100, 176
character 2, 4–7, 12, 16, 19–24, 26, 28–38, 40, 47, 49, 52, 54–56, 58–59, 63, 68, 72–81, 85–87, 101–104, 106–107, 114, 117, 124–133, 135–136, 138–142, 144–145, 147, 149, 151, 155–162, 166–169, 172–173, 175–176, 181*n*69, 183*ch*6*n*3, 185*n*21
Chesterton 134
The Chez Ami 17, 32, 106, 118, 123, 126

chiasmus 38, 158, 161
Chief Justice (character) 75, 101, 116, 119, 124
"Childish Things" (episode) 75, 97–98, 177
children 18, 79, 81, 86, 121–122, 126, 151–152, 164, 167
The Chorus 2, 25, 137, 140, 142
civil war 12, 20, 24, 51, 62, 143, 155–156, 164
Claggett, Magistrate 68
Cochran, Doc (character) 31, 48, 84, 119–120, 124, 145, 154, 167, 171
Cochran, Doc (real person) 15
Cohen, Derek 27, 181, 187
comedy 31, 110, 142–144
comic 16, 25, 77, 84, 105, 107, 121, 123–124, 134–135, 147, 155–156
communication 5, 24, 52, 65, 67, 93, 154, 175
community 2, 4, 10, 12, 19–20, 26, 28–30, 34–36, 40, 46, 54, 57–58, 63, 67, 82, 90, 101, 107, 131, 133, 135–136, 142, 144–145, 147, 151–152, 154, 156–157, 172, 181n69, 184n50
compassion 53, 118–120, 141, 150, 160, 185n2
"Complications" (episode) 65, 81, 94–96, 154, 177
"A Constant Throb" (episode) 176
Cook, Diane 32, 34–35, 48, 118, 169, 181n73, 187
corruption 7, 10, 20–21, 24, 28, 59, 69, 70, 72, 74, 78, 80, 86, 92, 109, 117, 130, 132, 137, 146, 162, 172, 176
Cramed, Andy 155
Crook, General 45
The Crown 13
culture 2–5, 7, 9–10, 16–17, 22, 26–27, 29, 82, 103, 105, 126, 129, 174–175

danger 21, 32–33, 42–43, 45, 60, 63, 66–67, 75, 78, 92, 107, 114–115, 120, 140–141, 143, 160–161, 166–168
"Deadwood" (episode) 17, 30, 39–40, 62–63, 83, 96, 109, 149–150, 167, 177, 180n57
"Deep Water" (episode) 40, 44, 70, 77, 84, 86–87, 124, 139, 141, 150, 177
devil 72–73
Dickens, Charles 1
Diffrient, David Scott 33, 67, 188
Directed by John Ford 188
disability 1, 77, 120
Doherty, Dan (real person) 15
Dolly 93, 107, 169–171
Dority, Dan (character) 32, 45, 52, 57, 61, 63, 65, 74, 77, 89, 91, 99, 115, 120, 134–135, 149–150, 154, 161, 167
doublings 129, 135, 142, 157, 160–161; *see also* mirror
Draper, Don 176
Driscoll, Tim 61, 65, 149–150, 167
Drysdale, David 24, 28, 32, 141, 188
Dudley, John 26, 116, 125, 127, 130, 168, 172, 181n68, 188

The Earps 53, 99
Easthope, Anthony 70, 82, 188
"E.B. Was Left Out" (episode) 23, 77, 97, 177
Edgerton, Gary 188, 190
Edmondson, Henry T., III 49, 55, 188
Ellsworth, Whitney 19, 63, 69, 74, 89, 98, 111–112, 118–119, 126, 138, 150–151, 156, 161, 171, 180n36
empathy 31, 34, 53
Epilogue 2, 140, 142
Essential Shakespeare Handbook 188
ethics 12, 32–33, 78, 95, 135, 182ch3n17, 184n60
evil 22, 32, 34, 117, 120
Eyre, Richard 188

Falstaff, Sir John 2, 5, 18, 21–22, 25, 33, 46–47, 49, 56, 58–59, 61, 72–77, 80, 87, 89, 92, 94, 101, 104, 107, 112, 114–116, 119, 122–124, 132–133, 140, 144, 159–160, 174–175
Farnum, E.B. (character) 19, 23, 31, 44, 56, 61, 65–66, 68, 70–71, 74, 76–77, 89, 90, 97, 124, 149, 177
Farnum, E.B. (real person) 15
fathers 56, 80–82, 84, 93, 101–102, 152–153
Faust 53
fear 43, 48, 63, 64, 67, 69, 85, 92, 96, 100, 109, 111–112, 118, 121, 123, 128, 140, 153, 163, 170–172
Feeley, Matt 188
Feinstein, Jessica 188
femininity 33, 92, 125, 148
Fields, Samuel (character) 124, 161
Fields, Samuel (real person) 15
film 1–4, 10–13, 20, 23–25, 27–28, 34, 81–82, 84, 117, 122, 130–131, 136, 139–140, 143, 149, 175, 179ch1n1, 187–188, 190–191
The First Four Books of the Civil Wars 14
Flora 118, 120, 161
Ford, John 12, 34, 183n41, 188, 190
Freud, Sigmund 31
fuck 23, 36, 44–45, 48, 53–54, 65–66, 68, 71, 78–79, 81, 83, 86, 90–100, 115, 149, 154, 159, 168–171
"Full Faith and Credit" (episode) 170–171, 178

Garber, Marjorie 3, 20, 52–53, 56, 60, 62, 70, 72–74, 77–78, 88, 132, 188
Garret Ellsworth, Alma 15, 17, 19, 31, 40–41, 44–45, 48, 50, 56–57, 68–69, 77–78, 89–94, 98, 103–104, 106–113, 115, 117–121, 125–127, 136, 139, 142, 150–151, 161, 168, 171
Garret, Brom 19, 41, 61, 65, 75–76, 104, 106, 108, 110–113, 149–151
Gaunt, John of 22, 106, 108, 112–113, 118–119, 137, 155, 162, 166
The Gem Saloon 29, 44, 52, 63–64, 67–70, 83, 90, 92–93, 97–100, 104, 123–124, 126, 132, 135, 138, 181n69

Index

gender roles 1, 6–7, 176, 191
genre 2, 4–6, 9–14, 18, 23, 25–27, 31–32, 34–35, 81, 115, 130, 138, 140, 142, 167, 174, 179ch1n1, 183ch6n3, 187–189, 191
Gloucester, Duchess of 106, 108, 110, 112, 119
Gloucester, Duke of 60, 108
good 10, 16, 18, 21, 23–24, 26, 28, 32–34, 42, 54–55, 58, 70, 72, 75–76, 82, 94, 97, 104, 117–119, 123, 126, 130, 143, 145–146, 150, 165, 167
Goold, Rupert 141, 190
Graulich, Melody 4, 31, 52, 77, 139, 188–191
grief 5, 53, 103, 108, 110–113, 122, 128, 137, 153, 164–165, 169, 175
gunfighter/gunslinger 18, 22–23, 30, 139, 144, 191
Gustave 151

Hagelin, Sarah 125, 135–136, 138, 147, 151, 167, 181n74, 184n50, 184n60, 188
Hall, Edward 14
Hamilton 24
Hamlet 31, 56
Hamlet (character) 15, 54
Hark, Ina Rae 28, 114, 118, 120, 123, 125, 188
Hattaway, Michael 63, 143, 188
Havrilesky, Heather 188
Hawkins, Sherman 129, 155, 160, 172, 188
Hawks, Howard 25, 34, 190
Hearst, George (character) 29, 31, 34–35, 41, 45, 52–53, 55–56, 65–66, 68–69, 71, 76, 79, 88, 93, 97–101, 112, 117–120, 124, 135, 145, 147, 150, 156, 161, 166, 170–172
Hearst, George (real person) 15
HBO 1–4, 10, 13, 17, 35, 132, 156, 177
Henry IV (character) 2, 4–5, 10, 14, 16, 18, 21–22, 26, 29, 32, 36–37, 41–42, 47, 55, 58–60, 62, 64, 67, 70–73, 76–81, 84–86, 88, 99–101, 106, 114, 118–119, 124, 132–133, 137, 152–154, 159, 175, 187
1 Henry IV 2–3, 5, 16, 18, 21, 36–38, 40–52, 54–55, 57, 68–70, 72–76, 78, 80, 84–87, 91–92, 95, 103, 107, 112–116, 122, 132–134, 143–144, 147–149, 159, 181, 189–190
2 Henry IV 2–3, 16, 22, 25, 40, 60, 64, 66, 71–72, 74–75, 80, 84, 86, 91, 94, 101, 103, 110–112, 114, 116, 124, 134, 140, 143, 152–153, 155, 166
Henry V 2–3, 14, 16, 19, 25, 28–29, 34, 51, 58, 103, 107, 112, 116–117, 121–122, 124, 137, 140, 143–144, 146, 153, 156, 183n26, 187–188
Henry V (character) 10–11, 14, 18, 24, 32, 34–35, 51, 56–58, 94, 101, 115–116, 119–121, 137, 144, 155, 176
"Here Was a Man" (episode) 40–41, 70–71, 110, 136, 177
hero 13, 20, 28, 32–33, 51–54, 81, 115, 130, 144–145, 147, 149–150, 156, 160, 167, 172
Hickok, Wild Bill (character) 17–18, 20, 23, 30, 40–41, 44, 48, 49, 57, 64, 68, 70, 82–83, 86–89, 96, 104, 110, 119, 124–125, 133, 136, 138–139, 144, 149–150, 160–161, 168, 180n57, 189
Hickok, Wild Bill (real person) 14–15, 17
Hill, Walter 63, 177
Historia Anglica 14
history 2–4, 6–7, 9–16, 18–21, 24–27, 29, 32, 35, 38, 51, 57, 63, 80–81, 88, 102–105, 111–112, 114, 121, 123–125, 127, 129–130, 133, 137–138, 140–141, 143–144, 146–147, 155–156, 160–161, 172, 174–176, 179intro.n4, 180n20, 181n74, 187–191
Holinshed, Raphael 14, 18
The Hollow Crown 116, 122, 137, 141, 188–190
honor/honour 5, 7, 15, 21–22, 23, 34–37, 40–44, 48–51, 53, 58–59, 68, 71, 73, 77–78, 80, 83–89, 94, 100–101, 110, 119–120, 130, 138, 142, 153, 160, 166, 176
Hostetler 35, 44, 124, 134, 161
Howard, Jean 25–26, 190
human condition 9, 31–32, 34–35

"I Am Not the Fine Man You Mistake Me For" (episode) 76, 99, 178
identity 4, 6, 9, 11–12, 17, 20, 25, 54, 62, 82, 88, 95–96, 126, 128, 151, 165, 189
illness 32, 94, 96, 141, 152, 169, 171
Isabel/the Queen 18, 105, 109–111, 132
Isringhausen, Miss 119

Jacobs, Jason: "Al Swearengen, Philosopher King" 64, 74–75; *Deadwood* 19, 25–26, 32, 46, 52, 55, 115, 119, 127, 132, 138–139, 189
Jarry, Hugo 95, 98
Jason, Peter 134
Jen 100, 120, 126, 161
Jewel 31, 75, 77–78, 107, 112, 120, 145, 161, 171
"Jewel's Boot Is Made for Walking" (episode) 31, 41, 44, 64, 90–91, 103, 107, 111, 168–170, 177
Johnson, Michael 139
Julius Caesar 82–83, 190

Kahn, Coppelia 189
Keidel, James 180n12, 189
kidney stones 32, 94, 152–153, 171–172
kindness 31, 34, 83, 145, 160, 171
King James Bible 2, 12
King John 104, 143
Klein, Amanda Ann 15, 20, 189
Krims, Marvin 125, 189
Kristeva, Julia 127
Kurtz, Martha 14, 18, 127, 189
The L Word 17

Lacroix, Celeste 33–34, 191
Lancasters 21, 61, 145
Landsberg, Alison 13, 179intro.n4, 189
Langrishe, Jack 50, 52–53, 78–79, 134, 151, 156

language 1–3, 12, 20, 27, 30, 37–38, 45, 47, 50, 52, 67, 70, 73, 76–78, 88, 97, 107, 120, 127, 129, 131, 136, 147, 150, 152, 155, 159, 180n36, 180n64, 183n26
laudanum 57, 108–109, 113, 117, 119, 126, 168
Lavery, David 179, 188–191
law 12, 15, 19–20, 22–23, 26, 30, 34, 36, 39, 46–49, 55–57, 70, 73, 81, 83, 88, 90–91, 96, 99, 101, 130, 132–134, 138, 145–147, 156, 159, 166
Lee, Mr. 117–119, 123–124
legitimate 9, 21–22, 26, 33, 39, 105, 119, 166
Leon 123
lesbians 17
"Leviathan Smiles" (episode) 53, 99, 178
Lewis, Nathaniel 189
"A Lie Agreed Upon, Part I" (episode) 50, 57, 76, 92–93, 115, 118, 142, 177
"A Lie Agreed Upon, Part II" (episode) 74, 94, 177
literature 1, 4–5, 12–13, 26, 92, 179intro.n4, 187–191
lying (deceit) 73–75, 119, 168

Macbeth 78, 113, 191
Machiavelli, Nicolo/Machiavellian 55, 76, 146, 182ch3n17, 190
mad 37, 42–44, 97, 114, 175; *see also* anger
Mad Men 13, 175, 189
The Man Who Shot Liberty Valance 23
Manifest Destiny 20, 27
manipulation 55, 64–65, 77, 92, 149
Marlowe, Christopher 53–54
Marsden, Michael 188
masculinity 3, 33, 82, 89, 92, 95, 107, 127, 130, 143, 147–148, 151, 155–156
Mason, Ned 30, 39–40, 44, 64, 82, 96, 144, 167–168
Mason, Tom 20, 65, 82, 167–168
McCabe, Janet 1
McCall, Jack (character) 17, 41, 44–45, 48, 68, 70, 168, 177
McGee, Patrick 28–29, 84
McIntosh, Shawn 65
McShane, Ian 63
mercy killing 19, 169
Merrick, A.W. (character) 53, 70, 134
Merten, Jennilyn 31, 34, 130
Metz, Sofia 89, 104, 107, 117, 125, 142
The Metz family 15, 30, 40, 62, 82, 167
Milch, David 1, 4–5, 7, 10, 13–15, 19–20, 25, 32–35, 56, 72, 75, 81–82, 84, 94, 100, 103, 107, 120, 135, 146, 149, 156, 172, 174, 177–178, 179intro.n4, 180n64, 187, 189, 191
Miles 118, 161, 168
Millichap, Joseph 20, 75, 174, 189
Miranda, Lin-Manuel 24
mirror 110, 142, 157, 160–161
A Mirror for Magistrates 14
misogyny 5, 161

"Mr. Wu" (episode) 44, 69, 78, 124, 177, 183
Mitchell, Giles 99, 182, 190
Mittell, Jason: *Complex TV* 3, 6, 11–12, 78–79, 129, 132, 183ch6n3, 190; *Television and American Culture* 4, 11, 129–130, 138–140, 190
Mizejewski, Linda 17–18, 190
monologue 32, 88, 131
motivation 4–5, 32, 45, 50–51, 75, 79–80, 88, 126, 131, 136, 139, 145, 153, 158, 173, 176
Much Ado About Nothing 31, 111, 191
murder 15, 19, 23, 29, 34, 41, 45, 48, 52–53, 60, 62–64, 67–70, 74, 78–79, 98, 106, 108, 110, 118, 134, 136–138, 141, 147, 151, 153, 156, 162–163, 167–168

narrative 1–7, 12, 15, 18–19, 23, 33–35, 62, 126, 129–132, 136, 138, 140, 143, 145–147, 151, 155–158, 173–174, 176, 181n69, 183ch6n3, 188
national mythology 3–4, 9, 12, 21
"New Money" (episode) 94, 106, 177, 182, 184
New York 13, 90, 149–150
Newcomb, Horace 27, 181, 190
"No Other Sons or Daughters" (episode) 49, 68, 177
Northumberland, Duke of 18, 37, 40, 42, 62, 66, 86, 88, 100, 112, 118–119, 162, 165
The No. 10 Saloon 30, 39, 82, 133, 136, 168
Nuttall, Tom 64

Olyphant, Timothy 136
order (legal) 4, 7, 9, 19, 20–21, 23–24, 26, 33, 42, 46, 55–56, 72–74, 82, 91–92, 94, 105, 131, 133, 146–147, 155–156, 176
orphanage 169–170
The Oxford English Dictionary 16, 43, 180n36, 190

parallel 2–7, 12, 15–16, 27, 35–36, 67, 69, 73, 81, 88, 100, 129, 132, 143–144, 147, 156, 172–174, 176
passivity 5, 103, 110, 112, 128, 175
Percy, Henry: "Hotspur" 2, 5, 16, 18, 22, 29, 33, 35–45, 48–58, 70, 73, 78, 84–88, 92, 95–96, 99–101, 103, 106–107, 110, 112–115, 120, 148–149, 151, 159–160, 175, 188–191
performance 2, 10, 13, 24, 54, 61, 76–77, 96, 99, 104, 122, 134, 137, 140, 160, 164
Perlman, Allison 67, 182, 190
Persimmon Phil 65, 167
perspective 3, 6, 11, 13–14, 21, 26, 28–30, 32, 35, 50, 64, 68, 78, 80, 83, 87, 92, 105, 107, 128–129, 131, 135, 137–142, 144, 157, 167, 174–175, 181n98, 184n23
Petersen, Anne Helen 108–109, 123, 190
Pippin, Robert 12, 23–24, 34, 139, 179ch1n1, 183n41, 190
"Plague" (episode) 68, 167, 177
Plantagenet 21, 86, 146
political 3–5, 7, 9, 11–12, 14, 19–24, 26–28,

31–33, 35, 37, 45, 47, 50, 52, 55–56, 59, 60–61, 64, 68, 70, 72, 77, 79–80, 85, 88, 94, 96–98, 100–101, 103–105, 107, 109–110, 114–115, 119, 121, 125, 130, 134–135, 137–138, 143–144, 146–147, 152–154, 156, 167, 171, 175–176, 182ch3n17, 190
power 4–7, 10–14, 18–21, 24–25, 27–28, 31–35, 51–54, 56, 59–60, 62, 64–71, 77, 79–80, 84, 94, 96, 98, 101, 104–105, 110–116, 118, 121, 123, 127–133, 136–139, 141–143, 146–147, 151–152, 154–155, 159–167, 170–172, 175–176, 188, 190–191
primogeniture 22, 162, 166
Prince Hal 2, 16, 18, 21–22, 33–39, 41, 46–52, 54–58, 64, 68, 71–78, 81, 85–87, 89, 91–92, 100–101, 114–116, 118–119, 121–122, 133–134, 144, 146, 148, 152–154, 156, 159–160, 175–176
profanity 1, 17, 69, 126, 150, 183
propaganda 10, 12, 18
prostitutes 29, 74, 92, 103–104, 106–107, 115–119, 122–124, 126, 132, 134–135; *see also* whores
psychology 5, 26, 34, 56, 175

Queen Elizabeth I 10–11, 19, 22, 29, 155, 174
Queen Elizabeth II 13
Quickly, Mistress 103, 106–107, 115–116, 119, 124

rack-focus shot 30, 138–139
Rackin, Phyllis: "Anti-Historians" 105–106, 190; *Engendering a Nation* 16, 26, 104, 190; "Historical/Sexual Differences" 105, 190; *Shakespeare and Women* 79–81, 103, 190; *Stages of History* 15–16, 25, 111, 180n29, 190
Rauchut, E.A. 86, 190
Reading Deadwood 179, 188–191
"Reconnoitering the Rim" (episode) 17, 40, 76, 113, 149–150, 177
Red Cloud (character) 15
Red River 23, 28, 82, 84
regicide 22, 24, 62, 65
Reiman, Donald 190
"Requiem for a Gleet" (episode) 177
respect 5, 34, 39–42, 53, 60, 62, 67, 79, 85–86, 90, 93, 118–120, 126, 130, 138, 145, 148, 151, 154–155, 166–167
Ribner, Irving: "Bolingbroke" 61, 67, 71, 182ch3n17, 190; "The Political Problem in Shakespeare's Lancastrian Tetralogy" 67, 190
"A Rich Find" (episode) 66, 76, 93, 124, 178
Richard II 2, 4–5, 10, 14, 16, 18, 20, 21–22, 29, 32–33, 59–62, 65–67, 69, 71, 73, 80–81, 84, 103, 105–106, 108–109, 111–114, 124, 130–131, 133, 137–138, 141, 143, 146, 154–155, 159, 161–167, 172, 175, 187, 190–191
Richard II (character) 10–11, 14, 18, 33, 42, 48, 60–62, 64, 66–69, 70–71, 78–80, 84, 86, 88, 100, 105–106, 109–112, 118–119, 131–133, 137–138, 141, 143–144, 154–155, 158–167, 172, 187
Richard III 22, 33, 104, 143, 176
Richard III (character) 11, 16, 19, 24, 33, 78, 155
Richardson (character) 35
Roosevelt, Teddy 13–14, 156
Rumor (character) 2, 25, 66, 140, 142
rumor/rumors 25, 66, 97–98, 116, 140, 147, 156, 166
Russell, Otis 44–45, 49, 52, 88, 91, 168

Salerno, Daniel 20, 72, 77, 190
Satan 63, 73
Sawyer, Eddie 17, 119
The Searchers 23, 84
Sepinwall, Alan: *The Revolution Was Televised* 1, 179, 190; *TV (The Book)* 156, 190
Shapiro, Michael 13, 180n20, 191
Shephard, Alexandra 191
silence 48, 80 97, 105, 114
Singer, Mark 180n64, 191
Slotkin, Richard 23, 191
Smith, Bruce 95, 191
Smith, Kathleen 191
Smith, Reverend Henry (character) 19, 33–34, 40, 48, 78, 84, 145, 169–171, 181
Smith, Reverent Henry (real person) 15
"Sold Under Sin" (episode) 36, 44–45, 52, 54, 82, 91, 150, 177
soliloquy 2, 37, 47, 54, 66, 87, 92, 133, 163, 173, 176
"Something Very Expensive" (episode) 118, 171, 177
sons 49, 68, 81–81, 84, 93, 105–106, 115–116, 152–153, 177
Soprano, Tony 175
The Sopranos 1, 175, 189
Spotted Elk (character) 15
Stagecoach 13, 183n41
Stanford Friedman, Susan 4, 191
Stapleton, Con 41, 64,90, 123, 134
Star, Sol (character) 17, 31, 36, 39–41, 44–46, 48–49, 57, 70, 83, 86–87, 89, 94, 118–119, 126, 134, 156, 161, 168–169, 175
Star, Sol (real person) 15
Steckline, Tim 185n21, 191
storytelling 6, 11, 33, 81, 129–130, 132, 183ch6n3, 190
structure 2, 4–7, 27, 87, 128–134, 142–147, 157–158, 161, 173, 176, 191
Stubbs, Joanie 17–19, 32, 104, 106–107, 117–119, 123, 125–126, 161
"Suffer the Little Children" (episode) 68, 89–90, 117, 136, 168, 177
suicide 117, 123, 135–136
suspense 135, 143
Swearengen, Al (character) 2, 5, 14–15, 17, 19, 23, 27, 29, 31–35, 41, 43–45, 49–53, 56, 58–

59, 61–81, 83–84, 86–101, 104, 110, 112–113, 115–116, 119–121, 124, 132–136, 138, 141–142, 145, 147, 149–156, 158–161, 166–172, 174–176, 184n60, 185n21, 189, 191
Swearengen, Al (real person) 15
sympathy 18, 33, 52–53, 67, 126, 128, 161, 164, 169, 171

Tearsheet, Doll 107
television 1–6, 9–13, 17, 21, 24, 27, 29–31, 33, 35, 57, 65, 101, 103–104, 116, 122–125, 129–132, 135–136, 138, 140–141, 143, 146–147, 156, 167, 174–176, 181n73, 183ch6n3, 187–190
"Tell Him Something Pretty" (episode) 56, 59, 62, 66, 78–79, 100–101, 178
"Tell Your God to Ready for Blood" (episode) 45, 52, 56, 66, 71, 98, 117, 178
tension 16, 30, 34, 83, 86–87, 93, 95–96, 135, 143
tetralogy 2–4, 14, 16,19, 21–22, 27, 103–104, 143, 145, 156–157, 160, 175, 190
Thomas of Woodstock 14
3 Bad Men 13
3:10 to Yuma 24
Tolliver, Cy 17, 19, 31, 68, 69, 78, 95, 115–118, 123–124, 134–135, 145, 155, 160–161, 166, 168, 170, 171, 184n60
"The Trial of Jack McCall" (episode) 44, 48, 70, 177
Trixie 17, 19, 31, 35, 44, 50, 63, 65, 77–79, 87, 100, 104, 107, 112, 117, 119–120, 123, 125–127, 134, 136, 145, 150, 154, 156, 161, 167–171, 180n36
"True Colors" (episode) 52, 178
True Grit 24–25
Tudor/Tudors 10, 14, 18–20, 26–27, 174
Turner, Captain 32, 76, 98, 134–135, 170–171
"A Two-Headed Beast" (episode) 178

"Unauthorized Cinnamon" (episode) 53, 78–79, 126, 178
Unforgiven 24
usurpation 14, 22, 32, 59, 61–62, 64, 67, 69–70, 73, 78, 137, 164–166
Utter, Charlie (character) 18, 32, 40, 52, 55–56, 69, 83, 118, 120, 139, 150
Utter, Charlie (real person) 15

villain 33, 59, 62, 69, 72–73, 81, 84, 116, 130, 144–145, 147, 156, 160, 166–167, 171–172
violence 1–2, 5, 20, 22, 26–28, 31, 34, 36, 40, 44, 46, 52, 55–56, 58, 63, 68–69, 76, 87, 94, 96, 120, 127, 129, 135, 167, 171, 174, 191
vision 6, 10, 12, 30, 64, 109, 127, 129, 131, 133, 136–137, 141–142, 157, 161
vulnerability 79, 99, 123, 125, 128, 151, 166, 168–169, 171, 179n2

Watson, Clell 46, 138, 168
Westerfelhaus, Robert 33–34, 191
Western 1–4, 7, 9–13, 15, 20, 23–35, 52, 63, 81–82, 84, 115, 117, 123, 125, 136, 138–140, 143–145, 149, 156, 172, 174, 179ch1n1, 187, 188–191
Whishaw, Ben 141
White, Walter 175
whores 74, 98, 108, 118, 123, 178, 190–191; see also prostitutes
"The Whores Can Come" (episode) 98, 118, 178
Widdicombe, Toby 191
The Wire 1, 189, 191
Witherspoon, Wendy 13, 23, 54, 62, 191
Witschi, Nicolas 23, 141, 188–191
Wolcott, Francis 68, 96, 106, 117–119, 151, 166
women 2–3, 5, 7, 17, 19, 32, 36, 54, 57–59, 81, 92, 102–128, 148, 151, 172, 175–176, 183n41, 190–191
Worden, Daniel 26, 28–30, 191
Wright, Eugene 99, 190
Wright, Will 136, 144–145, 149, 191
Wu, Mr. 44, 68–69, 77–78, 118–119, 124, 161, 177

Yankton 31, 66, 71, 78, 95–97, 135, 147, 154
York, Duchess of 81–82, 84, 106, 119, 124
York, Duke of 33–34, 61–62, 84–85, 106, 109, 112, 114, 124, 162, 166
York, Elizabeth of 19
York, Richard of 11

Zoller-Seitz, Matt 156, 190
zoom 137, 139–140

www.ingramcontent.com/pod-product-compliance
Ingram Content Group UK Ltd.
Pitfield, Milton Keynes, MK11 3LW, UK
UKHW042008140426
5217IPUK00015B/1043